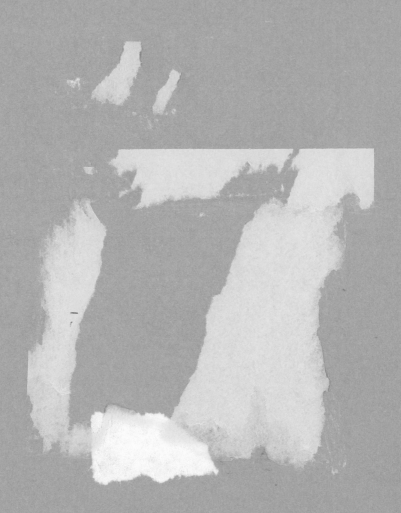

Elsa Schiaparelli

Elsa Schiaparelli: Empress of Paris Fashion

PALMER WHITE

with a foreword by Yves Saint Laurent

AURUM PRESS

A Eugene Braun-Munk Book

Copyright © Palmer White 1986

Foreword copyright © Yves Saint Laurent 1986

Published by Aurum Press Limited, 33 Museum Street, London WC1A 1LD

ISBN 0 948149 43 4

Phototypeset by Keyspools Ltd, Great Britain

Colour separations by Mandarin Offset Ltd.

Printed in Hong Kong by Mandarin Offset Marketing (H.K.) Ltd.

Contents

	Acknowledgements	9
	Foreword by Yves Saint Laurent	11
	Preface	17
1	The Fountainhead	19
2	Arethusa	25
3	Kerlor	31
4	The American Way	36
5	Gaby and Gogo	39
6	Poverty, Paris and Paul Poiret	44
7	'Display No. 1'	52
8	*Trompe-l'œil*	59
9	'Display No. 2'	63
10	A Comet in the Dark	70
11	'Madame'	79
12	Schiap	88
13	Schiaparelli Lady, by Day and by Night	93
14	The World Her Oyster	107
15	Such Stuff as Dreams Are Made On	122
16	Trimmings and Trappings	136
17	'Shocking': Pink and Perfume	152
18	Star of the Show	160
19	The 'Drôle de Guerre' and American Lecture Tour	180
20	M. Lelong Said, 'Non!'	189
21	The War Years in New York	197
22	The Tolling of the Bell	205
	Bibliography	219
	Index	221

TO

Gogo, for her warmth, humour and hospitality

Madeleine Ginsburg of the Victoria and Albert Museum, London, who has so significantly contributed to keeping dress alive and vibrant

Susan Frances Train, Paris Editor, American *Vogue*, constantly helpful, encouraging and tireless

TO

Monsieur Yves Saint Laurent, for everything

TO

All the unsung heroes – artists, craftsmen, skilled workers, photographers, collectors – who enable French fashion to maintain its place as the supreme world arbiter of feminine elegance and who collaborated most meaningfully with Elsa Schiaparelli

Acknowledgements

ARLETTY; Alex Balay, Société Bucol; Richard Bird; Stella Blum; John Cavanagh; Jean-Claude Colas; Hilaire Colcombet, Société Bucol; Irene Dana; Celestine Dars; Denise Dubois, Chambre Syndicale de la Couture Parisienne; Diana Edkins; Blanche Hays Fagan; Lilian Farley, 'Dinarzade', former Paris Editor, *Harper's Bazaar*; Hubert de Givenchy; Michèle Guégen (and for Jean Clément); Roger Jean-Pierre; Kyoto Costume Institute; Paulette Laperche; Hortense MacDonald; Mainbocher; Aroosiag ('Mike') Mikaëlian; Jacques Mouclier, Chambre Syndicale de la Couture Parisienne; John Newth; Philadelphia Museum of Art; Gabrielle Picabia-Buffet; Madame Paul Poiret; Robert Riley, New York Fashion Institute of Technology (Design Laboratory), New York City; Juliano Russo, Parfums Schiaparelli Paris; Bernardino and Guido Sassoli di Bianchi, Parfums Schiaparelli Paris; Jean Schlumberger; Yvonne Souquières; Union Française des Arts du Costume; Victoria and Albert Museum; Diana Vreeland; Marina Mestchersky Vorontzoff.

Particular thanks to Pierre Bergé, President of Yves Saint Laurent, President of the Chambre Syndicale du Prêt-à-Porter des Couturiers et des Créateurs de Mode, and President of the Institut Français de la Mode; Françoise Montenay, a career executive of whom Elsa would have been justly proud; Patton Campbell, whose talent as a stage costume designer is surpassed only by his genius in passing the flame through his teaching to his students; Walter Talevi for his research and advice on the Roman aspects; Gino Cacciapuoti di Giugliano, in every sense a Neapolitan aristocrat, who helped me to understand the Domenitis better; Ugo Bergese, a Piedmontese who enabled me to see into the Schiaparellis more deeply; the Chambre Syndicale de la Couture Parisienne, which entrusted me with Lucien Lelong's account of French fashion during the Occupation; Francisque des Garets, a grand French gentleman and a rare friend; François Lesage, the embroiderer, of a generosity surpassed only by his artistry; Luc Bouchage for Jean Schlumberger; Guillaume Garnier, curator, Musée de la Mode et du Costume, Palais Galliera, Paris; Eugene Braun-Munk, Angela Dyer, my editor, and Alison Rivett, designer, of Aurum Press, with great affection; and Gabrielle Buchaert, Monsieur Yves Saint Laurent's press attaché, always so patient and attentive, an unsung heroine deserving from Paris fashion a special tribute, hereby paid.

Madame Schiaparelli

S HE slapped Paris. She smacked it. She tortured it. She bewitched it. And it fell madly in love with her.

She disembarked – enigmatic, spectral – trying to slip unnoticed through the crowd with her trunks full of episcopal silks, cardinal scarlets and toreador jackets. Rolls of pompon-patterned edging, candy bags stuffed with gold nuggets and silver sequins, ottomans and papal moiré failles as sharp as scimitars, oriental dressing-gowns, army-officer brandenburgs and braids. Commedia dell'arte accessories, a Harlequin costume, sprays of stiff, fierce vulture feathers, frolicking little circus-horse plumes. An entire world of strange, disquieting and fascinating things. The customs official had a good mind to question her about that little ruby heart still beating in a vermilion goblet, but when he raised his head he could only see two eyes more piercing than any bird of prey's and, terrified, he motioned to let them through, all those cases slashed with a trenchant, shattering signature that did not brook the slightest contention.

Once settled in, Madame Schiaparelli, shrouded in a smuggler's cape, plotted, conspired and schemed. Caught in the nets and intrigues she was weaving, she forgot the time the curtain was scheduled to rise. She did not have a gown to wear. She was in a terrible hurry. She tore down one of the Venetian glass chandeliers in her drawing-room and spattered the stage, auditorium, galleries, corridors and lobby with its crystals, the sparkle of which reflected in the eyes of the ladies in the audience and lent them an incomparable radiance they had never had before, and she beguiled, subjugated, captivated, enraptured. The following day there was a mad dash for her doors. They all came, those ladies. They wanted to know everything about the secret of the lustre that had made them so astonishing the previous night at the theatre. They had worked havoc. They could no longer live without continuing to do so. Madame Schiaparelli did not divulge the secret but had all the chandeliers in her house smashed and for years cut, evened, filed, chiselled, bevelled, faceted, set those little fragments of crystal and

Few of the many artists and craftsmen brought into fashion by Schiaparelli more brilliantly reflected her sense of theatricality than did Christian Bérard. These three grande soirée ensembles are from the Astrology Collection of August 1938.

made them scintillate, not hesitating to mix them with glassware or plexiglass, which lit up Paris and foreign parts with the bold glow of their iridescence.

'How she exaggerates!' shrilled her enemies. But she went even further – she bolted, galloped, scaled the walls of convention and won the race, a black-sequined filly adorned with plumes like a horse on parade caracoling to the roll of drums and the clash of cymbals.

'It's nothing but a circus! Sheer clowning! All that isn't worth a damn! It's only tinsel, trash, hardware, street fair, showing off!' What to answer? It was true, there *were* those pointed hats, plumes, tufts and crests, a shoe balanced over the forehead and a siren's face embedded in a mother-of-pearl shell, circus clown's trousers and waistcoats, a shower of confetti, a riot of streamers. Conveniences and facilities? She couldn't have cared less. You're right, her jackets *were* comical – but of an elegance that caused a commotion. So don't go too fast. Under those stage effects that lent women originality, insolence and assurance and reanimated their bodies with new gestures, was concealed the simplest, plainest, most magical of sheaths, which the flaming flight of the bodice allowed to come into view like an ebony arrow.

iti 1965

Madame Schiaparelli trampled down everything that was commonplace. With great kicks of varnished hooves, she sent whatever was trite about its business, knocked down the customary and crashed into the boring, incapable as she was of resisting the most shocking of her impulses. She always ended up having the final word. She wheedled, she inveigled, she manoeuvred – and thwarted all the most subtle stratagems by the mobility of her surprising antennae.

Abruptly, she would turn her back to the show, its passing fancies, its pranks, and in a spirit of abandon transform herself into a languorous vestal draped in the luxurious flow of a crêpe printed with sensual, pliant creepers amongst which were scattered delicate butterflies.

'And her fingernails! Have you seen those fingernails? Red! Yes, bright red! A spy's claws. She's a wolf! A werewolf! A wildcat! She's a night bird! A twilight hawkmoth! An onyx serpent, a conch shell, a Borgia ring, a philtre! Mightn't she be a sorceress?'

And why not? She would have transformed you in less time than it takes to tell – and saved you. She was a bouquet of spells. She was a conspiration of the stars, a fireworks display. Watch out! Or be hypnotized.

1965
Printemps

'She's a Renaissance poisoner. She's Leonora Galigai!' From her phials and stills gushed singular colours, venomous greens, sinister violets, velvety garnets, strange medieval manuscript illuminations. And one fine day, suddenly roaring like a great wild beast in anger, she smashed her entire magician's laboratory and with an ogress's frenzied laughter managed to grab the formula for that explosive, astounding, flabbergasting Pink! A sort of cyclamen, a magenta, a

1968
Vté

Elsa was quick to realize the genius of Yves Saint Laurent. After he had opened his own house in 1962 he regularly designed clothes for her to wear – some of which, shown here and on page 217, were sketched by him for the Schiaparelli exhibition in Paris, 1984.

flaming, a defiance, a panic. She alone could have given to a pink the nerve of a red. A pink that went on to devour everything in its path, invade everything by ricocheting, make everything quake. A neon pink, an unreal pink, an aggressive, brawling, warrior pink, as intense as a Doge's wife red. Shocking Pink!

She cheated and tricked by inventing. How to hold it against her? Once she had added that electric she-devil's colour to the range of pinks, she shut herself up in black. She burrowed underground. Was it possible she had become uneasy about the fire she had just lit? She became gloomy. She rested. She dabbled in her faithful ink, knowing full well it would never betray her, certain that the colonnade of long night sheaths and boleros adorned with arabesques, braid, epaulettes, tassels, fringes, gold and jet black pompons – through the alluring contrast which emanated from their femininity and categorical severity and the setting of their re-embroidered contours, fascinating for their implacable perfection – would make of her its pantheon.

Madame Elsa Schiaparelli was incomparable. There is no equivalence to be found. Her imagination knew no bounds. She alone might have had the audacity to get married in black. In tulle-beclouded veils and ostrich plumes, a grandiose catafalque, she would have stalked down the steps of the church drawing up her duenna's gown to disclose legs swathed in a casino dancer's fish-net stockings. 'Whose funeral is it?' the crowd would have asked as it dropped to its knees, staggered by that tragic, eerie apparition, that monument of inordinacy. It would not have displeased her in the least to observe all those people kneeling around her. She would have blessed them and in her heavy black lacquer and chrome hearse set off on her honeymoon in China only to come back to us with a dragon instead of a dog that she would have at once entwined around her tunics.

Her particular charm? Her brutality, her arrogance, her self-possession, disdain, storms of anger, odd whims, her Gorgon's mask. 'You're describing a monster!' Not at all, you haven't understood anything about her. She was a barbarian queen, a tyrant, a tsar, a margrave. She didn't wish to please. She wanted to dominate, to grab the reins, win battles, terrorize at times, charge through snow-covered forests wrapped in sables, horse-whip the trees. And with nightfall, during a great feast, she would tear off her mounds of jewellery, precious stones, coils of gold and diamonds, tallow-drop emeralds and rubies and fling them across the table at her faithful boyars as a sign of reward, only to end up stripped of all her badges, insignia, decorations and emblems down to her tiara, which she would hurl to the ground, trample on and mortify before she anointed herself Empress by crowning herself with a ridiculous mutton chop.

'But she couldn't have been a tsarina! She was an Italian!' What difference does that make? She wasn't an Italian any longer, she was a Parisienne. Paris had adopted her. And Paris was wrong, for she proceeded to devour it. But Paris was right. She kept shaking it more and more until, exasperated, it spit flames, glittered, shone, radiated, turned the world upside down, and became – thanks to that toreador wearing a costume of light with Shocking Pink stockings – a conqueror yet another time.

Then, like all those galaxies that have made the dull sky crackle with a spray of stars, the great black she-eagle disappeared in her mere of pebbles and tarnished mirrors, shielded in her velvet chaise-longue by ramparts of piles and piles of books, the ground strewed with magazines telling of her triumphs. Was that incense already swirling in vaporous layers or dust meandering in trails of grey? Singular and colossal, she still had eyes that could pierce through this mysterious pollen. She spied on you, an old bird-of-prey trick. Her wings gave off their last gleams of dimmed sheen and fluttered from time to time, irritably.

When she died, Chic closed her eyes. Chic alone could have done so. She would not have allowed anyone else.

Yves Saint Laurent

Automne Hiver
1972

'I remember, when I was so small I could hardly read, seeing a cartoon of two men bathing on a solitary beach. They started to talk, got along splendidly, and after sunning themselves for a long time went behind different rocks to dress. One came out all smartness with a dangling lorgnette and a silver stick; the other in rags. Stupefied, they looked at each other, and with a cold nod each turned and went his separate way. They had nothing more to say to one another.'

'I am reminded of the sad prince who, to obtain happiness for himself, was told to wear the shirt of an entirely happy man. He went all round the world until he found working in a field a man who appeared to him completely happy. "My kingdom for your shirt," cried the prince in ecstasy. But the old man answered: "I have never possessed a shirt."'

ELSA SCHIAPARELLI

Preface

ELSA SCHIAPARELLI was brought up in a rigid social and religious context and given the narrowest of educations. Yet she broke out to represent what was most avant-garde and individualistic between the two world wars, attaining an exalted place in French fashion and, in the battle of the sexes, contributing signally to the social and professional advance of the modern woman whom she herself so vividly personified.

It took life almost forty years to transform Elsa, the sensitive, lyrical poetess, into Schiap, the staccato, impregnable career executive. That is why the fashion aspect of the Schiaparelli story may seem long in coming. But the lovely surroundings and the noble cultural atmosphere of her childhood and adolescence; the events, at times dramatic, that mark her early maturity; the developing artistic and industrial modernism which, more than any of her competitors, she understood and promoted; the gathering storms that she sensed long before they broke – all these contributed to Elsa's rich personality and unusual intelligence, and so to her accomplishments and to the excitement which she brought to haute couture. She was one of the rare designers to bring a background into fashion with her. This has to be understood.

Graced with an uncanny sense of anticipation, Elsa announced the look fashion would take half a century later: eccentric, individual to the extreme, easy to wear. Branded revolutionary, even at the outset anarchical, she came on loud and strong with her statements and knowingly attracted attention with her contradictions and witticisms. Her skeleton and crossword puzzle hand-knitted sweaters and her dresses using zips for the first time in haute couture scandalized as much as would punk fifty years later. Look now at the city streets, at schools and universities the world over: her experiments with fabrics and substances unheard of in fashion, strange prints, asymmetric proportions and shocking accessories are reflected there in riotous array.

Influenced in her adolescence by the Italian Futurists, by the French Fauves and Cubists, and by New York Dada while in

Elsa Schiaparelli in 1931.

America, on settling in Paris she joined forces with the Surrealists and then absorbed Art Deco to bring the spirit and principles of architecture, sculpture and painting into fashion, helping to break down the walls dividing these disciplines and anticipating today's eclectic approach to designing.

Through her clothes Elsa Schiaparelli used wit and shock tactics to arm modern women in their thrust towards equality and independence, brought make-believe, mystery and romance to their lives, and gave them a sense of star quality and triumph.

PALMER WHITE

Schiaparelli's delight in shock tactics found supreme expression in one of her most exotic collections based upon the circus theme, February 1938.

1

The Fountainhead

ON THE right bank of the River Tiber, not far from St Peter's in the oldest part of the holy city of Rome, stands a marvel of Renaissance architecture, Palazzo Corsini. Erasmus and Michelangelo were received as guests there. Queen Christina of Sweden lived there for thirty years after abdicating her throne. And there, on 10 September 1890, Elsa Luisa Maria Schiaparelli was born.

In unifying Italy twenty years before, the head of the House of Savoy, Victor Emmanuel II, had moved his court from Turin, the capital of Piedmont, down to Rome. He undertook to transform Rome from a quiet little country town of religious institutions and craftsmen into a setting worthy of a king, and in organizing his government he 'imported' many personally faithful Piedmontese. To his royal purple he annexed the cultural brilliance of the Royal Academy of the Lincei (today the Italian Academy of Sciences), the oldest and most prestigious association serving the humanities in Europe. In 1875 the King appointed Celestino Schiaparelli, a man of thirty-four from a family of well-to-do Piedmontese intellectuals, to head the magnificent Lincei Library. The library was housed in Palazzo Corsini, and Celestino, Elsa's father, was given one of the palace's splendid apartments to live in.

Historically, the House of Savoy had been linked to France rather than to Italy; French was widely spoken in Piedmont. The Piedmontese, manufacturers, statesmen and scholars as well as farmers and shepherds, were withdrawn, conventional and extremely hard-working mountain people accustomed to withstanding a rigorous climate and warring European factions who used their country as a passage or a battleground. Celestino, though every inch the stern patriarch of his times, was kind, gentle and profoundly attached to his family; if he was introspective and undemonstrative, he was also noble, the essence of integrity, and an energetic, patriotic and deeply religious man. His cultural interests ranged widely, and, as what was then considered something of a literary adventure, he translated monumental works by Arab poets and writers. Later he went on to research Persian and Sanskrit. In his retirement he

Alberto de Dominitis, Elsa's grandfather, with her mother Maria-Luisa (left) and uncle, Vicenzo, her childhood hero. The other child is Zia, Elsa's Aunt Lily, a renowned beauty who travelled widely and sent Elsa exotic presents from all over the world.

devoted himself to his superb collection of old coins and made exchanges with the King, another fanatical numismatist, who regularly invited him to Court functions.

Celestino's family was equally distinguished. His older brother Giovanni was an astronomer of great repute who, as director of the Brera Observatory in Milan, was first to observe the canals on Mars and discovered the association between comets and meteors. The two brothers had a sister, Emma, who became head of all the convents of Italy, and also two remarkable cousins, Luigi and Ernesto. Luigi, a historian who specialized in palaeography, set up the Schiaparelli Foundation and travelled all over the world organizing some hundred schools in missions, convents and monasteries. Ernesto was a noted archaeologist who founded the Turin Museum of Egyptology, today second only to that in Alexandria.

In sharp contrast, Elsa's mother's family, southern aristocrats from Naples descended from the Dukes of Tuscany, were extrovert, inventive, poetic, superstitious, inclined to melancholia and, in their way, just as adventurous as the Schiaparellis. This maternal side of Elsa's parental story begins in the mid-nineteenth century when the young Marquis de Domenitis was named Italian Consul in Malta. While there he married the daughter of the British Governor, a Scot; the youngest of their four children was Elsa's mother, Maria-Luisa. One of her brothers became Elsa's first hero: with the Domenitis' penchant for adventure he joined the secret society of the Carbonieri, fought to unify Italy with Garibaldi, was imprisoned by the Bourbons, escaped and went into exile in Egypt, where he took up law and became an adviser to the Khedive.

To understand Elsa Schiaparelli it is vital to keep in mind the opposite but complementary sources supplying the current within: the intellectual, reserved Piedmontese and the sensitive, outgoing Neapolitan imbued with the culture of Rome.

When Elsa was born her father was almost fifty and her mother thirty-five. In those days that was thought to be old. Nowadays the offspring of older parents often prove to be the most intelligent; then Elsa was considered 'difficult'. She had a much older sister, Beatrice, a violently religious girl who was already threatening to upset the family's rigid matrimonial traditions by taking the veil. Under great pressure from her parents Beatrice finally acquiesced to marriage and the raising of children, but thereafter devoted herself to decorating churches and writing and illustrating a Bible for young people.

St Peter's was the backdrop for Elsa's childhood. What images to stamp on a receptive infant mind! The great sheltering dome. The piazza graced by the long and gently curving colonnade-arms of the church mother, open wide to offer solace and protection to lost souls. The Swiss guards in their red, black and yellow uniforms designed by Michelangelo. Inside, precious marbles, gold, silver and bronze; the cardinals in their magnificent scarlet and violet vestments. There in that immensity Elsa was christened, and there, amid the sumptuous tentures and colours, she attended Mass.

Forty-five years later Schiaparelli featured in the prints for her Celestial Silhouette a leitmotif of the keys to paradise as held by St Peter in traditional representations of him; and the last of her typically mannish designs before the lights went out in France in 1940 was a choir-boy jacket in stiffened handkerchief linen.

In Palazzo Corsini, the young Elsa's home, again what images! Granite columns, spacious rooms, gilding, tapestries and frescoes, Roman statuary, vaulted ceilings depicting Graeco-Roman mythology – all contributed to the serene atmosphere of history and enlightenment. The palace with its eighteenth-century façade stood among heavy-smelling magnolia trees, its lovely garden set out in squares with rows of tangerine and lemon trees.

Little wonder that Schiaparelli the fashion designer never ran dry of inspiration: all she had to do was dip into the well-spring of images and colours of her childhood memories. The celestial globe in the Lincei Library showing the planets in their zodiacal houses (a Renaissance example was always to be found in the drawing-room of Elsa's own home) was undoubtedly the inspiration for her Astrological or Zodiac Collection, considered one of her most brilliant presentations. When she was old enough, her father allowed her to examine illuminated medieval manuscripts filled with fanciful figures hand-painted under blue and blood-red skies, and guided her through his illustrated books of saints. Among Schiaparelli's most striking uptilted hats of 1935 were to be found the Saints' Halos, little and big, transparent and opaque, straight and saintly or slightly cock-eyed, and she would also use mantillas, Fra Angelico hoods and monastic cowls. For the young girl, Celestino's great private collection, which on his death went to the Italian National Library, became another haven and joy. In the pages of these rare, exquisitely illustrated books she entered into the mythological worlds of Homer and Aesop, explored strange and colourful cultures and shared oriental exploits with Marco Polo and Scheherazade, both to be remembered in her designs. Especially she liked to accompany Pizarro on his conquest of the sun- and planet-worshipping Incas, fascinating for their jewellery, ceramics, weaving and dyes, and addicted to the vibrant Peruvian pink which Elsa was later to make her own.

At the turn of the century – when Elsa was ten – the influence of the Church was still pre-eminent in Italy. Innovative ideas were shunned, and the people of Rome, so open-minded by nature, continued to be uninformed, prudish and provincial. Rome proper, with its streets full of scurrying priests and nuns in black and white robes and wimples which Elsa would later adapt to haute couture, was still confined within its walls. Beyond these stretched Campagna Romana, the flat surrounding countryside whose melancholy and austerity would always underlie the fun and futurism of Schiaparelli designs. With her German governess Elsa went for long walks in

Palazzo Corsini, where Elsa was born and lived for the first twenty years of her life.

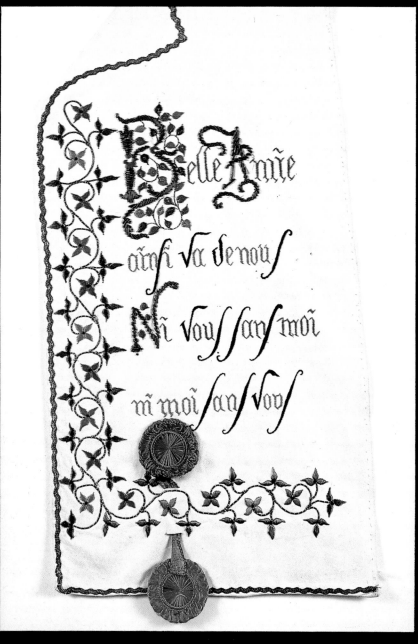

Elsa used the images and colours of her rich childhood surroundings in Rome as a constant source of inspiration. Sometimes they became almost direct representations, as in these embroideries depicting an illuminated manuscript used on a waist-coat, and a stained glass window which framed the neckline of a dress.

Campagna Romana, where, against the rich orange Latium sun, the images of parasol pines and of men and women severely dressed in straight black lines were imprinted on her mind.

When Rome was too hot, the Schiaparellis went up to Tivoli, a little town overlooking the Villa d'Este, of the thousand super-imposed fountains, and Hadrian's Villa, where the Emperor had reproduced monuments of places that had impressed him during his foreign travels. Now being excavated, these remains stimulated Elsa's interest in faraway places and ancient artefacts, which she was later to collect in the course of her own travels. Sometimes the family went north to visit Celestino's brother, who owned a Napoleonic villa near Milan on the shores of Lake Como. Uncle Giovanni befriended his unusual niece, whom he appreciated for her intellectual curiosity. He took her to look at the heavens through his great telescope, holding her up to it in his arms and explaining why he believed that Mars was peopled by human beings who harvested their own crops.

In those days only the daughters of well-to-do families in Italy were sent to school. The first one Elsa attended – parochial and single-sex – was a dreary cell of Establishment instruction and fierce discipline. Friction arose with her teachers almost at once and her parents soon sent her to a Protestant school, which differed from the preceding Catholic one only in being stricter in order to prove that it was better. At that time young ladies were never told anything about 'the facts of life'. To relieve her tormented conscience after a first innocent kiss, Elsa babbled a confession to a priest, who concluded that she had sinned and upbraided the ultra-sensitive girl so clumsily that it seems to have marked her for life. From then on she fiercely protected her innermost feelings from violation, an attitude reflected in the clothes she designed and the feminist viewpoint they represented.

Maria-Luisa had a habit of drawing unfavourable comparisons between Elsa and the older daughter, Beatrice, a lushly dark beauty. For an Italian, Elsa was unfashionably thin, with enormous dark brown eyes and long brown hair, and she suffered from the lasting conviction that she was plain. This, added to her basic shyness, partly accounted for her brusqueness in adult life. But, just as she would always react to adversity by fighting back, she now pondered ways of making herself beautiful. Weren't flowers beautiful? Well, if they covered your face like an enchanted garden, you too would become a Helen of Troy, she reasoned. She wheedled nasturtium, daisy and morning glory seeds out of the gardener, planted them in her throat, nose, ears and mouth and sat down to wait for them to bloom. She almost suffocated before a doctor on emergency call put an end to the botanical dream. Forty years later, fashionable ladies sported Schiaparelli seed-pod buttons and boutonnières of tiny flower seed packets. One of her brightest dresses came in a 'Seed Catalogue' print composed of packets of flower seeds.

Happily Uncle Giovanni, the astronomer, understood and sympathized. When she bemoaned some moles on her cheek, he assured her that they were beauty marks and that they had the form of the Great Bear, or Big Dipper, constellation, which meant that she would always be lucky as well as alluring. Elsa never forgot this, and later designed as a good-luck piece for her own everyday wear a diamond pin in the shape of the Great Bear, decorated the drawing-room of her Paris mansion in sky-blue cotton woven with black stars in the same motif, and used a Great Bear design for one of her most striking prints.

After listening to a description of parachuting and seeing sketches of this strange new sport and of Icarus wings in Leonardo da Vinci's notebooks, Elsa launched a personal experiment by opening an umbrella, leaping into space from a second-storey window of Palazzo Corsini and landing, unharmed, on a heap of soft earth. Forty years later she was to incorporate the parachute and Icarus wing images into her 'Stratospheric' and 'Aeroplane' fashion styles.

In 1908 an earthquake destroyed a large part of Calabria and Sicily, and a relief fund was set up for the homeless. Huge open carts were driven through Rome to pick up any spare clothing the Romans might have to contribute. Alone in Palazzo Corsini, Elsa raced through the rooms, catching up mounds of garments belonging to all the members of the family and showering them on the carts from an upper window. All her life she would give things away impetuously. When, half a century later, Madeleine Ginsburg came to her Paris home to ask for items for the Victoria and Albert Museum's costume and fashion collection, Elsa ran into her bedroom and came out with great armfuls of Schiaparelli wonders that she hurled over the banisters to the young Englishwoman gazing up in astonishment. Not long afterwards, flattered by the idea of an exhibition at the Philadelphia Art Museum, she gave outright to the museum over sixty of the originals of her great period from 1935 to 1939, most of which she had worn herself.

Elsa wears her good-luck piece in the form of the Great Bear at a garden party with Salvador Dali (right).

2

Arethusa

WHEN she was eighteen and considered old enough to receive a monthly allowance, Elsa began to choose her own clothes. Bored by her mother's taste – tartans with black velvet collars and a large brown hat trimmed with a wide yellow bow – she started to vary this 'uniform' by adding more startling colours. She was inspired by the scarlet moiré robes of the princes of the Vatican, and became so fond of mauve that she insisted on her escorts wearing mauve ties and mauve handkerchiefs in their breast pockets; her use of scarlet and mauve, combined with the Peruvian pink of the Incas recalled from her father's books, was to become one of her hallmarks. Even then she appreciated the idea of 'separates', choosing simple, fine, white lace-edged blouses to be worn interchangeably with various skirts. Later, when launching herself in Paris, she continued to use this economical principle which has now become part and parcel of every woman's wardrobe. 'It's when you can't be extravagant,' the head of the House of Schiaparelli would remind her customers, 'that you become ingenious.'

Celestino began taking his daughter – hatted, gloved and dressed in a high-necked frock with long sleeves – to the theatre. At the time Verismo, the subdued Italian counterpart of the violent French Realist movement in literature and music, was claiming its right to represent truth openly. In opera the epics and dramas of Rossini, Bellini, Donizetti and Verdi were popular, but it was Puccini's operas, *La Bohème, Tosca* and *Madam Butterfly,* with their frank approach to contemporary matters, which appealed most to an adolescent who would later stage fashion collections reminiscent of theatrical presentations.

Even in prudish Italy, the impact of Ibsen had inspired timid attempts to depict the evils of woman's enslavement by men, a concept not beyond the understanding of one young member of the single-standard system. At the height of his powers Gabriele D'Annunzio, the great literary figure of the time, was poetically proclaiming the artist as a superman, a Nietzschian belief shared by Elsa all her life. In this he was supported by his mistress, Eleonora

Duse, one of the greatest tragediennes of her age. Elsa worshipped this actress, who was intelligent, exquisitely feminine and very modern. Before her death in 1973, Elsa designed her own tombstone, her florid signature on graphite, to resemble the tombstone of La Duse, dead fifty years before.

La Duse ran her own company, but Elsa's first exposure to anything like the woman business manager in the modern sense came with Maria Montessori, a young physician, psychiatrist and educator who founded a series of homes in which she gave deprived children the freedom and training required to help them enjoy a relatively normal life. This dedicated woman's strength and perseverance with children inspired Elsa when she later had to cope with her own daughter's physical difficulties. Moreover, throughout her busy life she never hesitated to assist children in need – a dedication which helped her to endure the sad, lonely years of the Second World War in New York.

During Elsa's youth the new accent on the machine – in photography, motion pictures, gramophone recording, transport and communication – greatly influenced her. She was in her early impressionable teens when two races, Il Giro d'Italia and Il Gran Premio d'Italia, fired Italian bicycling and motor-racing enthusiasts. The two Italians who won the Peking to Paris motor race organized by the *New York Times* and *Le Matin* in 1907 were acclaimed as heroes, and Elsa devoured the accounts of their colourful exploits across southern Imperialist Russia. At the same time Italian pictorial artists were prefiguring the new twentieth-century ideal of objects and figures moving in space. Elsa Schiaparelli was to support the liberated woman releasing her energy in physical activity, business as well as sports.

Then impassioned young Filippo Marinetti tossed his bomb of Futurism, glorifying the speed and danger of the Machine Age. No one was better prepared temperamentally than young Elsa to respond to a summons for earnest, feverish living and revolt. No one was keener to carry out Marinetti's injunction to use only the materials and images of the new twentieth century. Elsa was still only eighteen when, to her delight, the Futurists, shocking conventional artistic circles to the roots, heralded the combustion engine as being a thing of beauty to match the master works of antiquity. This anticipated the new realism that would glorify the mundane and everyday during the early decades of the Century of Progress, not only in such monuments as the Orient Express, luxury liners and skyscrapers, but also in the industrial objects to be given artistic treatment – and later in Schiaparelli designs for Paris fashion. Unfortunately, before Elsa could become involved in the Futurist current, it was dammed. The Church persecuted Marinetti for offending morals, and he fled from Italy.

Time dragged by. Elsa, aged nineteen, lonely, bored and increasingly apart, sought a means of expressing herself. She started

The new liberated woman of the late twenties found the freedom and panache she craved in sportswear by Schiaparelli. In this photograph by George Hoyningen-Huené taken in July 1928 the black and white striped knitted vest is teamed with black flannel shorts and matching striped socks.

to write articles on the music she was hearing in recitals and concerts and at the opera. She had no technical knowledge and the articles could hardly be classed as criticism, but they enabled her to air her unconventional views, and one or two found their way into little magazines. A career as an actress might have tempted her, but Celestino would no more have permitted a daughter of his to set foot on a stage than he would, had he been alive at the time, have let her take up a profession or a trade. All her life Elsa regretted being unable to sing, and her comment about this after she had retired indicates her basic outlook on life as applied to her clothes: 'How wonderful to liberate oneself in what appears such an easy way, but at the same time retain the privacy of one's feelings.'

Casting about for something which would give her a sense of fulfilment, and finding nothing in religion, she wondered if philosophy might hold some interest. She started a course at the University of Rome and to her surprise, as she had always been annoyed by anything academic, she loved it. Her roving, mystical mind found the intellectual discipline it needed. Bossuet and Spinoza entranced her, for years St Augustine's *Confessions* took the place of a prayer book for her, and throughout her life the study of philosophy stimulated and renewed her.

When Elsa was approaching twenty, Celestino left the Lincei Library to take up the chair of Arabic languages and literature and to lecture in Oriental studies at the University of Rome. The family moved from Palazzo Corsini across the Tiber to a sprawling apartment overlooking the newly constructed Via Nazionale, which thrust across Rome from one side to the other. During the long still nights in spring, shepherds carrying crooks, wearing large black hats and wrapped in heavy black capes (which Schiaparelli the fashion designer was to remember) guided their bleating flocks across the city on Via Nazionale to pastures up in the wild, volcanic Alban hills; in the autumn they drove them back down to the Campagna Romana plains. Elsa never tired of watching from her bedroom window this enchanting tableau illuminated by the Roman moon. Sensitive to the poetry of the scene and influenced by D'Annunzio's poetic dramas, she now began to find an outlet in composing verse. In the new apartment there was nowhere for her to be alone, so beside the linen room in the back hall, in front of a window overlooking an ugly courtyard, she placed a table and a chair and around them a monstrous Japanese screen. There, away from the bustle of the household, she dwelt for hours on sorrow, love, sensuality and mysticism. 'I was possessed,' she recorded when over sixty. 'Never since have I experienced such complete pleasure. No achievement since has given me such satisfaction.'

An older cousin, Giustino, an art critic and collector, took for her the place of his father, Uncle Giovanni, as a friend. Knowing that Giustino would not laugh at her, she shared with him her attempts at poetry. He was so impressed that he showed some to a Milan publisher, Riccardo Quintieri, who enthusiastically offered to publish a whole book of her verse. Elsa was overwhelmed with joy at the prospect but prudently decided not to tell her family. Racking her brains for an appropriate title, she finally thought of an ancient Greek myth which represented her growing obsession with the female protecting herself from the male aggressor. In the myth, the nymph Arethusa avoids the crude advances of a rapacious young hunting god by fleeing to Sicily, where the goddess Diana grants her prayer and transforms her into a lovely fountain. In representations over the ages Arethusa has been associated with water and thus with purity.

Arethusa was reviewed in most of the Italian papers and was mentioned in English and German periodicals. Some of the verse, translated into Spanish, was included in an anthology of Italian poems published in Madrid. Despite receiving some criticism for being too abstract, speculative and pessimistic, the collection was acknowledged to be lively and elegant. 'Salomé', the first and best of the poems, was praised as a lyrical meditation on love, the soul and the problems of the mind and spirit. *Roma Litteraria* spoke of 'new and stupendous pathos'. *Populo Romano* commented: 'All Elsa Schiaparelli's poetry is profoundly human and essentially emotional. She looks for beauty in every drop of rain, every ray of sun, every leaf that trembles, every flame that scintillates.'

Remember that this was 1911, yet here was a young poetess of twenty publicly exalting passion, however philosophically. The Schiaparelli family were shocked by *Arethusa* and Celestino refused to read it. Instead, he packed the sinner off to rue her transgressions and calm her unholy ardours in a German-Swiss convent, but had to remove her when she went on a hunger strike that threatened her life.

Two years went by. Elsa was of marriageable age, but none of the eligible young men proposed by her family interested her even faintly. Most notable was a wealthy, charming but ugly Russian prince, who when rejected retired into solitude, wrote her tender letters and offered to leave her all his possessions. 'This was one of the few occasions in my life,' she later remarked, 'when a man offered me something of value.' On the other hand, none of the men she found attractive met with parental approval. On a trip with her father to Tunis she became despondent when Celestino turned away a dashing and wealthy young Tunisian. Tunisia remained indelibly stamped on Elsa's mind and she was often to use its particular and vivid colours in her designs. Some twenty years later, she spent a summer there studying Tunisian methods of sewing, draping and veil-twisting. Back to Paris fashion she brought the strange Arab breeches and embroidered shirts, suavely wrapped turbans, enormous pompon-rimmed hats, barbaric belts and jewellery and, most notably, the two-inch sole shoes that were to run throughout the century as 'wedgies'. Later Elsa bought a house in Hammamet.

After returning to Rome with her father the young Elsa was

attracted to a painter who had a studio outside the city walls in Campagna Romana and who offered her port and wine in the shadow of parasol pines. When her parents found out that he was already engaged, that was that. Then she met her first true love: Pino, a warm-hearted and intelligent Neapolitan, who would come all the way from Naples to Rome just to spend a few hours with her. Alas, her parents discovered that Pino was poor, and she was forced to part from him. She never forgot him.

Increasingly Celestino, now well over seventy and still active as the dean of the University of Rome, and Maria-Luisa, almost sixty, worried about their younger daughter. Unmarried, unoccupied, obviously unhappy – what were they to do with her? Destiny took a hand. Maria-Luisa received a letter from an Englishwoman who had been at school with her in Florence and had married well. She was planning to turn her country house in Kent into a home where orphans could be brought up in a progressive way. Did Maria-Luisa know of any bright, willing Italian girl who would like to come and help with the children and learn English at the same time?

3

Kerlor

For this photograph by Hoyningen-Huené of a long beaded evening jacket striped in satin on velvet, Elsa specified that the background should be one of her favourite Bianchini fabrics designed by Raoul Dufy.

Aㅁㅁㅁ a thirty-four hour journey from Rome, a young Italian woman chaperoned by family friends alighted from a train at the bustling Gare de Lyon in Paris en route for London. This was Elsa Schiaparelli's first taste of what would always be to her the most beautiful, exciting metropolis in the world. An unsophisticated twenty-two-year-old, she was awestruck by the City of Light in 1913. Isadora Duncan was dancing naked and untrammelled under transparent tunics. The Ballet Russe was exploding with colours, sensuality and savage rhythms. The Ecole de Paris, the Fauves, Picasso, the Cubists – all were flourishing. Elsa's ostracized fellow-countryman, Filippo Marinetti, had seen his Futurist Manifesto published in *Le Figaro* and was influencing young artists with his glorification of modern materials, machines and images. Sonia Delaunay especially was espousing the futuristic cause, and her 'simultaneist' clothes, made of fabrics of complementary colours, had an impact on Elsa, who twenty years later would adapt some of Sonia's ideas for her own designs.

Here too Elsa encountered *Les Soirées de Paris*, the magazine just founded by Guillaume Apollinaire which was the mouthpiece of the avant-garde. This introduced her to the principal developments of Cubism and its disciples, as did Apollinaire's 'Les Peintres Cubistes: Méditations Esthétiques', a brilliantly perceptive essay. Thanks to the two publications, Elsa became acquainted with the names of Francis Picabia and his wife Gabrielle, *née* Buffet. Gabrielle was to have an important influence on Elsa.

The young girl from Rome also discovered that women in France were asserting their equality with men. Marie Curie, the Nobel Prize winner (whose daughter Eve was to be dressed fifteen years later by the House of Schiaparelli), lectured at the Sorbonne, and Sarah Bernhardt gave lessons at the National Conservatory of Dramatic Arts. These were great names; but Elsa also noted a woman stage manager at the Opéra-Comique, a woman astronomer at the National Observatory, a woman farmer receiving the Ribbon of Agricultural Merit, women cab and motor-car drivers, and a woman pilot decorated with the Légion d'Honneur.

On this first brief visit to Paris – she was there for only ten days – Elsa was enchanted by the rue de la Paix. It was much more than a street: it was an international meeting place, the focal point of good taste, a temple dedicated to the worship of beautiful, fashionable ladies. All the riches of French haute couture – the jewels, the silks and satins, the hats, shoes, boots, plumes and furs – were contained in those buildings with their balconies garlanded in roses and geraniums. Everywhere she heard ladies discussing the colourful and thrilling new styles of Paul Poiret, who was later to give her so much help. In 1913 Poiret, who had brought the feminine figure of the twentieth century to life through his wife Denise, was at his zenith, and Elsa seized her first opportunity to follow his dictates when, to celebrate her last night in Paris, one of her father's friends invited her to attend a costume ball. Since she did not possess an evening gown, she devised for herself a Zouave (French Algerian military) version of the Poiret pantaloon, which she was to revive and adapt as lounging pyjamas in the thirties. She draped and pinned yards of dark blue crêpe de Chine around herself and, à la Poiret, used one length of orange silk as a sash to form a high waist and wove another into a turban, which she was also to bring back and to wear so frequently herself that it became almost a trademark.

When Elsa arrived at the ball with her escort, the dancers were gliding to the sensuous strains of that latest rage, the tango. The most

Schiaparelli's treatment of lounging pyjamas began a rage for women wearing trousers that has never since waned. The taffeta Pagliacci trousers (above) are designed to be worn with a changeable orchid coat, while the corduroy ones (opposite page) are teamed with a tweed jacket embroidered with sequins.

up-to-date dancing school in Rome had taught her only quadrilles. But, sallying forth bravely, she tangoed so enthusiastically that the pins of her costume began to give away, and had her partner not trotted her off the floor, her first encounter with Paris society might have ended like a number at the Folies-Bergère. Never mind, she had had the time of her life, and when next morning she made for the Gare du Nord and a train to London, she knew without any doubt that Paris had the climate in which she could bloom.

If Elsa felt at home in Paris, she was very much a stranger in an England not long emerged from the Victorian age, despite its similarity to her own bourgeois background. However, any homesickness she felt was dispelled at once by the countryside. 'Who has ever been in an English country house,' she wrote forty years later, 'without falling under its spell?' So she set about her duties helping her hostess with the orphan children, but escaping as often as she could to visit London. She was impressed by George V and Queen Mary, compared Buckingham Palace not too unfavourably to the Quirinale, and developed a crush on the dashing young Prince of Wales, the future Edward VIII (she was later to design clothes for his wife, the Duchess of Windsor). She wandered through the British Museum and the Victoria and Albert, and attended the exhibitions of British artists and defenders of modernism previously unknown to her. Unfortunately, the brilliant post–Ibsen theatre was denied her by her limited command of the language, but she could appreciate grand opera at Covent Garden as well as enjoying the light operas of Gilbert and Sullivan, the popular songs of the English music-halls and spectacular musical comedies like *Chu-Chin-Chow*. English-women, like Frenchwomen, were on the march towards independence, she noted, and she never forgot the sight of Piccadilly Circus being invaded by the suffragettes led by Emmeline Pankhurst.

One afternoon Elsa got lost in a London pea-soup fog, and as a result almost missed a meeting of the greatest significance to her life. Interested as ever in anything philosophical, she had seen a poster announcing a young theologian and writer scheduled to speak in French on theosophy, and had bought a ticket for the lecture. The lecturer was Comte William de Wendt de Kerlor. In his early thirties, he was Breton French on his father's side (there is a village named Kerlor in southern Brittany) and French-Swiss on his mother's (in Geneva, where he was born, there is a Boulevard de Wendt). He had inherited a Slav look from his maternal grand-parents, Poles from Cracow. This contrasted strikingly with the Italians to whom Elsa had been accustomed, and she found the tall, slim, elegant man with his magnetic eyes very attractive. He also appealed to her mysticism as he dwelt on Buddhism, and when he went on to talk of the power of the soul over the body, of magic and eternal youth, she became spellbound. If she heard the applause at the end, she forgot to get up when the audience left and only came to her senses when an attendant asked if she wished to meet the lecturer.

Comte William de Wendt de Kerlor in 1914, the year of his marriage to Elsa.

Oh, yes, she did wish to. They became engaged the next day.

At the announcement, her aged parents toiled all the way to London to disrupt the union. But this time they failed. The wedding took place in a register office in early 1914, with no fuss and no white wedding dress. When she returned from the ceremony to the tiny mews house her husband had rented, the new Comtesse de Kerlor discovered that seven mirrors had been inexplicably smashed. Superstitious as she was, she might have taken this for the sinister augury it proved to be. But she was too happy to pay attention.

In Kerlor Elsa had found her master, an extension of her Catholic patriarch father, but also her mate. If he was a man she could love and desire, he was also an intellectual she could look up to, a virile and decisive protector and someone to fear a little, for he could be egotistical and vain. The first, all too brief months of their marriage were surely the most satisfying private moments Elsa was ever to know. But, inexorably, the world was moving towards war.

Since Kerlor had been born in Switzerland he was exempt from military service, but life in London nevertheless became difficult for the couple after August 1914. Not that they wanted for money: Celestino, though far from rich, had given his daughter a respectable dowry. But under the circumstances few people were attracted to lectures on theosophy in French, and Kerlor, instead of understanding the dwindling attendance, lost faith in himself. As Elsa herself put it, he began to act like a cloud drifting in the sky. To boost his morale, and fully aware of the effect of his mixture of Slav charm and Gallic manners, he responded to the approaches of other women and began to neglect his wife. Since Elsa had few friends in London and her English was still not good, she began to wonder if she belonged anywhere in this wide world – and to whom. Eventually Kerlor was no longer able to remain in England as a youngish foreigner without work and exempt from military service, so in 1915 they moved to Nice, where his family had once lived and which was a safe distance from the scene of battle. They rented a small flat overlooking some gardens, which gave Elsa much pleasure. She was enchanted by the then unspoiled beauty of the Riviera, which before the war had been a smart winter resort for princes, maharajahs and millionaires. But though no longer handicapped by language barriers, Elsa did not put down any deeper roots there than she had in London. Kerlor again began absenting himself, and to fill in her time Elsa took to traipsing off to Monte Carlo and the gaming rooms. Of course she lost what little money she had and was one day sent back to Nice without a sou, on a railway voucher bearing the words, 'With the compliments of the Casino'.

And here, with Elsa strolling alone up and down the Promenade des Anglais in the autumn of the year 1915 and contemplating the empty beaches of wartime Nice, the images blur. For she never revealed, either in conversation or in her autobiography, what happened during the next three and a half years of her life.

4

The American Way

ARLY one spring morning in 1919 Comte and Comtesse de Kerlor arrived in New York City harbour aboard a battered old steamer, *L'Espagne*. He was a tall, distinguished-looking man of about thirty-five with light brown hair, deep-set, penetrating blue eyes and high cheekbones. She was a dark, voluptuous woman in her late twenties, dressed in an extravagant, somehow medieval way, with long black hair streaming in the wind.

No one was waiting to meet the couple. After presenting their papers to inspectors and undergoing a short medical examination, they left the pier in a taxi. Instantly and from all sides Elsa was assailed by the new images, materials and sounds of the twentieth century that she was to absorb and then reproduce in French fashion. Streets in a gridiron pattern: broad, parallel and sharply perpendicular. Skyscrapers, testimony to American faith in technology and progress mixed with American theatricality: stark vertical lines, all-steel skeleton structures, brick, concrete, gleaming glass. Brooklyn Bridge and Williamsburg Bridge: long, light, open to the sunlight in a scaffold of voids. The giganticism of Pennsylvania Station, Yankee Stadium. The rackety Third Avenue El. Cops' whistles, police-car and ambulance sirens, fire engine bells. Red fire hydrants, green letter-boxes, peppermint-stick barber shop poles. Posters and stills of 'movies' glorifying danger and armed violence (the Wild West), machines (locomotives and automobiles) and speed (chases).

Even before they arrived at the famous old Brevoort Hotel in Greenwich Village, Comtesse de Kerlor realized that provincial Rome, where she was born and raised, artistic and fashionable Paris, which she had visited, and insular London, where she had lived, were all three hidebound and outdated, and that here in the United States the technological future, which in Europe had been glimpsed only by intellectuals and artists, was the present.

The general status of American women, so far in advance of the austere bourgeois-Catholic double standard under which Elsa had grown up, greatly impressed her. If true equality had not actually been achieved, universal suffrage had nevertheless just become law, household appliances did away with much drudgery, divorce was easy and fashions were freed. American women, who now played tennis and golf, went bicycling, roller and ice skating, drove motorcars and wore corsetless garments, were enjoying a physical liberation illustrated by the movies and prefigured by Futurist artists. Middle-class girls were beginning to escape from old, staid patterns into the professions, the arts and business; the daughters of labourer immigrants could climb the social ladder through becoming stenographers and then secretaries. These were startlingly new concepts to Elsa and, together with the sights and sounds of New York City in 1919, would have a decisive influence on her career and her development as a designer.

While living there, Elsa complained that America had no Old World tradition, but after she started in business she thanked God for that lack because she was able to turn it to her own use. She would impose on the States a new European mode, Parisian of course but in essence her own, that fitted conventional demands yet incorporated many novel artistic aspects which were in tune with the shapes, sounds and trends of the American Way. Elsa never failed to express her gratitude. 'America has always been more than hospitable and friendly to me,' she wrote nearly thirty-five years later. 'She made it possible for me to obtain a unique place in the world. France gave me the inspiration, America the sympathetic approval and result.'

Her stay in the United States also determined the pattern of her private life. In the hope of clinging to his youth and fitness, her husband had become a strict vegetarian, did not drink and led a Spartan lifestyle. However, he never became physically or psychologically strong enough to cope with the pressure of New York, and travelled further and further afield. In addition to lecturing and

A diminutive Elsa (far right) addresses a packed stadium at St Paul, Minnesota, in November 1940 at the end of her triumphant lecture tour of America.

writing articles on theology, Kerlor started offering private consultations on philosophy as the universal panacea to ever-increasing numbers of moonstruck American ladies and had a torrid affair with Isadora Duncan. At this point, Elsa became pregnant.

All but rejected by Kerlor, she spent most of her time in their room at the Brevoort Hotel, which was noted for its French cuisine, living on oysters and ice-cream because they were the cheapest items on the menu. One evening as she was stretched on the bed alone resting, her father materialized and sat down beside her. Neither he nor she moved. In silence she looked at his pale, drawn face as he gazed at her and then little by little faded from view. Next day, 26 October 1919, a cable arrived: Celestino Schiaparelli had died the day before. 'A light of knowledge, energy, rectitude and benevolence has been extinguished,' mourned the Roman daily *Il Piccolo Giornale* on the front page. 'Thus I lost my strongest attachment,' Elsa wrote. 'In the realm of love, everything is possible. Perhaps at the moment of death we are granted a last wish before taking the next step in our destiny. Is the body, upon reaching the wilderness of the end, allowed to stop and look back for a second at the most loved person or the most in need? Thus my father visited me to give me strength and courage.' She would require both.

The only child Elsa was to have, a girl, given the name of Yvonne but to become known as 'Gogo', came into the world with considerable difficulty. Before fading from the picture entirely, Kerlor had the name Radha added to her birth certificate in memory of the goddess who had brought manna to Buddha under the banyan tree. Elsa was now almost thirty, a forsaken wife without a profession, an almost penniless foreigner in a tough town in an alien land, and without any faith to cling to. In the strugggle to keep her baby and herself she had no alternative but to master her loneliness and fear. Coinciding with the death of her father, the disintegration of her marriage freed her for ever of any dominating influence, masculine or otherwise. Disillusion and bitterness – and the need of money – obliged her to repress her natural sensitivity and shyness. Thus began the hardening process which ultimately transformed vulnerable Elsa into the impregnable 'Schiap' of fame and fortune.

5

Gaby and Gogo

SEVEN years earlier, in 1913, when Elsa left Italy for England, apparently unrelated events on the American side of the Atlantic were conspiring to shape her destiny. The first International Exhibition of Modern Art, the most scandalous, important and exciting art exhibition ever held in the United States, was opened in New York City on 17 February in the enormous barracks of the 67th Infantry Regiment at 26th Street and Lexington Avenue. Old Europe overwhelmed the New World with an avalanche of intellectual, incomprehensible works by witty, anarchic artists. Among the most controversial were two who had themselves brought their paintings over from France, Marcel Duchamp and Francis Picabia. The latter, a childhood friend of Paul Poiret, was accompanied by his wife, Gabrielle.

Remaining in New York during the ensuing war, Duchamp and Picabia, with 'Gaby' in attendance, formed the nucleus of a small artistic group; like Gaby, this coterie was to be of great importance to Elsa. It included Alfred Stieglitz, the revolutionary American artist-photographer. At 291 Fifth Avenue he organized exhibitions in the pointedly named Photo-Secessionist Gallery, also called 291 Gallery, which he managed as well as owned, and he put out a correspondingly ultra-modern magazine, *Camera Work*. In his circle were the great originators of fashion photography: a European refugee lionized in Paris, Baron Adolf de Meyer; the American Edward Steichen, born in Luxemburg and brought into Paris fashion by Paul Poiret; and young Man Ray, fresh from Philadelphia.

Meanwhile, on the other side of the Atlantic, exiles, agitators and artists took refuge in neutral Switzerland. In Zurich one day in 1916, a group of shock-method painters stuck a penknife into a French dictionary. It hit 'dada' (defined as a fixation, or child language for a horse), and Dada became the name of their new movement. No correspondence or communication existed between Zurich Dada and the anti-art Parisians in New York, Duchamp and Picabia, but when Picabia returned with Gaby to France soon after the Armistice and happened to visit Zurich, he realized the similarities, united the

Elsa always admired Baron de Meyer's work, even after others had decided that he was outmoded. This photograph by him shows the Peiping (Peking) red quilted cape, worn here over a grey satin sheath, in which Elsa startled the audience at a concert at the Théâtre des Champs-Elysées in 1933.

two currents and in 1920 brought Dada to Paris. All this was to have a bearing on Elsa's future.

Gabrielle Picabia, a musician in her own right, was an intelligent, perceptive and generous woman. In 1919, estranged from her husband and needing money to raise their children, she returned to the United States. She was counting on friends she had made there during her previous stay to support her new business, selling Paris-designed clothes in New York, especially those of Nicole Groult, Paul Poiret's youngest sister and competitor, with whom Gaby had become friendly through her husband. Aboard *L'Espagne* she met Comte and Comtesse de Kerlor. Elsa reminded her of a Burne-Jones woman looking dreamily into the past, the fitting companion of a magus, as she put it. Gaby also observed that while the young Italian deferred to her husband, she was well informed about the arts, though her knowledge was mostly academic, and could speak intelligently if briefly, in excellent French and picturesque English, about Fauvism, Cubism and Futurism – no mean achievement to the mind of the older Frenchwoman, who had lived in the centre of these movements in Paris before the war.

During the following months in New York, Gaby failed to work up a clientele for her Paris models. Appealing to her friends for contacts, she spoke to an elderly American doctor, who said he was taking an interest in the plight of a new patient, a well-born Italian woman with many contacts who might be able to help Gaby find customers. When he mentioned her name, Comtesse Kerlor, Gaby remembered her with pleasure from the Atlantic crossing, and the doctor brought them together. Elsa, the Frenchwoman found, was much thinner. A sharp scrutiny had replaced the dreamy look. No longer dressed in an extravagant way, she had cut her hair short and had adopted a manner that was brisk and to the point. She was living in a cheap hotel where, unable to afford a pram, she put her baby in the sunshine on the fire escape in an orange-crate obtained from the grocer next door. Gaby asked Elsa to work with her, offered her a share of her own room at the Brevoort, and found a nursery for the baby.

Gaby had struck up relations again with the little artistic circle she had previously frequented in New York: Marcel Duchamp and Alfred Stieglitz and his group, which still included Baron de Meyer, Edward Steichen and Man Ray. She introduced Elsa into their midst. Charmed by her intellectual inquisitiveness, warmth and humour, they adopted her. De Meyer let her pore over the files of his impressionistic work. Steichen sharpened her visual appreciation of modern architecture by showing her how to look at the studies of Manhattan structures that had inspired him, particularly the curious Flatiron Building, then the symbol of skyscrapers. Man Ray had just published the one and only issue of *New York Dada* and, with Duchamp and Katherine Dreier, was now founding La Société Anonyme, the first American organization designed to promote

If Schiaparelli was drawn to the Surrealists, they were also attracted to the bold clarity of her lines as shown in this Daliesque photograph by André Durst.

modern arts. When he invited Elsa to take a hand in its launch by helping to draw up mailing lists of prospective members and to make arrangements for the first meeting and exhibitions, an entire new artistic direction opened up for her.

The business association between Gaby and Elsa was not a happy one. The Frenchwoman's modest methods did not suit her Italian assistant, who saw things in much more ambitious terms. Elsa's contacts demanded a wider choice of garments than Gaby had available. Moreover, she wanted a more spectacular promotional set-up than Gaby's finances permitted, and she possessed persuasion and patience that the other annoyingly lacked. However, they finally sold all their clothes and Gaby returned to Paris, but her influence on her associate's life was far from over.

Elsa's struggle for existence once more became desperate. To pay the mounting hotel bills, she swallowed her pride and wrote to her mother in Rome for help. When a little allowance started to arrive, she put her baby into the hands of an old nurse in a cottage in the woods near Stamford, Connecticut, believing that the fresh air and natural surroundings would do her good. Patchen Place, Greenwich Village, with its crooked houses and rows of trees, reminded her of Paris and London. There she took a room so small that when she had filled it with dilapidated European antiques, she had to sit on the bed to dress.

Right after the war, America's pent-up culture exploded in Greenwich Village, which became a centre of English-speaking literary work. Elsa was surrounded by artists, writers, intellectuals, theatre people and poets, and among these she made many new bohemian friends.

To make ends meet during the winter of 1920-21, Elsa did translations and part-time work for importing houses, then managed to get herself hired by a Wall Street broker to watch the ticker-tape. That job did not last long, as her reports of share movements kept reflecting unexpected, dangerous and wholly inaccurate shocks to the market. For a short period she helped out at the American Relief Association which, headed by future President Herbert Hoover, was raising funds to feed ten million starving Russians.

In time she made the acquaintance of the soprano Ganna Walska, a flaming Polish beauty who was tone-deaf and married only millionaires willing to back her operatic career. The singer was to perform in Havana and, delighted by the prospect of some warm weather, Elsa agreed to accompany her there. Elsa loved Cuba, where she found Spanish rigidity counterbalanced by a graceful sense of humour – which did not, however, prevent Cuban music-lovers from howling the Pole off the stage and out of the country. Several years later, Ganna Walska became the owner of the magnificent Théâtre des Champs-Elysées in Paris, and Madame Schiaparelli often had to invent excuses for declining invitations to her former employer's unintentionally hilarious recitals. This did not prevent

her from welcoming the singer as a customer, and when Ganna Walska died (at the age of ninety-nine) she left her stupendous wardrobe, which included numerous Schiaparellis, to the Los Angeles County Museum.

Upon Elsa's return to New York early in the spring of 1921, Stieglitz told her about some wonderful new experiments in colour photography for the movies, and she got a stand-in job in some New Jersey studios. Here her eyes were burned so badly that she remained blind for days, which did not help her sinking morale. Mercifully, a benevolent soul lent her a well-provisioned cottage in Woodstock, New York, for a few weeks of peace and rest. At that time Woodstock was a fashionable resort for artists, and Elsa soon struck up a friendship with a young Italian tenor from the Metropolitan Opera. He too was unhappy because of a broken marriage, and in each other they found respite and even some measure of happiness. It lasted only until the singer's wife arrived, charging adultery. Shortly afterwards he died suddenly of meningitis. Elsa saw to all the formalities and funeral arrangements, for his wife, certain of inheriting, had vanished.

During this winter of 1921-22 Gaby Picabia returned to New York with some new Nicole Groult gowns and, despite past differences, enlisted Elsa's assistance anew. On her return to Paris, Elsa supplemented the small allowance she received from her mother by selling, from her home, dresses consigned to her by other Paris houses through Gaby Picabia's influence. Unfortunately, she could not reach any wide buying public with such expensive originals, and the representations dwindled to an end.

Alone once more, Elsa began to feel the pinch of poverty again: the little she received from home went to the baby's nurse, and she herself was often without the money for food. Everything now seemed drab and hopeless. She became profoundly depressed, but she had not touched rock bottom yet. Her baby began to toddle but oddly, like a crab. Elsa consulted a specialist, who diagnosed infantile paralysis. No treatment would be good enough for Gogo, who was to endure operations, plaster casts and crutches for over ten years. All of it had to be paid for.

The soaring vertical planes of New York's buildings made a lasting impact on Elsa and were to be mirrored in many of her designs.

6

Poverty, Paris and Paul Poiret

IN EARLY 1922 Elsa had been in New York for three years. By then at the end of her tether, she felt that the doors of life had banged shut against her and her ailing baby. But she was mistaken, for at this lowest point the opportunity arose for her to return to Paris. During the previous summer in Woodstock a young American woman, Blanche Hays, had rented the house next to Elsa's. Blanche, also upset over an unhappy marriage and also having an only daughter to raise, understood and sympathized with her neighbour, whom she found colourful, artistic and intelligent. During the miserable winter that followed, Blanche became Elsa's confidante and refuge.

Blanche had for some time been wanting a Paris divorce but, having little French, hesitated to go to France alone. Combining forces with Elsa seemed the natural solution to both their problems, particularly since living in France was so cheap by American standards that Blanche's substantial private income would keep both of them. They sailed in June 1922. 'If I have become what I am,' the head of the House of Schiaparelli was quoted as declaring in *Constellation* for March 1954, 'I owe it to two distinct things – poverty and Paris. Poverty forced me to work, and Paris gave me a liking for it and courage.'

Gaby Picabia invited Elsa and Gogo to stay with her until they got settled, while Blanche and her daughter Lora went to a hotel. Through Gaby, Elsa found a French doctor who suggested that Gogo should live with him and his family so that she could have, under the most favourable conditions, the daily electric treatments that she needed. This arrangement worked very well, and Gogo lived happily for several years in this family, who loved her dearly. Elsa's allowance from her mother was enough to cover the expense, and Blanche lent her whatever little she needed in addition.

Maria-Luisa was delighted at the prospect of welcoming her prodigal daughter back to Europe and helping to care for her baby granddaughter. Elsa duly hurried down to see her mother and rediscover Rome with Blanche and Lora, but she refused to remain in

When Mrs Reginald (Daisy) Fellowes, one of the world's best-dressed women, wrote a long fashion article for Femina *in February 1938, she devoted several pages to Schiaparelli, with particular emphasis on her use of embroidery. Here a black woollen evening cape (above) is embroidered with heavy sequined bows, the jacket of an evening suit in dark green velvet (right) has gold embroidery in deep relief, and on the collar of the black wool suit (right, above) are sunbursts of gold and strass.*

Italy. Doing so might have solved her material problems, but for Elsa it was important to go on fighting to be free, no matter how hard that might prove. Back in Paris, she and Blanche found a large, old-fashioned, furnished apartment on the Boulevard Latour-Maubourg near the Eiffel Tower and not far from Gogo, where Elsa engaged a cook and a maid and ran the household.

Although Elsa enjoyed the pleasant months of theatres, concerts, art shows and small dinner parties that followed, she was anxious to reduce her dependency on Blanche. Always prompt to lend a helping hand, Gaby introduced her to a clever antique dealer who began taking her with him to auction sales and antique shops in Paris and the provinces; soon he allowed her to go on her own. To help out with the bills for Gogo's treatment and the costs of the divorce from Kerlor, Maria-Luisa gave Elsa Celestino's superb coin collection to sell, and Gaby put her in touch with a French businessman who bought it for a good price. Soon Gogo had improved so much that she could go out for short walks.

Through Blanche, Elsa soon realized, she would only remain within the confines of the American colony, and she was keen to meet Parisians, artists and foreigners. Once again Gaby came to the rescue. She brought Elsa into the Dada group, by now in decline. Elsa already knew Marcel Duchamp and she now met Gaby's ex-husband and life-long companion, Francis Picabia, as well as Tristan Tzara, the Swiss-born founder of Dada, and his group of poets and writers. It was Man Ray who first escorted her to the den of international sophisticated debauchery then in vogue, Le Bœuf sur le Toit. This was a bar plus a tiny dance floor promoted by the young Jean Cocteau, who fifteen years later was to design embroidery for Schiaparelli as well as being the most sensitive and perceptive contemporary analyst of her place in fashion. Le Bœuf, the pulse of Les Années Folles and the granddaddy of gay bars, had little black columns, a ceiling of iridescent glass and Raoul Dufy lithographs on the walls; behind the bar was Picabia's *L'Œil Cacodylate*, named after a patent medicine, an eye-like montage of unrelated inscriptions signed by the artist's friends.

Many people who were to figure prominently in Elsa's life frequented Le Bœuf. Here in a red sweater was Picasso, who would one day paint an allegorical picture of her. There in a black-sequined man's dinner jacket was the Honourable Mrs Reginald (Daisy) Fellowes, heiress of the Singer sewing machine millions, the best-dressed woman in Europe and the fashion leader of Paris. Nearby was Nancy Cunard, the most flamboyant siren and man-eater among the post-war English exiles. Both women were to leave Chanel for Schiaparelli. There was Chanel herself, Maurice Chevalier, André Gide, Artur Rubinstein, Prince Youssoupoff (who had killed Rasputin) and the Prince of Wales, the future Edward VIII, for whom Elsa had felt a weakness since living in London ten years before. There too was Igor Stravinsky, who had acquired some jazz band instruments; while presiding over Les Six, a group of innovative young composers, was Erik Satie, whose introduction of the sounds of contemporary life into music – typewriters, movie set clap-sticks, lottery wheels, factory whistles, steamship and automobile horns – appealed to the young woman about to bring like objects into fashion.

Paul Poiret, returning to civilian life after the ruinous war years, had proceeded to capitalize on everything he had left in order to finance the reopening of his business. For several summers he ran the Oasis, a night club and then theatre, in the vast garden of his eighteenth-century mansion. Knowing that Gaby, the ex-wife of his old friend Picabia, needed money, he asked her to receive for him

Although Jean Cocteau drew compulsively all his life, it took Elsa Schiaparelli to persude him to sketch designs for embroidery. The typical Cocteau profile on this coarse linen jacket has flowing hair of gold bugle beads and sequins. Note the artist's signature embroidered to lower right of the jacket.

there in the summer of 1922. But she had only one evening gown, dating from before the war. Elsa, though inexpert in dressmaking, offered to make a new gown for her. It was little in itself, but it did so much for Gaby that Poiret noticed the change and asked her to compliment the 'designer'. Encouraged by the great Poiret's reaction and unable to afford expensive clothes, Elsa decided to make some simple dresses for herself. Although she knew nothing about dressmaking, she proved to have a flair, for these clothes turned out to be quite presentable. The climax came when she browbeat Blanche Hays into sewing a coat for herself. Blanche never forgot watching her lay some grey cloth on the dining-room table and cut into it without a pattern. The coat ended up as a full-length one lined with patterned silk. Elsa solved the problem of obvious defects in her cutting and Blanche's sewing of the neck and shoulders by cunningly hiding them under a shawl collar of long-haired grey fur.

For evening Elsa wears a knitted beret interwoven with metal thread.

Blanche's satisfaction with the coat and the compliments of friends encouraged Elsa in some ideas she was beginning to entertain about being able to invent clothes. She dashed off some sketches and with them approached a few people in haute couture. Among these, at the house of Maggy Rouff, was a gentleman who told her she would do better to plant potatoes! At this discouraging point a rich American friend of Blanche's asked Elsa to act as a guide on a buying spree of clothes. Naturally this had to include the latest Poirets, and Elsa asked Gaby to call the great man's secretary to make sure that they would be given good seats at a showing.

Paul Poiret's collection, the first collection Elsa had ever seen, was a riot of colour and invention that remained alive in her memory for ever. After the show, waiting behind the scenes for the American woman who had decided to try on some of the clothes, Elsa stared moonstruck at the models hanging on a rack. Gingerly she fingered them, thrilling to the texture. Then, with a daring she could never later explain, she slipped into a coat of large, loose-cut velvet – black, with vivid stripes and lined with bright blue crêpe de Chine. As she gazed at herself in it, feeling glorious, she sensed that someone was watching her. Turning, she saw Paul Poiret himself standing there. Smiling broadly, he said, 'Why don't you buy it? It might have been made just for you.'

That magnificent coat, made for the plain woman she thought she was! 'I cannot buy it,' she replied. 'It is certainly too expensive, and where could I wear it?'

'Don't worry about money,' said Poiret (who never did himself), 'and *you* could wear anything anywhere.' With a charming bow he offered her the coat.

Being appreciated by this connoisseur of women overwhelmed Elsa as much as the gift. But Poiret, superbly generous as he was, did not stop there, especially when he learned that she was the one who had designed Gaby's evening dress. He befriended her. Over the years he lavished enchanting clothes on her whenever and for whatever occasion she needed them – and when she did not – so that she soon possessed a large Poiret wardrobe which she kept into old age.

It is no mere coincidence that Paul Poiret played such a significant part in the life and career of Elsa Schiaparelli. Who was more suitable to be his successor in originality, intelligence and sympathy for the avant-garde? 'For colours,' *Harper's Bazaar* would comment in November 1934, 'she is the feminine Paul Poiret.' Her friend and benefactor was long dead by the time Elsa wrote her autobiography in 1954. Yet she took pains to acknowledge her personal debt to him, to note the ideas which she had borrowed from him and which had contributed to her success, and to insist on according him the accolade of 'the Leonardo of Fashion' – this in a profession riddled by envy, spite, satisfaction over the misfortunes of rivals, and easy ungratefulness.

Overleaf: Schiaparelli caught much of her friend Paul Poiret's exuberance for rich colours and materials, as shown in the bold chequer-board evening coat in satin and velvet and the striped taffeta and satin evening dress with cape and bustle. The rich velvet evening gown (far right) was a 1950s development of a practical wartime idea – the Transformable Dress.

7

'Display No. 1'

THE First World War gave women the role in life for which they had been rehearsing since the 1890s. While the men were at the front, they learned to be independent and assumed new responsibilities, driving ambulances, nursing, running their husbands' or brothers' businesses. After the war they saw no reason to relinquish these gains and started defending their new right to a permanent place in what threatened to become a man's world once again. They wanted to walk and move briskly, hop easily in and out of vehicles and change clothes only once a day, in the evening. So, while maintaining the long and slender pre-war Poiret silhouette, couturiers of the twenties simplified fashions and placed the accent on youth, simplicity and freedom of movement, shortening skirts and cutting them on the bias.

There were sound financial reasons for changing the styles. Of the major industries in France, dressmaking – which brought in eighty million francs annually in exports before 1914 – suffered the most from the increased cost of labour caused by the war. Tailors demanded twenty-five per cent rises in salary, seamstresses went on strike. A yard of velvet that formerly cost six to eight francs might now only be had for twenty-five or thirty; and the price of silks, worsteds, woollen goods, linen and ribbons had risen to a similar degreee. Since manufacturers did not dare to increase the prices of finished products proportionately, their profits diminished. The cost of cloth naturally intensified research into the possibilities of artificial fabrics.

Little wonder therefore that Poiret's splendour now became excessive and his star waned. Later he would say that Jean Patou was the challenger who had done him the most harm. Patou dominated the twenties, although it was Coco Chanel who, in popularizing them, came to personify their spirit. Patou drew his clientele from the sporty international café society, whereas Chanel catered to the young and not so young women who wanted to look modern. Chanel viewed her customers, exemplified by the erratic and bohemian Nancy Cunard, as youthful, uncomplicated thorough-

The mermaid outline of these early Schiaparelli designs is amusingly echoed in this drawing by Charles Martin for Harper's Bazaar, *1930. The black velvet suit on the left has a vest blouse in white antelope with a shawl collar. The three-quarter length coat in heavy black serge with a standing collar of shaved lamb accompanies a dress in lighter serge with insets of black crêpe de Chine.*

breds, ready for any sporting activity; sleek and asexual, with hair bobbed and hips and breasts flattened, they blended coolly into their environment. Chanel's clothes were designed to be worn all day and thus to look appropriate on all sorts of occasions. They were made of Linton tweed and silk jersey fabrics which moved with the body and were supremely practical because they did not crease.

During the twenties only one factor – an entirely new one – influenced fashion more than art: women's growing participation in sports. Rarely has the theory that the popular sportswear of today becomes the town and country wear of tomorrow been better illustrated. It all started with Suzanne Lenglen, the great tennis player. Emerging in 1921, she replaced Madame Poiret as the typical twentieth-century woman, adding an athletic note to the slim, elegant, androgynous figure. Before Suzanne, women who played tennis wore instep-length dresses over corsets and starched petticoats, and their hair was firmly covered with a hat. An elongated mousy brunette, Suzanne was transformed by Jean Patou into the *élégante* who led to 'la Garçonne' and to women trying to look as if they had scarcely emerged from puberty. She came running out on to public tennis courts in a white dress with no petticoat, the pleated skirt fluttering barely below her knees, and on top a short-sleeved vest adapted from a man's cloth waistcoat, her white silk stockings held up by garters above the knees and an orange or green bandeau à la Denise Poiret round her hair.

Sportswear first became smart in the form of a two-piece dress with a calf-length skirt. Thanks to Patou and Chanel, its role was soon widened. Patou developed his tennis sweater into Cubist sweaters, then adapted Cubism to all sportswear, later extending the craze to sports accessories and bathing costumes made from a new unshrinkable jersey. He introduced twinsets, added skirts and accessories to the sweaters and launched the knitting industry. The machine-made knitted sweater in silk or soft wool responded perfectly to the many practical demands of modern elegance and could be combined with skirts in an almost infinite number of ways.

The only point of similarity between Chanel and Schiaparelli is that both their extraordinary careers began with this emblem of the twenties, the sweater. In the mountains with Blanche Hays during the winter of 1923-24 Elsa was dissatisfied with her unbecoming appearance in the sports clothes available. What could she do? All ready-made sweaters looked awful on her and the custom-made ones were too expensive. She designed her first sweater for herself. It was in black and white, and when she appeared in it, the colour combination was hailed by her friends and acquaintances as a happy novelty in sportswear. An American friend of Blanche's, a Mrs Hartley, wanted to invest in a French business; impressed by the success of Elsa's sweater, she persuaded her to produce a small collection, mainly of sports clothes. In late 1925 she bought a tiny dress house, Maison Lambal, located not far from Place Vendôme on the corner of rue Saint Honoré and rue du 29 Juillet.

'Part of the enchantment of Paris in the twenties,' Scott Fitzgerald remarked, 'was that everything which happened there seemed to have something to do with art.' But in the early twenties, artists in Europe and even the United States, weary of the nervous rapidity of pre-war trends – Futurism, Expressionism, Cubism – were doubting the value of modernist experimentation. Perhaps, they began to think, the usual and commonplace were not so ugly and boring after all. Might it not be intelligent to make the best of things as they were? They began reverting to realism, in Dada, in geometrical abstraction, in Surrealism. In what came to be known as the New Realism – that aspect of the general movement glorifying machines and using axles, valves, nuts, bolts and so on, satirized by Charlie Chaplin in *Modern Times* (1936) – they mirrored the technical invasion of the environment. In Paris, Salvador Dali used watches graphically to suggest the uncanny, while Picabia was elevating machines to the level of works of art and Fernand Léger was putting finishing touches to factories. As artists they transformed the mundane; it became interesting, and the next logical step was to

A startling colour combination for the ski slopes in this highly practical but elegant outfit of topcoat, knee breeches, jerkin with front pockets, and Peruvian chullo hood.

commercialize it and, in so doing, glorify it. Of this trend Elsa Schiaparelli was the most brilliant example. Influenced by the Italian Futurists in her youth, impressed in the United States by the objects and gadgets of modern daily life, she would introduce the banal into fashion and, by an indefinable personal magic, work it into something beautiful, compelling, even mysterious.

In 1925 the Exposition des Arts Décoratifs et Industriels Modernes, 'Art Deco', was opened in Paris, a stupendous exhibition that brought to the notice of many millions of visitors the new developments in the decorative arts and demonstrated their application to industrial products. The basic aim was to persuade the French to buy French and to revitalize exports, but the exhibition had far-reaching effects. Romantic in spirit though businesslike in appearance, it marked both a renewal and a point of departure in the vigorous search for an authentic twentieth-century style of living. It sought to reconcile man and machine to ensure greater harmony, concerting the efforts of past antagonists – engineers and architects, artists and artisans – to combine beauty, efficiency and economic necessity, and apply them to industry. Art Deco stressed the practical and functional: the style was classical, symmetrical and rectilinear. Much of it reflected the geometric forms which had so impressed Elsa in New York City.

At the 1900 Paris World Fair, French elegance was represented by twenty-one couturiers. At the Art Deco exhibition twenty-five years later there were seventy-two. Fashion had been recognized on an artistic level.

When one considers the long list of dressmakers in Paris at the time, it is a tribute to Elsa's inventiveness that *Women's Wear Daily* in January 1926 devoted a whole article to Maison Lambal's sports models and daytime ensembles. In words that summed up, even at this early stage, the Schiaparelli style, the article went: 'The collection, although not large, is carefully conceived and executed. Each mode maintains an individuality and reveals interest. They are all simple and direct with very fine detail work and pleasing colour combinations.' Public attendance and reactions were also pleasing, but Mrs Hartley, the sponsor, soon realized that continuing to finance a dress house with Elsa, who could not see things in any way but big, was beyond her modest means, and she closed down the business.

For once adversity did not cause Elsa to despair. If she had not made much money for her work, it had paid off in other ways: she had proved something to herself and to others. Several people who had seen the collection offered to back her in her own business, and as a sleeping partner she chose M. Kahn, a successful businessman, because he was French, knew about fashion through being associated in the backing of Vionnet, and had large holdings in the Galéries Lafayette department store.

Elsa had by this time left Blanche and was living in her own small apartment, two rooms on two floors in a former eighteenth-century mansion at 20 rue de l'Université near St Germain-des-Prés. Here in January 1927 she spread out on tables and held up for show by hand her 'Display No. 1'. Although confined to what was to become known as 'spectator sportswear', the limited number of articles anticipated the Schiaparelli revolutions in handiwork, materials,

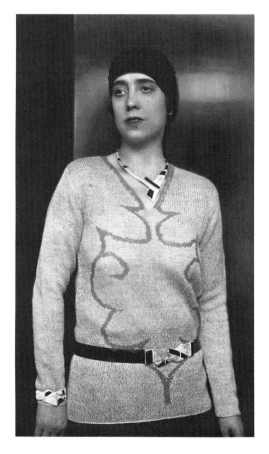

Elsa goes Art Deco: the geometrical design of one of her new sweaters is echoed in the metal accessories she wears.

colours, designs and accessories. Emboldened by Poiret's example and her own origins, she had tossed in the bright canary, deep ochre and rich orange of the Latium sun in a protest against the sober pastels, beiges and navies then in vogue. The sweaters, unlike Patou's and Chanel's, were hand-made and would soon prove to be so popular that all the great couturiers copied the idea. In several of these she made her first revolutionary use of the emerging materials of the century with 'kasha'; this very elastic new woollen fabric, just patented by Rodier and introduced by Patou, was resistant to wear and tear and designed to make the figure appear slimmer. To the by now somewhat over-familiar pullover or sweater she added cardigans, perking them up with the first of her striking buttons. Then, exploiting the idea of interchangeable separates whose possibilities she had realized as a girl in Rome, she added knitted jackets, and skirts generally of crêpe de Chine in colours matching the sweaters. The scarf became an integral part of the sweater, an innovation of her own. She also offered matching scarves and socks that repeated the sweater design on their cuff. Metal thread was woven into the knit to lend a slightly sparkling effect to the surface and gold and silver thread was combined with the wool to suggest brocade.

'Display No. 1', modest as it was, reflected Schiaparelli's Futuristic convictions. The speed of the automobile, the locomotive and the aeroplane was modifying the way objects registered on one's sight. For maximum impact on a viewer tearing past something – whether a billboard or a smartly dressed woman standing on the pavement – lines had to be simpler, forms bolder and colours stronger. Schiaparelli's were. 'Display No. 1' also, in its simple practicality and use of artistically treated fabrics, announced her coming contribution to the new relationship between artists, craftsmen and industry pioneered by Art Deco. In her designs she used spots, revived balanced patterns and combined ultra-modern geometrical abstractions and Futuristic treatments with the stark simplicity and angularity then being taken from Cubism by the decorative artists of the period. Some of her articles had asymmetrical arrangements of stripes, others motifs in the form of diagonal lines, others had the horizontal and vertical lines – the grid structure inspired by Mondrian and Manhattan – in contrasting colours forming rectangles.

As patrons were not coming to 20 rue de l'Université thick and fast enough to satisfy her, Elsa went out in search of them. Sometimes she lugged suitcases full of sweaters to display to foreign visitors in their hotel suites. But already French *Vogue* had scented a newcomer to be watched. In February 1927, scarcely a month after she had presented 'Display No. 1', it devoted a page of photographs by the great Hoyningen-Huené to her designs, and only six months later, a full page of sketches. Customers started to swarm to her.

'I have to move into something bigger,' she told M. Kahn, her backer.

'Very well. We'll find a shop for you in a nice neighbourhood.'

'I want to be on rue de la Paix.'

'Not to begin with?'

'Yes, to begin with. I don't care how small, but it is rue de la Paix or nothing.'

On 1 January 1928 she moved to 4 rue de la Paix. Here, in a sordid garret, were the tiny bedroom, sitting-room, workroom and salesroom in which for the next seven years she would combine living with work. The ceilings hung low. The rooms, equipped with fitful coal stoves, were cold in winter and, under the sun-drenched roof, boiling in summer. Rats and mice scampered around her bed. She got a small fox terrier to keep them away, but he was even more terrified of them than she was, and at the first squeak of a mouse crawled into bed with her. As she had no fitting rooms, she put up some screens; as she had no chairs, customers were obliged to stand around a table on which her wares were displayed. And as the lift in the building never worked, they were already exhausted from having toiled up six flights of steep, narrow stairs.

As soon as she earned some money, Elsa had the place decorated simply: pure white walls with black furnishings and brilliant carpets. On the front door she hung up her name in what was now the typical Schiaparelli colour combination, black and white, adding below, 'Pour le Sport'. In February 1928 French *Vogue* carried her first advertisement, a quarter page in the form of a simple black block with white lettering, 'Schiaparelli Sweaters Tous les Sports', on a wide white background. In the same month, the New York *Sun* pointed out that Schiaparelli was now showing items other than sweaters – frocks, bathing suits, shantung seaside pyjamas and tailored jackets featuring geometric and futuristic patterns, some suggesting an insert belt or collar. Even the lofty *New Yorker* announced her coming 'Display No. 2', adding, 'She is hardly established and is a good bet as a growing influence on the Paris world of sport.'

8

Trompe-l'œil

ONE DAY in April 1927 Elsa noticed a smart American woman in Paris wearing an unusual knitted pullover. Though plain, it was different from anything she had ever seen: it had a steady, consistent appearance and, while elastic, did not stretch and so lose its shape like ordinary sweaters. This she found was due to the unusual stitch, for although the knitting had been done with the normal two needles and two identical strands of wool, these were not intertwined but were caught up at every fourth stitch by a third needle. Thus one strand remained underneath, reinforcing the other like a sort of lining.

'Who did this knitting, please?' Elsa asked the startled American.

'An Armenian peasant, a refugee from the Turkish massacres in East Anatolia.'

'Would it be possible for me to meet her?'

A meeting was arranged and the woman, knowing only her native tongue, appealed to a fellow-Armenian who spoke English and understood knitting techniques to come and translate. This was Aroosiag Mikaëlian, a young girl who was to become Elsa's mascot. 'Mike' (so nicknamed by Elsa for obvious reasons) had been spared from death by the Turks because she was enrolled in the local American high school and they concluded that she was a foreigner. The American Relief Committee had spirited her away to safety with other orphans, and when she met Elsa she had just received a state diploma in England as a newly qualified nurse and was taking a short holiday before starting her first job.

As she discussed the 'Armenian stitch' with the two women, an idea hit Elsa: *trompe-l'œil.* 'Can you knit with two threads that are not of the same colour?'

'Yes, of course.'

'If I give you a design, could you copy it?'

'I don't know. I can try.'

In two minutes Elsa sketched a large butterfly bow to look like a scarf tied round the neck and requested in the knitting a white overweave on a black ground with white underneath. The first try:

To Dr Charitzher Elsa Schiaparelli

lopsided. The second: unattractive. The third: sensational. Besides the unusual and intriguing effect of the *trompe-l'œil* bow, there was something smart about the way the white understitches showed discreetly through the black, breaking the monotony of the background.

Invited to lunch at the Ritz on an occasion when fashion leaders would be present, Elsa deliberately arrived late wearing the sweater. Conversation stopped as she proceeded to her place. ('My professional life,' she liked to say later, 'hung by a thread.') All the ladies present asked for copies and told their friends, but it was an order for forty copies from the buyer for Lord and Taylor Fifth Avenue that was the beginning of real business. There was one condition: they had to be ready for shipment in two weeks, along with forty matching skirts. Mike was already so struck with Elsa that, to help out, she temporarily gave up her plans to return to England. ('Temporarily' would be until Elsa's death.) She ransacked Paris for Armenian knitters, found half a dozen, organized and supervised their work in her little hotel room in a working-men's suburb and herself sewed up the sweaters. Deciding to eschew all fantasy in the skirts so that they would not divert attention from the sweaters, Elsa bought some sturdy, plain materials on sale at the Galéries Lafayette. The order was completed, shipped and paid for within the set time, and a sketch promptly appeared in American *Vogue* for 15 December 1927 with the words, 'artistic masterpiece'.

After designing some asymmetrical arrangements of stripes which caught the attention of the British magazine *Liberty* for 24 March 1928, Elsa quickly followed up the butterfly bow with designs of men's ties and perky handkerchiefs around the throat or hips. She went on to produce crossword puzzle and bridge sweaters with caps to match, noted by *Women's Wear Daily* for 17 September 1928, and bow knots which were sold by Wanamaker's in January 1929 for $19.50 a piece. As a variant she had the sweaters knitted with large needles to give a diaphanous effect hitherto unknown. Next, she combined the *trompe-l'œil* with a reality that was an extension of the knitting: a knitted-in handkerchief that had real ends tied on the side, a knitted-in belt with a genuine buckle. Within a year, rich women the world over were wearing the black and white, soft and cosy Schiaparelli *trompe-l'œil* sweater. At the four smart Knox the Hatter shops in New York a sweater set plus crêpe skirt and belt to match went like hot cakes for $95 – about $700 in 1986 – quite a price for a near unknown.

In the glow of success, Elsa felt that the moment had come to dare to be daring. Having followed her friends of Dada days into Surrealism, whose pictorial elements attracted her more than the expression of the subconscious, she touched off the first of her shocking effects by presenting the Schiaparelli skeleton sweater. This was patterned with white lines that reproduced the bone-structure of the thorax so that the wearer gave the appearance of being seen

Elsa wearing her innovative butterfly bow trompe-l'œil *sweater in 1927. The photograph is dedicated to Lilian Fisher (Farley), known as 'Dinarzade', the American Patou mannequin who became Paris editor of* Harper's Bazaar.

through an X-ray machine. The ladies of the Establishment were outraged, but the newspapers, which in those days usually took scant notice of fashion, cackled and crowed.

In the twenties, everything black came into vogue, thanks to the French Colonial Art Exhibition of 1922 which introduced the eroticism of African sculpture to a wider French if not international public. In 1925 the Art Deco exhibition reflected the influence of black African art on weaving, carpets, drapes and many other furnishings. This greatly appealed to Elsa, and she adapted the savage colours and forms to her hand-knitted sweaters, now sometimes collarless and cuffless. She added masks and idols from various countries in French Equatorial Africa, and magical symbols from the French Congo. She also incorporated into her sweaters designs of her own invention: one such, composed of pierced hearts and snakes, resembled the tattooing on a sailor's chest. She then used these sweaters as backgrounds for barbaric accessories, from which emerged the striking Schiaparelli-style jewellery. Still meant for sportswear alone, this consisted of carved, tinted and lacquered pieces (reflecting the Art Deco trend in the artistic treatment of new substances) and – a strikingly novel idea of Elsa's own – strand necklaces and bracelets made of horsehair.

'As for hand-knit sweaters,' reported the *New Yorker* for 15 February 1928, '... [the couturiers] all annexed the idea from Elsa Schiaparelli.' None became identified with them like the House of Schiaparelli, which never stopped producing the articles that had helped to make its name. But although they became world-famous and the demand was tremendous, Elsa was careful to maintain the snob value of owning one of these sweaters at the exorbitant prices, and accepted orders only for limited quantities. Progressively she expanded her handknits to the most unusual items: bathing suits, socks, sports jackets, sandals, long stockings, bonnets, gloves, skirts and even evening dresses. After she herself wore the first knitted turban in public, demand became such that she repeated it in cotton.

In due course Mike had a workroom of her own, and here – unheard of for knits – she fitted customers individually. At Elsa's request she improved on the Armenian stitch, and devised some new ones. She also mastered a very complicated construction that Elsa had found on a piece of seventeenth-century wool.

9

'Display No. 2'

Undressing this woman, posing provocatively in her new Bermudas, would in Cocteau's words be 'an undertaking tantamount to moving house'. As well as the long woollies covering her arms and legs, she wears a scarf that entirely masks her face and neck. On her head is a motorman's cap.

THE warming-up period was over. Now Elsa took the field. Her goal was to capture those who wintered on the Riviera or in Florida or southern California, or who went on winter cruises in sunny climes. She opened their eyes wide. Soon a surrealistic scarlet fish was seen wriggling on the stomach of a bright blue bathing suit, coupled with a beach robe in reversible scarlet shantung worn with hand-knitted wool slippers. These were the first items Elsa showed in late July 1928 in her 'Display No. 2', reviewed by the New York *Sun* on 4 August right after Vionnet's collection. And the rest of the beach ensembles – which, as before, she laid on tables or held up by hand – caused just as great a stir. Take for example a swimsuit in, of all fabrics, celanese, and accompanied by, of all features, a hooded cape. Or wrap-around skirts, which were to reappear in coats and dresses throughout the thirties. Or hand-knitted tunics with modernistic motifs and jersey shorts with a woven waistband designed for Saks Fifth Avenue: 'We moderns,' ran the Saks advertisement, 'have been eagerly awaiting their arrival.' Or divided skirts (later called culottes), destined, as 'play suits', to become a universal feature of sports clothes. All were accompanied by the startling hand-knitted pancake beret, thenceforward to be found in many forms, even for evening wear. These variations included the popular tam-o'-shanter and, in 1934, 'Luck', shaped like a horseshoe.

On the front, bathing suits sported patterns of anchors, stars, linked hearts and affectionate legends. That was surprising enough. But turn round! There was her 'nude sunburn back': a backline lowered almost to the last vertebra with transparent straps to let the shoulders tan smoothly, thus avoiding the hard line of brown and white that ruined *décolletages*. On Fifth Avenue in New York young women were soon streaming into James McCreery's, which sold the scandalous article in jersey copies for $12.75, whereas Patou's famous swimsuit went for $9.75.

The following season young Americans also went wild over one bathing costume that had straps looking like men's suspenders and

another consisting of four one-armhole half-dresses in four shades of tussor and tied on the side like an apron. 'Comfort, perfect suitability and undeniable smartness are qualities not often happily united in garments really designed for sports,' opined the *New York Herald* on 7 August 1928, a fortnight after Elsa had revealed 'Display No. 2', 'but all Schiaparelli sports clothes are admirably adapted to the use for which they are made.' Adding seduction to agility, she brought more original ideas into sportswear than all the other designers put together.

In its use of pigskin and ponyskin 'Display No. 2' foreshadowed the special Schiaparelli way with trimmings and linings. It also showed Schiaparelli's gift for applying a garment with a special association to a quite different use: for example the jodhpur suit, which featured riding breeches adapted to winter sports. 'Display No. 2' also introduced fabrics in forms never before connected with women's clothes, such as homespun trimmed with astrakhan, horse blanket for waistcoats (to be worn later with severe suits), whipcord, and a cellular cotton yoke previously confined to men's shirts.

In 'Display No. 2' Elsa announced a wide range of beauty products to come, with sponges bearing Tahitian patterns and cotton articles lined with white sponge. To accompany these, she launched her first perfume, 'S', in black and white packaging. Deliberately, she had chosen a fresh and invigorating fragrance to offset the somewhat insipid sweetness of most contemporary scents. Sold by Lord and Taylor Fifth Avenue for a bold $21 an ounce, 'S' represented absolutely new ideas which would only come into their own half a century later: it was unisex, and was designed not only for travel but for life in the open air, i.e. sports. Elsa also produced 'S' in an eau de cologne (later renaming both 'Schiap'), and this was followed only in 1933 by l'Eau de Lanvin and in 1969 by Patou's Eau de Sport until the idea finally caught on.

For 'Display No. 2' Elsa wanted to extend her scope from beach, sports and country clothes to suits and dresses for town wear. She therefore hired some cutters and fitters and took to dressmaking. Already she was commanding a new look: 'Up with your shoulders! Bring that bust back! What's that waist still doing down there? Raise it to its original place! Stop slinking and slouching, girls! Stand up straight, dammit!' Mischievously, she presented a white frock adorned surrealistically with two black man's gloves, one on the bosom, the other low on the back. She also enlarged on the possibilities of her interchangeable separates introduced in 'Display No. 1', notably, as described by *Harper's Bazaar* for 1928, in a six-piece ensemble – knitted coat, knitted waistcoat, Rodier kasha skirt, wool skirt, and skirt and culottes in crêpe de Chine. Another combination involved a jacket in three or four colours to be worn with a skirt in one of the colours. For the simple, fresh-looking jackets and skirts harmonizing with her sweaters, she used hand-woven fabrics so thick that they could stand up on their own.

A new look for the beach in 1931 – one-piece pyjamas in black jersey resembling knitted wool.

The first Schiaparelli fur appeared at this time. Not only did she use fur to line and trim, she faced long scarves with fur and turned up one end to form a muff. Next she launched scarves wholly of fur, sometimes formed into triangles. She herself wore one in public of ermine to go with a black tweed suit, a revolutionary idea. Franklin Simon and Co. of Fifth Avenue was featuring this as early as August 1928. Soon she was designing fur wraps and sports coats of lapin – rabbit sheared and dyed – for Saks Fifth Avenue, which ran an advertisement in *Women's Wear Daily* on 19 August 1928. The following month she presented an exquisite reversible coat of soft, shiny kid lined with black ribbed silk. French *Vogue* in October 1928 began talking about 'typical examples' of Madame Schiaparelli's 'personal techniques', and her 'mark of great originality'.

'Display No. 2' also marked the appearance of Schiaparelli tweeds: tailored ensembles of coat and dress sometimes of two thicknesses and two weights and astonishingly interwoven with reversible jersey. This latter was hailed by the Chicago *Tribune* on 27 January 1929, and the same month Best and Co. of New York advertised a copy of a Schiaparelli jacket suit in tweed for $79.50. Within a few months they could not get enough of it, while a Chanel sold for $65.00. To her tailored ensembles Elsa later added trousers, thus anticipating the mix-and-match separates that would usher in the eighties half a century later.

Elsa now started to prepare her first major collection to be shown in January 1929. Simultaneously Gogo, at school in Lausanne and so much better that she was learning to ski and ride, came down with a serious illness. Elsa, distraught, practically designed the collection in trains between Paris and Lausanne. But Gogo got better and the collection was a great success. A new life was beginning for Elsa at forty.

The Paris *Times* deemed Schiaparelli in February 1929 'one of the rare creators'. It would not be long before her tweed evening gowns would astound fashion, and by August 1929 American *Vogue* noted a tweed that looked like a stringy rag rug, while *Harper's Bazaar* in September 1929 had a drawing of a very strict blue and brown open weave bouclé tweed designed exclusively for the magazine. Then there appeared the first of the exquisite Schiaparelli wools, particularly tweeds dyed according to her own ideas.

Quick to sense her ever growing potential, in November 1929 *Harper's* sharp-eyed artists took care to note her addition of lovely, simple frocks. Only five months later, the magazine ran a full-page advertisement worded with extraordinary foresight: 'Schiaparelli Selects Hanan Shoes to uphold the body in the sculptural planes of the New Silhouette'.

Accessories were always of the greatest importance to Schiaparelli. From the beginning she had invented myriad ways of making scarves interesting, and in mid-1929 she hit American fashion headlines with her removable fox or astrakhan 'horse' collars and

Tweed gets red carpet treatment in this drawing by Bérard of Schiaparelli's new silhouette with rigid shoulders and neat-waisted jacket, worn with a nose-diving hat.

Bérard

slip-on-and-off scarf collars. In 1930 came thigh-length triple scarves often in vibrant red, white and blue, colours equally patriotic for both the French and Americans. Attached together at the back, they were twisted or braided all the way down the front, a style that persisted, or twisted thickly around the throat with perky tab ends standing out at the side. They could be worn with ski suits, tennis frocks and pyjamas. Later she added them to suits and coats, using fabrics as unusual for scarves as crêpe satin and crêpe de Chine. Customers clamoured for Schiaparelli scarves developed into capes (Elsa would do variations for over thirty years), for two long scarves worn either crossing the bodice of an evening dress or falling down the back in a graceful sash, and for the unheard-of scarf belts launched by Sheila Hennessey of the cognac manufacturing company.

American *Vogue* for 15 April 1931 described her necklace scarves as 'Schiaparelli's really brilliant invention'. Another scarf, in 1933, was made of puffy material and adapted to the wearer in her shop (a hitherto unknown service) by a fitter snipping from a bolt. Then customers went wild over her collars of white horsehair braid (and later of latex), which tied at the back and resembled a baby's bib. In 1934 she added them in flat decorative feathery wool plaques to jackets launched by Tallulah Bankhead. Yet another hit, in 1935, was a big fox-edged scarf hanging like a cape, to be manipulated according to mood.

The Mad Cap in 1930 also did much to spread Elsa's name. It was a tiny knitted cap like a tube that took whatever shape the wearer desired. It created a furore after being adopted by Ina Claire, the dazzling, sophisticated and best-dressed American actress. Elsa became so tired of seeing the Mad Cap reproduced that she almost wished she had never thought of it, despite its contribution to her bank account. From all the shop windows, including five- and ten-cent stores, at the corner of every street, from every bus, in town and country, the thing dogged her. One day she saw one endangering the breathing of a bald-headed baby in a pram, and that day she gave her staff orders to destroy every single one in stock, to refuse to sell it and never to mention it to her again. In time she had second monetary thoughts about it, however, and in mid-1933 presented its successor, the Crazy Coxcomb.

Opposite page: A velvet collar finishes off this militaristic suit of horseguards' cloth. The epaulettes (here of fringed wool), huge buttons, and hat worn over a snood are other typical Schiaparelli touches.

The Mad Cap, worn here by Katharine Hepburn.

10

A Comet in the Dark

SINCE the First World War the international economy had been tottering. Customs regulations were severe, taxes on luxury items high. The symptons of upheaval were everywhere apparent but nobody seemed to care, and all anyone talked about was rising prices, profits and marvellous investments. In the United States 'prosperity' was the keyword. In France the Parisians, intoxicated by the 'violent hope' (as Apollinaire called it) of eternal peace and excited by the mirage of a life without periodic devastations, were revolting against bourgeois stuffiness and hypocrisy by wallowing in an atmosphere in which collective love, homosexuality, drug addiction, alcoholism and unmotivated suicides were commonplace. The sobering climax came in 1924 with the depreciation of the franc by 280 per cent.

From then on the cosmopolitan French substituted anxiety for insouciance and tranquillizers for opium, while foreigners, particularly North Americans, flocked to Paris to buy up everything – dresses, accessories, jewels and divorces. The City of Light became the hub of the world for luxury businesses, attracting the foreign investments that hauled France out of its antiquated provincialism into the industrial twentieth century. Paris fashion blossomed. In 1925 clothes, furs, lingerie and fabrics were collectively number 2 on the list of French exports. Yet ten years later they were number 27. Why was this?

First, the style of the twenties contributed to a slowdown in production: the austerity of the tailored suit, the simplicity of the robe chemise, the absence of lace and embroideries, the disappearance of trimmings on hats. People tended no longer to change for the theatre. It was smart to dress modestly in contrast to the growing vulgar display of the nouveaux riches, and it was *dans le vent* ('in') to affect the 'snobbism of mashed potatoes'. Moreover, a growing number of women absorbed in work were finding a rapid and economical answer to their dressing needs in ready-to-wear. And finally, haute couture, in essence a luxury industry, became a victim of the economic crisis which hit the Western world like a hurricane at the end of the twenties.

On 'Black Thursday', 14 October 1929, the New York Stock Exchange came crashing down, ending the 'Decade of Illusion' and bringing in its wake to both sides of the Atlantic the greatest depression in the history of capitalism. In the following five years American tourists in Paris decreased by 75 per cent. Young people deserted the 'in' cafés of Montparnasse, while Montmartre was ancient history and Le Bœuf sur le Toit a sparsely patronized reminder of merriment that now seemed distasteful. All the night clubs closed. The streets were empty in early evening. The smart Plaza Athenée Hotel was so forsaken that the management invited people to stay: all such 'guests' had to do was tip the personnel so that these would not leave.

An unrelenting series of bugbears came to plague French exports in general and bring the luxury businesses in particular to the brink of ruin. Not only had these lost the customers who came to France, but heated nationalism broke out in those customers' homelands. 'Buy American!' 'Buy British!' they were told. Customs barriers soared to hitherto unscaled heights, and quotas became prohibitive. Trade interests even made the British boycott the few French items that their government still allowed to be imported. It was not long before French industries were dying off, factories were idle and thousands were out of work. Obviously fashion was not spared. At the mid-season showings in December 1929 there was not one of the New York Seventh Avenue buyers who, representing retailing interests, had been transforming haute couture from a group of small businesses catering to rich private clients into an international industry. During the following years haute couture had to use up millions of francs of accumulated profits in trying to save the wages of 300,000 cutters and sewers, 150,000 embroiderers, beaders, makers of lace, gloves, bags, shoes, furs, buttons and jewels, not to mention weavers, spinners, dyers, milliners and local dressmakers. All over the world, hundreds of thousands of copyists trembled at the threatened collapse of the forty or fifty leading Paris dress houses.

Against this dark background, Elsa Schiaparelli's comet-like rise seems only the more incredible. Actually, it is simple to understand. First, she annexed all the rich private customers in Paris and London. Then she monopolized the export market, taking advantage of the lessons she had learned during her stay in the United States to cater so cunningly for the vast American middle class, lower as well as upper, that practically single-handed she established the throwaway elegance which became part of the American woman's lifestyle. 'Probably more than any other person,' American *Vogue* stated on 20 August 1935, 'she is responsible for the feeling of spontaneous youth that has crept into everything.'

To consolidate and enhance her reputation following 'Display No. 2', Elsa realized that she needed free publicity – from word-of-mouth recommendations, gossip columns, celebrities in the public eye who were daring in the same way that she was. The theatre was

Down the staircase of the new Place Vendôme premises sweeps this haughty herald of spring 1935 in a blue felt Skylarker hat and a blue wool suit of pre-war Viennese military cut.

an excellent hunting ground. Now, what actress was the ideal Schiaparelli type? When looking at a woman, Elsa first scrutinized her legs, particularly the ankles. Then, as in the classical Egyptian silhouette, she required a long neck, broad shoulders and slim hips. Of the stars of the French stage at the time, the only one who possessed the necessary physique, as well as a keen intelligence and sparkling wit, was Arletty. Fittingly enough, Arletty had begun her career as a mannequin for Poiret and had been first dressed in the theatre by him. Elsa approached her backstage one night and she agreed to come and have a look. After the visit Arletty left Lanvin for Schiaparelli.

Wooing famous actresses was one thing, but in the twenties leaders of high society disdained to appear in fashion magazines. The breakthrough for Elsa, however, came almost at once. American *Vogue* featured a sketch of the young Duchess of Sutherland in a black and white Schiaparelli frock in May 1928, three months before 'Display No. 2'. French *Vogue* for December 1928 published a sketch of young Comtesse M. de Polignac in a Schiaparelli ensemble that included a dress with a geometric design on the front and one of the new scarves. In December 1930 it followed with another sketch, of Princess Pignatelli, and then in December 1931 the mighty Comtesse Sixte de Bourbon-Parme was shown in two pages of Schiaparelli sketches.

By now Elsa's originality and audacity had also attracted the Hon. Mrs Reginald (Daisy) Fellowes, who abandoned Chanel for her. One of the great hostesses on the Paris scene, as outspoken as she was talkative, the elegant, witty and self-confident Daisy had for ten years been knocking people cold in England, France and Italy and doing much to shape lifestyles, fashion and conversation in high society. For her nothing was too extreme: she adored shocking people, wore black to be presented at Court, asked a man to prove his love for her by jumping into a swimming pool she had just emptied, and crossed herself every time she came upon an advertisement for the Singer Sewing Machine Company which supplied her wealth. Elsa and she became positive conspirators.

The next to arrive was Nancy Cunard, deserting Chanel as well as Patou. By now, to add to Elsa's admiration, Nancy Cunard had given up her *femme fatale* act, dared publicly to express her happiness with a black American jazz musician, and adopted a serious, even militant stand for both feminine and racial equality. Taking their cue from these women, many of the leading members of the *beau monde* now found their way to 4 rue de la Paix. Almost at once they became customers, to be followed by the ultra-smart and conservative wives of diplomats and bankers, millionaires and artists, North Americans and South Americans as well as French and British.

At the height of her creativity Elsa never looked back in time for inspiration, as do so many less masterful designers. She continually adapted modern foreign influences, and had a genius for translating

The Hon. Mrs Reginald Fellowes and her daughter the Comtesse A. de Castéja wearing saris by Schiaparelli, painted by Cecil Beaton for Vogue *in the drawing-room of Daisy Fellowes' house in Neuilly.*

Three 'Schiaparelli-isms' from Peru: a chullo (top), a hood worn in the mountains, for winter sports; a montera of wool and braid; and puños, lavishly embroidered armlets worn with evening dresses.

whatever she found wherever she went into fashionable articles – referred to as 'Schiaparelli-isms' – that had none of the spurious arty-crafty nature which so often besets garments with foreign inspiration. Her Tyrol peasant ornaments, Balkan coachmen's patch-pocketed jackets, North African skirt-pant trousers of the Tuareg tribe, all had a fresh vitality of their own. In 'Display No. 2' she had offered a Moroccan burnous for the beach, but for the same use in her first collection she produced a most significant item, a brown linen Mexican peon costume comprising, in addition to a jaunty sombrero, a jacket and brightly sashed peg-top trousers. The jacket, relieved of the Mexican touch, was to evolve into her famous line of boleros, while the trousers anticipated those in navy waterproof jersey to be launched in 1930 at St Moritz for après-ski wear. (Arletty was photographed wearing them in French *Vogue* for 31 December 1930.) A year before, Elsa had brought out slim skirts with so deep an inverted pleat in front that they could be taken for trousers when the wearer was standing still. Now she shocked everyone by dictating trousers for everyday wear, aided and abetted in America by Greta Garbo and Marlene Dietrich.

In 'Display No. 2', beach and resort pyjamas in sailcloth like a Dutch boy's costume and in black jersey like a monk's robe had introduced the Schiaparelli pyjama motif. They were so wide and voluminous that they resembled a skirt. Developing them, Elsa now presented a pyjama suit. When this caught on she refined the pyjamas, which were already in vogue for housewear and informal entertaining, by producing her own slim, straight lounging pyjamas, hostess pyjamas and evening pyjamas. She also introduced dinner slacks, so voluminous that the parting between the legs was not to be seen – the 'palazzo pyjamas' of the 1960s. Exercising her unrivalled genius for publicity, she herself wore a variant of the pyjama motif in black string, open-meshed like a fishing net. The beautiful and celebrated Lady Duff Cooper – as Diana Manners, star of Reinhardt's *The Miracle,* and wife of the British Ambassador to France – sat upright at the sight of pyjamas on a solo dancer in an operetta at the Cambridge Theatre and cabled to 4 rue de la Paix for a copy. A new rage started, and in her February 1932 collection Elsa added fuel to its flames with an 'overall' pyjama developed from the overall tops of ski trousers and cut all in one – utilitarian, comfortable and very smart. The ill-fated woman pilot Amelia Earhart wore a flying suit adaptation, during the Second World War women munitions workers took to it, and later generations of mothers put their infants into another version. At the beginning of the eighties, for dressy women everywhere, jumpsuits took their place beside jeans.

Combining the skirt-like pyjamas and the trousers, Schiaparelli's next move was to show trouser-skirts for every occasion – travelling, city wear, evening and sports. Less voluminous than the pyjamas and more tailored and slimmer than the divided skirts, thus more slender looking, they were graceful and feminine and to her mind much

Schiaparelli combines corduroy trousers with a Linton tweed jacket embroidered in gold and copper with appliquéd 'rubies'.

more modest than skirts. The revolutionary slogan, 'Trousers for Women', was soon blazoned in shop windows everywhere. 'The controversy was violent, and unexpected because it was not such a new idea,' Elsa acknowledged frankly. 'Poiret had tried it before.' And in his last house Poiret was still trying, looking hopelessly old-fashioned because he would not adapt his pantaloon gowns to the changed tastes. To support him, Schiaparelli defiantly brought them out too ('An achievement in dramatic lines!' cried *Harper's Bazaar* in June 1931), but to no avail for the ageing Poiret.

Elsa knew a good thing when she hit on it, and with trouser-skirts she had. Growing bolder, she took another theatrical leap forward by shortening the 'Display No. 2' divided skirt, at first for sports. Enter the culotte. In some variations she revealed the leg all the way up to the thigh. At last she had her first great scandal. When, for the first time since 1915, she went to London in April 1931 to promote her goods personally, she had (to her joy) to be protected from attack. Letters to the Editor came hurtling at the *Daily Mail*. 'I hope,' boomed one good lady, 'if any woman dares to appear at Wimbledon in that abomination she will be soundly beaten.' (The world champion, Lily Alvarez, did and wasn't.) One gentleman protested, 'It should be a penal offence to wear them.' 'We should retaliate by wearing skirts,' chimed in another man, 'but for us that means severe punishment.' A lady priding herself on broad-mindedness snapped, 'They are the last word in immodesty. Unfortunately, we are living in a depraved age.'

By way of reply, Elsa incorporated both trouser-skirts and the divided skirt into her interchangeable separates. To a deep orange crêpe blouse and orange crêpe de Chine trousers, she added a swirling orange divided skirt wrapped and tied around the waist by a narrow sash. The result: a long evening dress, enhanced by a waist-long cloth-of-gold coatee. All over the United States women adopted the divided skirt, so that in a few years it became known as the 'rural uniform'. It survived to such effect that in the early sixties Norman Norell based an entire suit collection on it.

In January 1930 Elsa herself publicly modelled her first evening gown. It caused an uproar. Starkly simple, it was a plain, figure-hugging, black crêpe de Chine sheath with the scandalously low 'sunburn' back of her famous bathing suit from 'Display No. 2'. It also had a short jacket in white crêpe de Chine with two long sashes that crossed at the back and could fasten in a bow either in front or on the side, and ended in a bunch of arrogant white cock's feathers. The idea of an evening dress with a short jacket staggered Paris fashion, and this design, Elsa noted later, proved to be the one most successful dress of her career. In variations that early in 1933 included the cock feathers sprouting from the shoulders or floating as an impertinent tail behind, the ensemble was reproduced all over the world and started a vogue for short, exquisitely brocaded evening jackets. These Elsa soon adapted into her well-known boleros, and later lengthened into revolutionary short evening coats and widened into short capes. She caused a sensation when she arrived in late 1933 at the Théâtre des Champs-Elysées for a Toscanini concert in a pale grey satin backless sheath with a short Chinese lacquer-red cape in quilted taffeta partially covered by one of her famous collars of ostrich feathers coated in glycerine to make them appear more lustrous.

Quickly taking advantage of the success of the first evening gown, Elsa combined it with trousers. *Harper's Bazaar* for March 1931 presented a drawing of the Schiaparelli trousered evening gown and cape in white georgette that had flabbergasted guests at a dazzling gala soirée in St Moritz. (Later on she was to do long at-home dresses with narrow 'tube' trousers and to dictate slacks for dining out as well as in.) The following month, *Harper's* European feature writer, covering the mid-season collections, declared of Schiaparelli's: 'I

Marlene Dietrich (right) wears an evening dress with sprouting black cock's feathers, a Schiaparelli speciality in the early 1930s.

should fill altogether too much space were I to recount all the originalities and clever novelties. This is called the House of Ideas, and it lives up to its reputation.' After hailing 'the unbeatable Schiaparelli knack' on 1 April 1931, American *Vogue* on 1 May 1931 announced, 'Schiaparelli, once famous largely for sports clothes, hereby steps into the limelight as a great evening designer.' 'Three years ago Madame Schiaparelli was unheard of,' observed the *Daily Mail* in England on 19 May 1931. 'Today she is recognised as the leading smart Paris designer.' Janet Flanner, the *New Yorker*'s 'Genet', a most perceptive observer of the French scene, did a long profile on Schiaparelli in the issue for 18 June 1932. Only two months later *Woman's World* remarked: 'The house has now sprung into the first rank of creative couturiers.' Three months after that, in its lead article, French *Vogue* named Schiaparelli along with the greatest designers for the first time. In a cover story on the world of Paris fashion and its celebrities, *Time* magazine declared on 13 August 1934: 'Madame Schiaparelli is the one to whom the word "genius" is applied most often.' By now, Elsa's four hundred employees were turning out between seven and eight thousand garments a year for the 'mother of invention'. With no previous experience and a work history of scarcely seven years, she was the most discussed fashion designer in the world.

Even so, Elsa had still only opened the side-shows. The main attractions were yet to come.

Elsa's novel combination of short jackets with evening dress caused a stir in the early thirties. In 1936 she shocks again by using felt for a copy of a man's smoking jacket in a blatantly masculine cut (right), and softened by pearl-beaded pockets (left). Both, in this drawing by Bérard, are worn over long crêpe sheaths.

11

'Madame'

EVERY morning Elsa rose at eight, no matter when she had gone to bed, sipped lemon-juice-and-water and a cup of tea for breakfast as she read the papers, handled private correspondence, made telephone calls and gave the menus of the day to the cook. Weather permitting, she often walked to work. 'Always on time, five minutes early' was a motto with her. Punctual to the second everywhere in the world and livid if anyone else was one minute late, winter and summer she arrived at her office on the dot of ten. There she slipped a double-breasted white tailored cotton smock over her skirt and blouse or simple frock and outworked everyone until seven in the evening with power-house energy. She herself opened every letter that came in, answered it and signed every cheque. She discussed every matter with her suppliers and businessmen. At her openings she personally tied each scarf and fastened each belt on the mannequins. When she was away on business trips or holidays, she rang Paris every morning to find out who had come in the day before, what they had bought, and what they had not bought and why not. In time she came to fear that she was nurturing a mania for detail, but convinced herself she was wrong. If she made mistakes, they were her own mistakes.

After the success of 'Display No. 2' Elsa was clever enough to realize that she needed ambitious young people to help her, and keen-sighted enough to detect winners. Although Jean Patou was at the height of his fame, Elsa induced one of his best tailors to defect to her, and he brought with him many of the Patou faithful. A month before her first collection in January 1929 she also persuaded two young Patou *vendeuses,* or saleswomen, to follow with their clientele, for whom like most Paris fashion *vendeuses* they acted as advisers and confidantes. One of those first saleswomen was a dynamic Breton in her mid-twenties, Michèle Guéguen, who was named *directrice* by 'Madame' within three months. Like Mike, she was to stay with Schiaparelli until the end, and she then finished her career in the same position with Hubert de Givenchy. For life also came young Yvonne Souquières, the private secretary of whom Elsa wrote, 'Her second name should be Faith.'

'Madame' at her desk, 1933.

Also important in Elsa's rise to fame was Bettina Jones, a young American who dealt with American customers and later devised many of the ingenious displays in the windows of the Schiaparelli Boutique. Another who joined the ranks was Hortense MacDonald. Elsa asked her to leave a promotion job with the Paris branch of the US Shipping Board to become her publicity director. 'But I know nothing about fashion,' Hortense said, when approached. 'Neither,' retorted Elsa, 'does the Princess [Thérèse de Caraman-Chimay] about the press.' From the word go both young women excelled at their new work, the one introducing unheard-of American savvy into the French fashion business scene, the other the snob value of a titled aristocrat in an original role in an unexpected milieu.

Princess Thérèse de Caraman-Chimay, of the great Belgian family related to the Dukes of Burgundy, was the first of a number of noblewomen and wealthy celebrities whom Elsa introduced into fashion: Princess Sonia Magaloff, Princess Cora Caetani, Princess Marina Mestchersky (later, as Countess Vorontzoff, to take over furs for Dior) modelled her collections. Princess Paulette Poniatowska, society mannequin *par excellence,* was to be seen wearing the latest Schiaparelli originals at all the fashionable events in all the smart Continental gathering places: Deauville, Biarritz, Cannes, Monte Carlo, Venice, St Moritz.

For the design of accessories and secondary items, Elsa from the outset chose remarkable artists and craftsmen. One of the most unusual was Jean Clément, whom she spotted and hired as early as 1927, when he was twenty-seven and virtually just out of school. Not only was he a painter graduated from l'Ecôle des Beaux Arts but he also had a degree in chemistry from the University of Paris. The combination gave him a remarkable expertise in the treatment of colours and the working of plastic materials. Jean Clément, who would share his life with Michèle Guéguen, was the greatest genius Paris accessory design has ever known. He created the astounding Schiaparelli purses, buttons, belts, much of the junk jewellery and other accessories, and all the items in plastic. Clément dedicated himself to fashion and to 'Madame' exclusively until his untimely death in 1949, despite alluring offers from Balenciaga in haute couture and from businessmen in many related activities who tempted him with the prospect of earning a fortune if he would agree to commercialize his talents. Indifferent to money and fascinated by his work for Elsa, he always refused.

Somewhat later Elsa entrusted the execution of Jean Clément's designs to one Roger Jean-Pierre, the young business manager of an atelier specializing in accessories and jewellery. This association also testified to Elsa's perspicacity. After founding his own house, Jean-Pierre worked with Christian Dior and later the young Yves Saint Laurent, became Balenciaga's main supplier, and rose to the presidency of the Chambre Syndicale de Paruriers de la Haute Couture (*parure* means adornment). Upon receiving the Nieman-Marcus Award in Dallas in 1962, he dutifully reported back to Elsa, who by then had retired.

'Madame, I owe it all to you.'

'And I,' she replied, 'feel I have received it myself.'

Rarely, if ever, has a couturier used people's gifts to greater effect than did Elsa Schiaparelli. Because she possessed the humility – and was shrewd enough – to face her weaknesses, she chose the best collaborators in each field. She had keen insight into their capacities, respected them as artists and human beings, and tacitly signed a moral contract with them that neither she nor they ever dishonoured or broke. Relentlessly, like a great orchestra conductor, she inspired, beguiled and drove this élite to surpass even itself in finding original uses for conventional substances and introducing into fashion the new materials of the time. She placed an unprecedented emphasis on the individual expression of the skilled personnel of haute couture, bringing these people into the limelight as never before. Ultimately, the Schiaparelli story is that of all the unsung heroes – the fabric manufacturers, embroiderers, furriers, dyers and designers of jewellery, trimmings and and accessories, as well as the workroom tailors, *premières* and seamstresses – without whom French fashion could never have achieved or maintained its unique place as the supreme arbiter of feminine elegance in the world. It is a tribute too to the many other men and women who, in costume centres, institutes, societies and the costume sections of museums everywhere, devote themselves to collecting, preserving and through exhibitions keeping alive the social and artistic legacy of this particular product of modern times.

If Elsa could be extremely difficult with her equals, she was also autocratic, high-handed, impatient and hasty with her employees – except Mike, for whom she never had a cross word. Reserved, even aloof, she never forgave inefficiency or fatigue, forbade any familiarity, loathed stupidity above all other things and found precious few people intelligent. On the other hand she was generous and very just. Each one always knew exactly where he or she stood with her. There was no gossiping, whispering or conjecturing about 'Madame' in the workrooms or corridors. She never uttered a word of encouragement or paid a compliment, but the employees sensed her approval when it was there. Of course, she realized how sensitive they could be. Sensing one day that she had somehow hurt Jean Clément's feelings, she called in Michèle Guéguen. 'Tell Clément I'm sorry, though I don't remember what I said or did.' Moreover, she recognized when she was wrong, although no one could ever tell 'Madame' that something she asked for was impossible. 'Impossible,' she would snap, repeating the old Gallic adage, 'isn't French.' It wasn't English or Italian for her, either.

As she had gone through hard times herself, she paid quite well at a time of shamefully low wages. She allowed the mannequins to buy any model dress and suit in a collection for less than the cost of the embroidery alone. Once a year she took all the fabrics left over and distributed them to the women and girls who sewed. To Thérèse de Caraman-Chimay she gave a leopard coat that Joan Crawford had left behind partially unpaid for. Well before any enforcing legislation, she gave her employees three weeks' paid holiday a year, and she always kept two beds available in the St Joseph Hospital for any who might fall ill. She did much to help her people raise their children and sent gifts every year to former employees, even after both they and she had retired. But she never made any allusion to her charitable acts. It was considered a privilege to work for her house. People rarely left her employ, at home or in business. Hours did not count; they thought nothing of working overtime without being paid or of coming in on Sundays unrequested. Moreover, when tough times came, they remained loyal.

Many great artists of the period worked with Elsa – Dali, Cocteau, Vertès, van Dongen, Giacometti and Christian Bérard – and fine fashion artists, notably the Swedish-American Carl Erickson ('Eric'), formerly a painter. As far as fashion photography was concerned, the giants she had met in New York remained important to her career. Man Ray was a constant friend and companion. Baron de Meyer had lost ground to Edward Steichen, who was ridding photography of impressionistic effects and, like Elsa in clothes design, drawing it on

Elsa herself wore this velvet jacket, em-broidered by Lesage with a grape motif in red, yellow and green gold lamé and thread with coloured glass pendants.

to a path parallel to the evolution of modern art, including the avant-garde; he emphasized the new type of woman, liberated, athletic and bold. Elsa, however, admired Baron de Meyer for his romantic though *dépassé* lighting, and authorized him to photograph some of her clothes as late as 1934. She also thought highly of Munckacsi for movement and Brodavitch for his portraits. She worked with other great fashion photographers such as George Hoyningen-Huené, remarkable for his choice of subject-matter, dissymetric architectonic composition and surrealist effects; also with Horst P. Horst and Cecil Beaton. She was among those to recognize the talent of the first significant young woman photographer, Margaret Bourke-White, who, like Elsa in her clothes, directed an artist's eye towards the beautiful new shapes in industry. After the Second World War Elsa was an early enthusiast of Richard Avedon for his expressions of fashion speeding through time (a prolongation of Italian Futurist pictorial artists at the beginning of the century). 'Thus surrounded,' she declared, looking back in late middle age, 'I felt supported and understood beyond the crude and boring reality of merely making a dress to sell.'

When she started her business, Elsa ran it on a simple system of autocracy from which she never swerved. She knew so little about commercial transactions that she was innocent of even the great guiding principles such as borrowing and falling into debt. However, she could think through and read contracts so well that, only a year after 'Display No. 2', she bought out her silent partner, M. Kahn, by pouncing on an ambiguous clause in their agreement. By this time she had already ensured better backing from the French banking branch of the Rothschilds, but she always remained sole owner of her business, an unusual case in haute couture.

Obviously she did not keep the ledgers herself. She hired an accountant, M. Meunier, who supervised the financial transactions and the book-keeping. The prodigal artist in her and the realistic guardian of the invoices in him often confronted one another.

'Meunier! Why did you cancel my order for this?'

'The fabric is too expensive, Madame.'

'Why?'

'You intend to do only one article and not copy it. We'll lose money on it.'

'So? Think of the publicity!'

But a brilliant businesswoman? Fundamentally indifferent to material values as she was, Elsa did not have a good head for business. If it had not been for M. Meunier, she would have been in trouble early on. As well as her general staff, there were many people who refrained from telling her the truth, largely because they were simply afraid of her furious reactions. Then, confronted by an error which had become too obvious to conceal any longer, she would go into a rage anyway and fire the offender on the spot. But by then the harm had been done.

This well-known œil-de-bœuf *portrait of Elsa in 1937 is by Horst.*

By 1931 the *découvreuses* (discoverers), as Elsa called them, the international celebrities, rich society beauties and stage and film stars, started to balk at climbing those six flights of stairs to the garret and crowding into the tiny rooms. Able now to pay a higher rent, she picked up her screens and descended to premises on the first and ground floors linked by a little inner spiral stairway, keeping the garret as workrooms for her growing dressmaking staff. From her tiny office overlooking rue de la Paix on the first floor she could catch a glimpse of Place Vendôme. Downstairs she arranged her new surroundings to look like a boat, hanging the walls with festoons of white fishing nets and stringing up ropes on which to display scarves, belts, sweaters and other articles in colourful disorder. The curtains were in unheard-of shiny black patent leather, the furniture in black wood with comfortable hammocky cushions, and a map of the Basque coast of France painted by Jean Clément stood out in vivid greens and blues on a wall covered in white moleskin. To receive customers the *vendeuses,* dressed as uniformed schoolgirls, sat at the entrance behind black school desks. There was so little space that Thérèse de Caraman-Chimay had to set up her office under the stairway. The words 'Pour la Ville – Pour le Soir' were added to the sign at the entrance, and this slogan was traced in white on a little black delivery van that Elsa bought, and in black on her white stationery.

Customers soon came in such numbers that she rented another small area on the ground floor at the back of the building to be run apart from the main establishment. She christened this prelude to her famous boutique 'Schiap' (pronounced 'Scap') and put on sale ready-made things at very reasonable prices: beach costumes, pyjamas, sweaters, bonnets, suits, separate skirts and jackets and some accessories. As customers made for 'Schiap' they passed a large showcase against the wall. In it were glass pickle jars decorated with eyelashes made of paper or feathers and red leather lips, and sporting Elsa's knitted hats and feather boas around the neck.

In designing her wares, Elsa might have been inclined towards intellectuality because of her knowledge of art history, familiarity with modern movements and involvement with contemporary forms. What saved her was the acknowledgement of her inexperience, which she wisely conserved, her taste for adventure, the thrill of taking a gamble and the glee of winning it. She was a gifted bull in a china shop whose ignorance prevented her from recognizing the impossible. Her courage was without limit, her approach fearless, even daredevil. When she began 'devising' she had, by her own confession, no idea what she was doing, she relied on her instinct and never knew what would result. She used colour with an artlessness that was the other side of genius. She was imbued by Paul Poiret with admiration for the technical skill of Jeanne Lanvin and the artistry of Madeleine Vionnet, but she never acquired any greater 'learning' than that. So she was hampered by none of the dressmak-

A black goffered mousseline sheath is crowned with a sequined gold mesh Ihram head-dress, here worn by Lady Lionel Earle in a photograph by Norman Parkinson.

ing traditions. Conventions held no restraint for her; rather, they were something to be ignored in her avoidance of the banal. What did she risk? She had no capital to speak of, no superiors, did not have to report to any shareholders and paid her backers regularly so they had no hold over her. The small freedom was hers.

Most of her designing Elsa did in her head, often while walking to work, alone in the countryside, driving or, later, riding in her chauffeur-driven Delage, lined in white pine and fitted with a bar. By nature a rebel who hated restrictions of any kind, she did not think well between walls. She held that 'twenty per cent of women have inferiority complexes and seventy have illusions', and on that basis she worked out her sales policy. She also trumpeted far and wide a new precept for buying clothes: 'Accepting cheap substitutes for real values will not bring about a return to prosperity. Everything that is cheap and quickly perishable is an extravagance no woman can afford. One well-cut, beautiful dress is the luxury allowed to a shaky budget.'

It never mattered to Elsa that her clothes were widely copied. The superb artists in her workrooms, she was fully aware, put them together so exquisitely, in such incomparable fabrics and colours, that when done elsewhere they looked completely different. 'The moment that people stop copying you,' she held, 'it means that you are no longer any good and that you have ceased to be news.' It was not long before every little dress factory in Manhattan was indeed copying her. From Third Avenue New York to Howard Street San Francisco, millions of American shopgirls who had never heard of Schiaparelli were proudly wearing her designs.

12

Schiap

IF YOU wanted to show you were 'in' with Elsa, and it was smart to be, you called her 'Schiap' – although, unusually for one in her profession, she could not bear small talk, did not hold court, had no mob of flatterers and shrouded herself in no mystery. Dark, and in build recalling an ancient little Tanagra statue, she had features that were somehow exotic and a tense, enigmatic expression. Her large, thoughtful eyes were often disturbing and she smiled only when she had time, commercial need, and in the company of her daughter and granddaughters. In the interest of sales she could make fools think that she appreciated their wit, nondescript people that she admired their beauty, and *nouveaux riches* that she respected their taste. On the other hand, she was frequently rude to important people to compensate for her timidity and to prove her independence. Outspokenness was a conscious part of the Schiap shock treatment. Once, having invited too many people to dine for the number of crystal glasses she had, she simply put out empty mustard bottle glasses.

'Surely you can afford a few more crystal glasses,' said a guest.

'Are you paying for your meal?' retorted Elsa.

She was naturally frank and faultlessly idiomatic in three languages, but sometimes her English was picturesque.

'There isn't such a word in English,' someone would tell her.

'Well, there ought to be,' she invariably replied, 'and I shall go on using it.'

And she did.

Behind all her fluency, however, she retained the secrecy of a talented child too gifted to attempt any explanation to adults. Larger than life, she was unpredictable but disarmingly simple, profoundly lazy but formidably hard-working, both generous and mean, hugely dependent on friendship but over-demanding, alternately charming and hateful. She saw deeply into people, sensed the future cannily, was passionately interested in astrology and constantly consulted fortune tellers, even at street fairs. Very superstitious, she believed in all kinds of omens and would detect symbols in what to most were

Elsa's daughter Gogo sketched for Vogue, *October 1945, in a beaver felt bonnet tied under the chin and trimmed with winter flowers.*

mere coincidences. The Capri goat's milk her father made her drink as a child, she always maintained, accounted for her being so stubborn, tenacious and revolutionary.

Elsa accepted sorrow and loss readily, but she never knew how to deal with happiness. Even to her intimates, she remained somewhat inexplicable. There was something severe, over-logical and distant – something Piedmontese – in her that prevented her from expressing her undeniable Neapolitan warmth to create intimacy. She was not demonstrative in either love or friendship (though she certainly knew what both meant) and did not tolerate being touched. Her only devotion went to her daughter, Gogo, but to do what she believed best for the girl's health, and also to comply with her own need to work untrammelled, she kept even Gogo at a distance.

At all times Elsa remained mistress of herself, displaying a touch of Roman hauteur, and no matter how hectic the pace she never bustled. From her study of philosophy and history came a keen sense of perspective. She could be witty in a French way, but she also had a self-deprecating sense of humour that helped to keep her on an even keel. Still, in her moments of greatest success it was sometimes difficult even for her to remain cool. What saved her then was a sense of detachment, a feeling of insecurity, a knowledge that so much in life was futile and vain, and an inbred Neapolitan melancholy.

'Many men admire strong women, but they do not love them,' she mused when approaching old age. 'Some women have achieved a combination of strength and tenderness, but most of those who have wanted to walk alone, have, in the course of the game, lost their happiness.' She had found her happiness with the only man she ever abandoned herself to, her husband, and later she forfeited the possibility of rediscovering it because she was afraid of suffering if ever she gave herself again. Stifling all thoughts of William de Kerlor, she refused any recall of the emotional devastation he had inflicted on her. Never did she spontaneously mention him to their daughter, and studiously avoided answering Gogo's questions about him. The girl only discovered what her striking father looked like when she was in her late teens and one of Elsa's friends gave her a photograph of him.

Over the years Elsa was attracted to various men, had several lovers and could have made advantageous marriages. But she avoided becoming attached. Although women were her main support she always got along better with men, yet no man could hold her completely. Her relationships with the opposite sex were a series of friendships, sometimes close, sometimes detached, always full of an anxiety for freedom and battles for small liberties. She attained her goal of financial security, even luxury, and adapted to world-wide fame with pleasure, but she had not without reason likened herself to the nymph Arethusa fleeing brutal male conquest; her emotional life was governed by a deep necessity to preserve her physical and spiritual privacy. She incorporated this necessity into her fashion

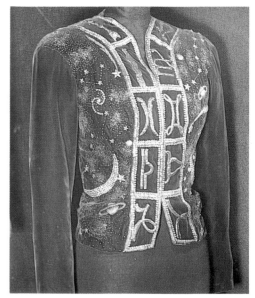

The night sky is perhaps not exactly as Elsa saw it through Uncle Giovanni's telescope, but the Great Bear and Little Bear are clearly to be seen, as are all the signs of the zodiac. This jacket, embroidered by Lesage, appeared in the Astrology Collection of 1938.

designs. 'In spite of success, glamour and despair, the only escape is oneself, and nobody can take that away,' she concluded late in life. 'It is stronger than jealousy, hardship or oppression.'

Many artists and photographers did portraits of Elsa, but she liked to think that the most singular and telling was a painting by Picasso. A cage is placed on a green carpet which recalls the baize of gaming tables and is strewn with playing cards, symbols of fortune and chance. Outside, an angry black bird flaps its wings defiantly at the sky: the professional woman challenging the universe. Inside, a dejected white dove gazes wistfully at some pomegranates: her pure inner nature contemplating normal, everyday happiness. Alas! the bars of the cage prevent the dove from pecking at the seeds.

The first generation couturiers, from 1860 to 1930, were considered by the *beau monde* whom they clothed to be just tradespeople – glorified dressmakers – and were accordingly shunned socially. This was true of Charles Frederic Worth, the first couturier, in spite of his being solicited by the crowned heads and leading noblewomen of Europe and Great Britain, of Jacques Doucet, the 'Grand Gentleman of Fashion' and art patron who adorned the *grandes bourgeoises* described by Marcel Proust, of Jeanne Lanvin and of Paul Poiret.

Chanel, largely because of her liaison with the Duke of Westminster, was the first to put a foot on the ladder of the élite, but it took her many years to get there and she did not expose herself much outside France. Elsa Schiaparelli, with her cultural background and life in England and New York, was socially acceptable from the beginning. A fixture in what was then international society, the former Comtesse de Kerlor was invited to the grandest homes everywhere, and in her own home gathered together the cream from the worlds of politics, art, the stage and cinema. Elsa's Italian nature craved colour, action and crowds. She was to be seen everywhere, and she sold her clothes by wearing them in public. In a crowd she was always noticeable, particularly in evening dress.

Elsa loved to entertain, and now had a proper place in which to do so: an apartment on the Boulevard St Germain between the Chamber of Deputies and St Germain-des-Prés. To furnish this home as she wished, or perhaps as she thought appropriate to the image she had been creating, she called in Jean-Michel Frank, the leading interior decorator of the time, to bring up to date the series of formal rooms dating from the 1890s by conceiving a contrasting setting as strict, neat and modern as her clothes. Frank commissioned designs from such well-known artists as Salvador Dali, the Giacometti brothers and Christian Bérard, but nevertheless he believed rooms should be designed for people, not as showcases for works of art. His method was simple: he emptied the chosen apartment of all its old furniture, reduced decoration to the simplest elements, and avoided unnecessary ornamentation. It was said of him that one had to pass through a suite of rooms stripped bare to find the mistress of the house sitting at her secrétaire opposite an ancient Greek statue.

Jean Cocteau called them 'burglared apartments', and it was true that Frank would adorn a room with only a single piece of African sculpture or one picture by Picasso.

Out of Elsa's new home he pulled everything save some fine arched bookcases. Her tiny lodging in Greenwich Village had been filled with little European antiques, but she now adopted the images and materials of the twentieth century. Pure white walls provided a background for touches of shock colour. In the inviting, casually arranged living-room were curtains of a stiff and gleaming rubber substance, chairs covered in yellow chintz, an enormous orange leather couch and two armchairs in emerald green rubber. In the dining-room, small black bridge-like tables with glass tops were set before almond-green divans. The bedroom was done in a blistered lavender blue fabric. A footstool was made from the hipbones of an Argentinian horse. There was a painting by Tchelichew, and Alberto Giacometti had provided the lamp bases, typically elongated.

Elsa's first dinner party at the apartment in Boulevard St Germain was a formal affair, and Gabrielle Chanel, who privately referred to her new competitor as 'that Italian who's making clothes', accepted an invitation. At the sight of the modern furniture and exotic black porcelain plates amidst modern Swedish silver, she shuddered, she later recounted, as if she were passing a cemetery. Elsa, who always alluded to Chanel as 'that dreary little bourgeoise', was gleeful over the reaction: 'Chanel,' she remarked, 'specializes in cemeteries.'

As the thirties progressed, Chanel, whose business like that of all the couturiers came to be threatened more and more by Schiaparelli, developed a positive obsession about Elsa. She even became physically dangerous. At photographer André Durst's Bal de la Forêt, one of the last great costume balls before the outbreak of war in 1939, Chanel, dressed as herself, dared Elsa, as a surrealist oak, to dance with her. Deliberately she steered the tree into some lighted candles, where the bark caught fire. With the aid of many soda siphons, guests managed to put out the fire.

Unlike so many of her contemporaries, Elsa openly acknowledged the success of other professional career women (Chanel apart), particularly if they met her criteria: they had to be intelligent, to possess the humour to avoid taking themselves too seriously and boring everyone to death with their presumptuousness, to dare to brave convention, to have battled their way to the top, and to contribute to feminine independence. She often attributed Mary Pickford's rags-to-riches rise not to the star but to the brilliant businesswoman, and she freely recognized the achievements of Helena Rubinstein, Elizabeth Arden and, after the Second World War, Estée Lauder, a positive tycoon, though Elsa preferred Rubinstein's more European approach to big business. Ultimately, however, she surpassed them all as an inventive spirit, a presiding executive and, quite simply, as a woman.

Schiaparelli spreads her wings in this gown of stiff shagreen satin as photographed by De Meyer.

13

Schiaparelli Lady, by Day and by Night

AT THE end of Les Années Folles most people were tired of reductive styles in dress as they were of interiors with rigid lines. They had wearied of the cardboard woman with a scooped and hollow silhouette, angular shoulders, flattened breasts and a low waistline. They were bored with the black that Patou and Chanel had imposed in reaction to Poiret's colours. Still, haute couture kept reflecting the atmosphere of the economic crisis during the early thirties by remaining demure and subdued – and somewhat dull. Soon wealthy people became impatient with the practicality that was so much the order of the day during the Depression. Recalling the madness of the early twenties, they yearned to dress up again and escape into the romantic and theatrical. They were longing to be jolted and swooped up into some fun and games. The moment was ripe for Elsa Schiaparelli, and she was ripe for it. Instinctively she knew that this was the time to be shocking, and the word became her theme. 'Schiaparelli never stopped hitting Paris in the face with the most ideal form of provocation,' noted Yves Saint Laurent in *Bravo Yves* (1982). In the history of fashion few designers have interpreted the mood of the day more accurately or energetically than did Elsa. Vibrantly in tune with her times, she foresaw needs before they were felt and answered them with a gift for anticipation that was at times uncanny.

By now, of course, she had learned a few principles about clothes. These principles she had laid down herself, helped by her memories of the beautiful surroundings of her childhood and all the strong, colourful images she had retained from her experiences afterwards, particularly in New York. Her concept of clothes was architectural: the body was to be used as the frame is used in a building. Instead of following the undulating curves of the flesh, she followed the length of the hard, bony structure. The variations in line and detail always had to keep a close relation to this frame. The more the planes of the body were respected, the more the garment acquired vitality. One could add or take away, lower or raise, modify and accentuate, but the harmony must remain. The Greeks understood this rule and gave to their goddesses the serenity of perfect form with the appearance of freedom. Much of this Elsa learned, at her own admission, from Paul Poiret. Like him she did not see a dress merely in terms of stitches: like him she never drew designs for models, but sketched new ideas in order to suggest them to her junior designers and then indicated what she wanted by draping cloth on and around dummies, as Poiret had on living women – herself included.

In the trade Elsa came to be called the 'Aesthete of the Machine', for she understood that cut was of first importance, that cut implied fit, and she always contended that garments perfectly cut and perfectly fitted would remain smart long after the fashion which they followed was forgotten. She understood the modern craving for colour and a forceful, slenderizing line, and duly produced clothes of stylized simplicity. Indeed she always proclaimed that simplicity of line was the key to the distinctive, elegant silhouette, and symmetry its stamp. In time she experimented with new means of attaining symmetry, as when in 1939 she balanced one ex-aggeratedly bouffant right shoulder with an over-large high hip pocket on the left side.

The eight years, 1921-29, separating Chanel's first collection and Schiaparelli's were decisive in Paris fashion, for the two women were more than competitors, they were antagonists. Chanel claimed that dress designing was a profession: Schiaparelli insisted that it was an art. Cristóbal Balenciaga, the designers' designer, the last great titan of haute couture save Grès and Yves Saint Laurent, was of Elsa's opinion. One of her first customers when buying designs for his dress houses in his native Spain in the early thirties, Balenciaga always said that Schiaparelli was the only true artist in fashion. His obsession with cut, and the architectural construction of his post-war designs, was to owe much to her own. Indeed, so grateful was he that to welcome her back to Paris after the Occupation he agreed, in a public gesture rare for him, to a request by American *Vogue* (15 November 1945) to share a page of sketches with her: for his part, he re-created three Schiaparelli '*greats*'.

Whereas Chanel stood for calculated ease and luxurious sim-plicity, Schiaparelli was tough and brash, offering sensational effects in bright and bold colours. This hard, highly individual femininity was personified by Tallulah Bankhead, bolt upright, prancing to a brass band on parade in the circus. Schiap brought daredevilry to the hitherto serious world of fashion, adding a touch of the Commedia dell'arte. She achieved the almost impossible marriage of eccentricity and commonsense, pulling off paradoxes and contradictions with brio. Thanks to her, the originality people were yearning after became the new *raison d'être*. The more eccentric and fanciful you were in the last years before the Second World War, the more likely you were to be accepted and the more fun you had. This calculated frivolity and extravagance was, as so often, to precede a holocaust.

At the beginning of the thirties the modernizing of the feminine

This yoked silk jacket has heavy clair-de-lune *embroideries and sequins in startling colour contrast.*

silhouette had been achieved. Through exercise and diet, women's bodies were more slender than ever before. Clothes no longer had to conceal physical deficiencies, but now they had to hide something else: the inner female. They had to protect the New Woman from counter-attacks by the male, whose superiority and domination she was challenging and whose territory she was invading. When she put on her clothes in the morning, this woman found safety in numbers: she was one of the many, uniformed, armed. In the evening, when she changed, she became a different person – truer to herself and her real nature, more conscious, even more cruel. That was Elsa's belief. In the battle of the sexes her clothes reflected an entire social revolution: defensive by day, and aggressively seductive by night. One of Schiaparelli's slyest, most deceptively feminine and most disturbing frocks (1935) was made of a print patterned with the rearing and prancing battle-geared horses of the god of war, Mars. The Schiaparelli Lady did not slink about like a siren or a flirt, as had her predecessors. She came charging furiously ahead, a horse dragging a chariot driven by whip-cracking warrior Elsa.

In the early twenties, Patou and Chanel had adapted some elements of the English gentleman's wardrobe such as cricketing coats and rowing blazers into sportswear for women, but this had nothing to do with fundamental feminine psychology. For Elsa the New Woman, fighting like herself for independence and equality, needed to be both protected and provided with weapons. Beauties had to be bulwarked, ugly women (the '*jolies laides*' among whom Elsa counted herself) be given confidence. In a new philosophy of dress she required her customers to look as if they had brains even when they hadn't, or knew how to use them even if they didn't.

As part of her tactics for reducing the gap between the sexes (half a century before unisex), Elsa adapted men's styles – golf suits, sports suits – to women's clothes. Her Aviatrix Coat and aviatrix flying suits were inspired by Charles Lindbergh's flight across the Atlantic in 1927. The young English pilot Amy Johnson, who set off from Croydon Aerodrome in May 1930 in a Gipsy Moth biplane on a harrowing twenty-day solo flight to Australia, took with her a number of Schiaparelli ensembles.

'By keeping men off,' Elsa held, 'you keep them.' Her daytime clothes, dubbed 'hard chic', had a militant, masculine quality. The New York-inspired Skyscraper Silhouette concealed feminine vulnerability in an almost belligerent manner: straight vertical lines and widened squared shoulders. The first of her 'defence measures' were a double-breasted coat and a wide shoulder yoke noted by American *Vogue* for 15 February 1930 and 3 August 1930 respectively. A coat of black crêpe (1 March 1930) had wildly enlarged lapels, which Elsa further emphasized by making them of a different colour, white, and a different substance, galiak. Only a few months later the same magazine for 1 January 1931 hailed a man's dinner-jacket coat with a sleek look achieved by using sequins. Eagle-eyed *Harper's Bazaar* for March 1931 did not fail to spy a jacket of an already acknowledged Schiaparelli style, 'the shoulders built up in Schiaparelli's special way, that looked for all the world like the costume of an apache at a Bal Musette.' This style made hips seem narrower, more like a man's. On 15 October 1931 American *Vogue* commented: '. . . clothes carpenter that she is, Schiaparelli builds up the shoulders, planes them off, and carves a decisive line from under the arms to the hip-bone, gouging in the waist.'

To ram the argument home Elsa padded, stiffened with canvas, epauletted and then built out the shoulders, sometimes jutting them (early 1933) into a form she called 'trays' and 'shelves'. On to them she heaped piles of fur, to their tips added bows, soutache braid, aigrettes, wide-spreading feathers, standing frills and anything else decorative or redoubtable, such as vertical points themselves accentuated by a pointed hat. To increase the volume, she emphasized upper arms and made them appear more muscular by padding ordinary sleeves, building up mutton-leg sleeves, already enlarged, inflating these in 1933 into gigantic cathedral-organ sleeves, pleated

*Individualistic Schiaparelli accessories —
snood, fingernail gloves and a mask —
accompany her dramatic evening coat in
Revolutionary red, drawn by Bérard,
1935.*

and corrugated, or 'fluted', then re-ordering the bulk into her pagoda shoulder-line and finally adding wings. Continue to ignore the armhole, disregarded historically because distasteful? Not Schiaparelli. She dignified it. After adapting bottle-neck and peasant sleeves to accommodate a very high armhole but providing it with visible roominess, she deliberately drew attention to it by the addition of circles or swirls of faggoting bands in fabric or fur. Aggressively, she dramatized other usually ordinary features of dressmaking to reinforce her hands-off effect: pleats, seams that went as far as arabesques, gathers and shirring.

Masculine uniforms which inspired Schiaparelli included Cossack jacket-coats, train guards' uniforms and red riding-coats which she adapted into evening redingotes and later into severe-looking hostess gowns. Soon she combined these with Chanel's vaporous tea-gowns, transforming them into a rage that became eternal, house-coats. The sumptuous cloaks of Venetian Doges came in perhaps the widest variety of silk weaves ever shown by Schiaparelli. The Dhoti, a draped skirt commonly worn by Hindu boy students in India, the Little Lord Fauntleroy suit, page-boys' outfits, toreadors' costumes with three-cornered hats – all were successful advances into male territory. Waxed materials and oilcloth gave the hardiest male antagonists pause, and thick quilted fabrics acted like shock absorbers to ward off their blows, notably the satin ribbon Beau Brummel waistcoat in 1932 and the synthetic Armada taffetas and velvets mounted on crinoline in 1933. Heavy embroidery fortified capes and scarf-capes and formed a coat of mail on the mannish jackets. Fur embroideries were often stationed high on the bosom or combined with pockets to protect the hips. Blazing Christian Bérard sunbursts like shields of armour also guarded the breasts, which were further defended by pugnacious I-dare-you-to falsies and (in 1937) brassières built into bodices, all too increasingly evident in British and American films until they became laughable in the fifties. The masculine Schiaparelli look finally became so pronounced that, claimed Elsa's detractors, a smart woman looked like a cross between an American football player and a hockey goalkeeper.

Elsa's sense of anticipation soon introduced a military look to her mannish mode. Already apprehending another world war, she designed a trim, horizon blue, metal-buttoned coat like the one Paul Poiret, as Chief Tailor of the French Army during the Fist World War, had reduced from the billowing red garment previously worn by the *poilus*. Significantly, in his final haute couture collection in August 1931, Poiret featured epaulette shoulders as Elsa brought out her Wooden Soldier Silhouette and an unusual military cape fastened by clamps in steel or copper. By 1939 the writing on the wall was only too clear, and all Paris fashion had taken on the hard military look anticipated by Schiaparelli.

As well as her body, the Schiaparelli Lady's head had to be protected. For years Elsa dictated the mesh-stocking snoods that became universal. These defeminized hair, classically a symbol of fertility. Schiaparelli turbans, often twisted, safeguarded hair from the risk of even being touched. So did the profusion of scarfs and headcoverings, masks and veils, particularly the Yashmak which rendered come-hither lips unassailable and revealed the beguiling eyes in an Oriental manner. While she ignored the sombre propriety then associated with hats, giving them a playful and sometimes even satanic dash of humour, Elsa nevertheless often made them serve her masculine look. Her Marco Polo hat, François Villon hat, Dick Whittington felt hat with a forward jutting brim (1934), huntsman's cap (or billycock), snappy black student beanies, toppers and bowlers – these were all immensely popular, as were her policeman's visor called 'Riot' (1934), hangman and moufflon hoods, Mongolian tribesman's hat, and stovepipes, which made the cover of American *Vogue* on 1 February 1936.

Schiaparelli's way with hair: evening accessories drawn by Valentine Hugo include a fluted visor, a carnival mask of gold sequins worn on the back of the head, and geisha-girl hairpins.

That same year, after the Socialist Front Populaire was voted in, strikes were declared throughout France. Chanel was picketed and occupied, but Elsa's employees, paid well enough, continued to work uninterrupted. With wry humour Elsa brought out her Phrygian Bonnet, symbol of freedom from enslavement, which Marianne (the French equivalent of Britannia or Uncle Sam) had been wearing since the Revolution and which the strikers had adopted.

It was natural that Schiaparelli should join forces with Antoine, the most progressive coiffeur in Paris, who not only cut hair strictly like a man's but stiffened it with lacquer. The best turned-out Hollywood film star of the early thirties, Kay Francis, an early Schiaparelli customer, looked entrancing in this style, as did the sometimes daring Norma Shearer, one of whose films was entitled *A Free Soul.* Perhaps Elsa's most striking early collaboration with Antoine developed from an idea she took from her friend Sonia Delaunay, the painter, 'grandmother of modern art', whose 'simultaneist' clothes Elsa had observed when passing through Paris on her way to London some twenty years before. Sonia had opened a little fashion house, and Elsa was struck by her adaptation of Cubism to clothes, her revolutionary cutting of coats from tapestries, her use of vivid bi-coloured hat veils, and especially her introduction of red and green wigs. Conspiring with Antoine in 1931 Elsa now concealed hair from the male eye altogether with silver, ash–blond and red wigs for evening wear and, later, waterproofed wigs as smooth as caps for sports. Certain of the stir to follow, she launched them in public herself – the first was black and shiny and looked like wrought-iron fern, another silver with curls on the top and on the temples – but wore them only with the plainest of dresses so that they became a part of the ensemble. She always defended wigs on the ground that in all periods of great sophistication both men and women wore them with supreme dignity and elegance and would not have been seen without them: 'Can you imagine Voltaire or Catherine of Russia or Louis XIV without a wig?'

When she sensed that the vogue for short hair was coming to an end she dictated upswept hair and upswept hats. For years the furies unleashed were literally hair-raising, masculine as well as feminine, and they gained Elsa the cover of *Vogue* on 15 September 1938. Gleefully, as an extra defence measure, she recruited mother-of-pearl, jewelled crystal and blond tortoiseshell combs. Then she pulled hair straight up on top of the head into a multitude of mean little curls like so many tightly clenched fists.

Just before the look that had become identified with her really went overboard, Elsa, guided by her sense of timing and the conviction that she had made her point conclusively, in 1933 reduced the lines of her Skyscraper Silhouette to a quiet and satisfying sanity. Shoulders were still square and padded but smoother, and customers adored looking as slim as a shaft in a combination of bold

A rampant cock's feather tops this Monkey Hat of felt, drawn by Vertès, 1938.

This hip-length Box Jacket in black wool is worn with a straw poke bonnet and a gold head on the shoulder.

individualism and austere styling, with measurements so accurate that a fraction of a centimetre could spoil them.

'Sober,' Elsa proclaimed, 'is not a synonym for sad.' Take the absolutely rectangular wool cape, for example, or 'Attention!', a strict, untrimmed, tailored black coat with high-banded pockets to indicate the waistline and squared shoulders enhanced by a series of darts on the sleeves: it remained in fashion for years, 'strong, man-scaled – clean, narrow lines', as American *Vogue* described an Ungaro equivalent in 1982. Customers who bought the 'Spartan' suits started feeling freer and easier in the perfect, severe black wool trouser suits that hit the front pages thanks to Marlene Dietrich's highly publicized example. Elsa softened the strictness or dramatized the dull classic colour of these tailored trousers and jackets by adding vividly checked or striped waistcoats, bright plaid blouses, blouses in new forms like the blouse culottes, step-in blouses, vest blouses and unusual tailored blouses as warm as sweaters, and through emphasizing dressmaking details such as seams, tucks and puckers. Capes falling straight in right angles from the shoulders and alpaca top-coats with square, underslung pockets suggested the lean and racy look of a sports tourer – and sold like hot cakes. As did the Box Coats and Box Suits: 'If,' opined American *Vogue* for 15 January 1933, 'there's anything new under the sun . . . ' it was the box clothes. *Vogue* added in 15 November 1934, 'Young Americans will probably live in them this winter,' along with the mad little visor newsboy cap. So enthusiastically were Schiaparelli coat dresses adopted that they soon became part of the British and American scene, as did small plain dresses in black.

'Why,' enquired *Harper's Bazaar* in March 1937, 'don't you realise that this wonderfully creative woman is expressing our life and times in her little suits and dresses and in her unique materials . . .?'

To many of her designs in 1930 Schiaparelli had added another device protecting the shoulders and bosom but also, on a simple dress or plain sheath, stressing the importance of the bust: the bolero. By 1931 some were so fitted that they looked like a coat or dress. In the next several years Elsa shortened them to a bust-length 'baby' version and then refined this into an over-the-shoulder yoke superimposed on a coat to look like a bolero jacket. A Schiaparelli hallmark, the glamorous and practical boleros and bolero-and-jacket suits became *de rigueur* the world over for all occasions, even on the beach. After bringing in shoulders that were still padded and smooth but rounded, in 1935 Elsa introduced the raglan style that enchanted women, British and American, for decades, and the full, loose and flaring fishtail-backed swagger-length 'braggart' coats in fur (even llama) and in flannel, cashmere, travelling-rug and saddle-blanket wool or camel hair. That year customers also became addicted to the pink shantung jacket fashioned like a labourer's shirt with the sleeves partially rolled up and the tails dangling over a white silk dress. This style spread so widely that by the fifties women factory workers were wearing it and it had also been adopted by men.

So much for the day. The evening mode was strikingly different, of luxurious splendour. In 1934 began the first of five years of unparalleled innovation. They started with long, narrow dinner dresses. These sheaths were usually barebacked, sometimes with revers outlining the décolleté, often black, and they could slide into tunics as cleanly as a sword slides into its scabbard. The sarongs, the directoire skirts, slim as Cleopatra's needle, were so simple they could be worn for ever. The gowns were accompanied by masculine smoking jackets, by sleeveless Tunisian jackets and by lamé jackets with coloured flecks: 'Schiaparelli fireworks', cried *Harper's Bazaar* for October 1937. Yet all were surpassed by the evening boleros, often lavishly embroidered and looking, said *Harper's* for December 1936, 'like jewels'.

There followed, in 1934 still, evening pyjamas of magical sophistication; the Cone Silhouette, an association of Poiret's Hoopskirt or Lampshade Tunic with reminiscences of the umbrella pines of childhood Rome; and the two-piece Moslem 'Ihram' gowns together with sumptuously jewelled, close-fitting protective Ihram headdresses. Then came the Indian silhouette, based on exquisite saris and their headscarves, all delicately coloured and muted.

The muteness was deceptive, the calm preceding a storm. For, like a female Aeolus, Elsa then unleashed (in 1934 again) the four winds of the Stormy Weather Silhouette, which she developed at once into the Typhoon Line. 'Forward! Backward! Upward! Downward! she ordered, whipping everything into motion, hurling it all into the fleet and windswept lines of a speedboat or aeroplane, into the swirls of sails caught in gusts, even blowing furs forward so that they strained out and up, anticipating the streamline. As the storm abated, there emerged later in 1934 the Bird Silhouette – winged berets, shoulder wings big enough to soar, winged capes on coats for day and evening wear, wing lapels, tail wings, the exotic colouring of the South Seas, and as trimming the plumage of flamingos, lovebirds and canaries. Fins (drapery to emphasize the narrowness of the silhouette in a slim-fitting sheath) were also to be seen amid the subsiding waves. All prefigured the radiant serenity of the Celestial Silhouette of February 1935, moulding the figure in soft spiral folds.

Never did Elsa rest on her laurels, and now in 1935 she swiftly took several more giant steps forward. Her long Dinner Suit became a uniform and, reaching a climax in the magnificent Persian Prince version, it relegated to ancient history all softer and more feminine costumes. Daisy Fellowes, who had easily slipped into Schiaparelli leopard-print pyjamas at a time of floating tea-gowns, all but stopped the horses during the first evening of summer night races at Lonchamp in a Schiaparelli midnight tailored suit in printed silk, and she disrupted an Orchestre de Paris concert in a Schiaparelli blue evening suit, both arms loaded with defiant, multi-coloured brace-lets which made so much noise that no one could concentrate on the

The sweeping lines of the Stormy Weather look are beautifully captured in this silhouette.

Right: The bolero became a Schiaparelli hallmark: this lavishly embroidered pair are from the Circus Collection of 1938. (There is a close-up of the embroideries on pages 168 and 169.) In sharp contrast is the long, lean line of the Persian Prince dinner suit, with rich gold-embroidered broadcloth jacket and Scheherazade turban.

string instruments. Mrs Fellowes also revelled in the sensation that she caused by arriving at a gala ballet performance at the Paris Opéra in a Schiaparelli evening gown with a decorous navy blue front and satanic red back.

Then, splash! Elsa threw automobile paint at Paris fashion. Everywhere she was to be seen wearing one of her mesmerizing gowns painted black and grey on white crêpe with a white, cock-feathered puffed cape. The paint seemed woven into the material and thus, as an integral part of the gown, complemented the cut. To imitate embroidery, she painted roses on sleeves and necklines. She also used paint for shock effect, as when she asked Salvador Dali to do a larger-than-life scarlet lobster amidst scattered seaweed on a white satin dress so romantic that it was an enchantment. Then came the sheaths showing the Etruscan and Egyptian influences, the revolutionary short evening gown, and its variant the short Schiaparelli cocktail dress, which went down in fashion history, as did the ballet-skirt version in which young American and British women whirled and danced for decades. *Les jeunnes femmes à la mode* also widely adopted the Schiaparelli short skirts worn with long coats, ensembles considered shocking by the Establishment. In what proved to be the culminating point (August 1939) the Cigarette and Mermaid Silhouettes accentuated youth and ease, height and slenderness all the more.

In its twenty-fifth birthday number in January 1961, *Life* magazine remarked: 'What strikes one in a panorama of twenty-five years of fashion is the absolutely riveting charm of the 1936 girl from top to toe, especially the model who wears a navy blue suit by Schiaparelli and one of Schiaparelli's doll-size hats ducked forward .... The whole fashion world might have a fling at reviving Elsa Schiaparelli's spirit.' The fashion world did indeed revive her styles at the end of the seventies, but how forced it all was. Her avant-garde had become the norm, her modernism was now conventional. Certainly, Paris couturiers continued to come up with amusements. But high jinks à la Elsa Schiaparelli? No. Consider the times. Her spirit was gone.

14

The World Her Oyster

To promote her clothes in person, Elsa returned to the United States early in 1933 for the first time in ten years. On this occasion, so unlike the previous one, she travelled in pomp on the *Ile de France*, was besieged upon arrival by a swarm of reporters and photographers, and made the headlines and radio broadcasts.

The catastrophic economic situation in the United States – twelve million jobless, Bonus Marchers turned back in Washington on an order from Congress and a three-day bank moratorium – determined the grim tone of Franklin D. Roosevelt's first Fireside Chat, the principles of his New Deal, and led to the US abandoning the Gold Standard. None of that put a damper on Elsa's exciting stay. Always on the lookout for the latest feminine achievements, she donned one of her severest suits and went to see a basketball game featuring Mildred 'Babe' Didrickson, an amazing athlete who emancipated her sex in many sports unheard of for women before her. Elsa made a point of attending a dance recital given by young Martha Graham, whom she came to admire greatly for being the first to depict contemporary American women in dance and for contributing to the glorification of the untrammelled body by inventing a new posture and sense of movement that corresponded with Elsa's own ideas on the matter.

America's main influence on fashion at this time was rooted not in New York but in Hollywood. Movie stars were the clothes-horses of the thirties. As Elsa herself declared in *Picturegoer Weekly* for 24 March 1934, 'It is a mistake to have extreme fashions, for they will date a film. Often films appear old because of their clothes, though they are quite modern in ideas. The dress designer must foresee the trend of fashions to come and give the clothes that classic touch which makes them last as long as required for the exhibition of the film. Also the film has such a wide public appeal that it influences fashion all over the world. A glamorous film star's lead is sure to be followed, so it is doubly important that film clothes should be in good taste.'

Of all the stars Elsa came to know, Greta Garbo (whom she called

Rosalind Russell in The Women *(1939) wears a Schiaparelli-inspired Box Suit and a doll-sized hat on her upswept hair.*

'*I'll be glad when I can afford things like this,*' *says Joan Fontaine to Norma Shearer in another scene from* The Women.

the Eleonora Duse of the screen) earned her greatest admiration – for keeping her personality intact and her inner life secret, and for never compromising or being untruthful. Garbo is generally credited with launching the masculine Schiaparelli style, and certainly she had the ideal figure for it: square shoulders, practically no indentation at the waist, straight hips and no curves anywhere.

It was, however, Joan Crawford who came to be the embodiment *par excellence* of the Schiaparelli Lady. Crawford triggered the Schiaparelli look in films, both because this suited her masculine figure and because of the nature of the roles she played. Having discovered Schiaparelli in Paris in 1930, Crawford returned to Hollywood where she persuaded the MGM costume designer, Gilbert Adrian, to stress the width of her back rather than try to hide it and to adapt the Schiaparelli designs for her. Crawford's broad shoulders, enhanced by padded and embroidered coats, jackets and gowns, became one of her physical trademarks. Such was the impact that all the other great Hollywood designers – Orry Kelly, Irene, Travis Banton, Howard Greer and wonderful Edith Head – had no choice but to follow the Schiaparelli trend set by Adrian, which lasted into the fifties.

By the thirties a few women had battled their way up to executive status, and films of the time reflected this victory, along with the entry of self-reliant females into fields hitherto reserved for men. As early as 1931 Crawford played a trainee reporter (*Dance, Fool,*

Dance), and was so modern as the secretary in *Grand Hotel* the following year that she may never look dated. *Vogue* for 15 June 1931 spoke of her 'astonishing metamorphosis' and transformation 'into one of the most brittle, exotic personalities of the [Hollywood] colony.' As she matured Crawford took on the aspect of a prow of a ship braving man-made storms, and indeed many of her roles could have been played by a man. Reluctantly she submitted to Elsa's dictate in the late forties to forgo the Schiaparelli Look, now outmoded, but dressed as a man in her last great starring part in *Johnny Guitar* and finally went in for playing the tough, successful, but loveless and lonely boss lady one might have expected of the Schiaparelli ideal and which, as the head of an international company, she actually became in old age.

Spiritually speaking, Bette Davis, a *jolie laide* par excellence, a highly intelligent woman and a brilliant actress specializing in independent and man-defying spitfires, best incarnated the Schiaparelli idea; but she did not portray women executives. The other stars who did – Jean Arthur, Barbara Stanwyck and Rosalind Russell (the sex of the male lead in *The Front Page* was changed so that she could become *My Girl Friday*) – were often dressed à la Schiaparelli: crisp and untouchable by day in tailored suits, their hair concealed by mannish hats or snoods, glamorous and seductive by night in evening dress or flimsy *déshabillés*, their hair down.

One day in 1933 a slim, sharp and husky-voiced young actress arrived at Schiaparelli's. She looked dowdy and gawky. She went away radiant and beautiful. Elsa had adapted designs to the unusual planes and angles of androgynous Katharine Hepburn, who emerged at just the right time to be canonized for having broad, blade-like shoulders and being flat-chested, wasp-waisted and lean-thighed. In one of her first films, *Sylvia Scarlett*, Hepburn dared to impersonate a boy. Later, to accentuate the androgynous silhouette, Elsa introduced Eurasian mannequins into Paris fashion collections; after the war they became standard.

Elsa clothed stars in a few unimportant films, and in 1935 she collaborated with René Clair on his British film, *The Ghost Goes West*. There was one curious episode in her relationship with the cinema. Unaccountably, Major Pictures, an independent company distributed by Paramount, commissioned her in 1937 to dress Mae West in *Every Day's a Holiday*. Apply modern Schiaparelli ideas to Diamond Lil's hour-glass figure and undulating walk in turn-of-the-century clothes? Elsa did not even try. To avoid having to go to Hollywood to cope with Mae, she informed Paramount that she would not be coming to the States. Mae would not hear of a trip to Paris. As a compromise, Paramount sent a dress dummy supposedly in Mae's famous dimensions, along with their requirements as to fabrics and colours. In due course Elsa's magnificent creations arrived in Hollywood. The studio's wardrobe department took one look at them and went into despair. It had failed to provide the dummy with

Joan Crawford, the epitome of the Schiaparelli Lady, photographed by Edward Steichen in a typically unusual combination of dark hyacinth-blue lacy knitted woollen dress with a jacket of heavy quilted crêpe in white and heliotrope.

sufficient padding to encompass Mae's curves, and at horrendous cost had to remake the costumes in order to add the extra inches. Not in the least put out, Elsa adapted the West shape to her most famous perfume bottle and designed Mae West hats.

Later in 1933 Elsa opened a branch in London, at 36 Upper Grosvenor Street. The house was typical of the area, narrow with four floors. She lived in the two top rooms when in town, and turned the rest into severely furnished showrooms and fitting rooms with concealed lighting and pale grey walls. Later, because of a need for more workrooms, she rented a tiny mews house nearby for herself; two rooms which she furnished in blue chintz and a garage that became the kitchen. This London experiment proved to be as entertaining as it was profitable, brought her invaluable publicity, and enabled her to form important friendships. It also made it easy for Elsa to visit Gogo, now at school in the fresh, green Hertfordshire countryside – having proved to be a natural athlete – and excelling in English outdoor sports.

The contrast between London, which Elsa thought the most masculine city in the world, and Paris, the most feminine, she found vastly stimulating. At that time the 'Buy British Only' campaign was at its most intense, tariff barriers at their highest and the press were promoting English designers such as Digby Morton, Lachasse, Hardy Amies and Norman Hartnell. Elsa's English trade was not,

Zsa-Zsa Gabor in John Huston's Moulin Rouge *dressed à la Schiaparelli.*

'Come up an' see me sometime . . .' Vertès catches the mood of Mae West, dressed by Schiaparelli for Every Day's a Holiday, *1937.*

however, in the least affected. The names of the famous who flocked to 36 Upper Grosvenor Street would have filled a small *Who's Who*. She was invited to all the smart parties at the Ritz, the Savoy, Quaglino's. She also enjoyed going to the more popular places, especially to a pub in Wapping where, with Noël Coward, Cecil Beaton or Alfred Hitchcock, she would munch bread and cheese and sip beer at the water's edge, watching the dark grey tugs and lighters as they threaded their way through the shipping in the haze of Whistler's Thames. On 21 May 1936 she complied with the *Daily Express*'s request for an 'Open Letter by Europe's Most Discussed Dress Designer to Her Daughter', the best-dressed young lady in the entire world and one of the most charming and sought-after members of the junior international set.

Dear Gogo,
Soon now you will be buying your own clothes, so, considering the time I spend worrying about clothes for women – some of whom I never even see – I suppose I ought to give you a little advice.

To begin with, you won't have a big dress allowance because I think it is a bad thing for young people (maybe for all women, I'm not sure). It takes them longer to acquire judgment if their mistakes cost them nothing. Up till now you have been wearing tailormades most of the time. Well, that is not a bad habit for anyone. Don't allow yourself to react from it too violently. Your first inclination will surely be to buy as much as you can for your money. Don't give in to it. . . .

You can only get to know good clothes from bad by looking at good ones. So, when you see a smart woman, study her. Only the rich can afford cheap clothes. If something you see looks worth twice its price, you may be sure the illusion will not last. What you buy must be good. Cut is of first importance, and cut of course implies fit. Suits, coats, dresses cut by an expert, fitting you perfectly, will stay smart long after the fashion which they follow is forgotten.

I will not give you a list of colors which 'will go' and those which will not because I believe that any one color will look well with any other provided (and this is, I think, the secret) that both are good clear, clean colors.

Two years later Elsa opened a Debutante Department in the London branch for teenagers who wanted to look as smart as their mothers. For the coronation of George VI on 12 May 1937, she rented the mezzanine floor of a bank to have a good view of the procession and served a champagne breakfast for friends from all over Europe. Little wonder that it was a particularly sad moment for her when the feeling of insecurity and the immense world problems on the eve of war compelled her in 1939 to close her London branch: 'My London years had been the happiest of my life.'

In 1935 Elsa took haute couture to the Soviet Union. Stalin, deciding to open Russian frontiers to the Western world, announced that the First Soviet Trade Fair would be held in December 1935, and that it signified a new plan to raise the Soviet standard of living. He invited the French Government to send displays from its light industries, from spinning mills, textile manufacturers, *parfumiers*, champagne producers and department stores. To show the Russian working girl what she should wear, the French sent Elsa Schiaparelli, accompanied by Cecil Beaton.

This caricature of Schiaparelli with Stalin, drawn by Covarrubias after Elsa's visit to Moscow in 1935, has serious political undertones: Elsa informs a despotic Stalin that women have the right to fantasy and independent status.

Black astrakhan for this Stormy Weather Silhouette in November 1934: the sloping shoulder-line is achieved by a jutting cape which covers a sleeveless wrap. The 'dachsund' muff, also in astrakhan, may be worn over one arm to look like a sleeve, or over both hands as a roly-poly.

In Moscow, Elsa lined her stand with brightly printed scarves and displayed French, American and British fashion magazines. Most Russian women had never seen a real fashion magazine, but Elsa noticed that they were more interested in how to make a dress than in what it looked like. That for her was a normal reaction: 'After all,' she later remarked, 'the thread and needle are in their way just as important as the hammer and sickle.' Everywhere she went in the Russian capital, she saw wide-awake women doing good jobs, apparently enjoying their increasing independence and appreciative of the efforts of the government to make them the equals of men. Keeping in mind that they were almost all employed outside the home and that their society, lacking a leisure class, had no time or inclination for whims and fads, she based her contribution on the idea of interchangeable separates. Leading the parade at the Fair, this exhibit – an exclusive outfit designed especially for Russian women and intended to be mass-produced – consisted of a one-piece dress in fine black washable jersey with a small, high, white Peter Pan collar; a black reversible jacket; a startlingly bright scarlet swagger coat of heavy felt reversible to black, with a few simple black buttons and with large mannish side pockets, which the Russians later rejected because of pickpockets on the trams; and a jaunty little black fishnet beret with a red tassel dangling from a concealed pocket, which the Russians again ruled out because of the pickpockets.

A few weeks after the Fair, Jennie Lee, wife of Aneurin Bevan, the British Cabinet Minister, went to the Soviet Union to write a series of articles for the *Daily Express*. English newspapers had carried the story of the Schiaparelli outfit for Russian women, and Jennie Lee set out to track it down. She found it in a corner of what had formerly been the Moscow Stock Exchange and was now a warehouse where samples of the goods from France for the Fair had been stored. So the story was true. Yet it remained unfinished, for the outfit stayed forlornly where it was, collecting dust. The plan for mass-producing it was abandoned, as were so many other Soviet plans involving outside influences.

A year before, Elsa had associated her recollections of Leonardo's parachute drawings and reminiscences of her own childhood attempts to master jumping by designing Parachute capes of back-jutting, buckram-stiffened tiers not unlike swept-back elements of the Stormy Weather line. Since they had not caught on very well, upon her return to Paris from Moscow she made it known how much she had been amused by the sight of Soviet citizens parachuting thick as flies from the tower set up by Lenin to train them to jump, and in February 1936 she produced her Stratospheric and Aeroplane Silhouettes. Into them she adapted the earlier capes and integrated another shorter one of bluish-purple wool with a collar representing Icarus wings of looped astrakhan. She also presented a parachute bonnet, sleeves imitating a parachute with rows of cording, and the light, airy Parachute Dress of billowing

The Parachute Dress, 1936, shown here in crêpe as drawn by Eric.

skirts cut in panels with seamed godets that made the wearer, when she moved, look like a flower floating on water. Falsely demure, she hid shorts in gay colours under them. *Vanity Fair* for 1936 had a cover drawing by Covarrubias of Elsa in red overalls chatting with Stalin in green overalls as they wafted down from the sky, hanging from parachutes.

Wherever her travels took her, part of Elsa's heart always remained at home, in the eighteen-room mansion that she had acquired in 1937 at 22 rue de Berri. Just yards from the Champs-Elysées, it was cut off from the street by a concierge's lodge and sheltered by massive walls overgrown with vines. In front it had a cobbled yard, at the back a deep, lush garden screened with overhanging trees and a shrubbery. It came to be known as 'the house of Schiaparelli's loves at first sight'. Since Elsa never acquired anything because of its value in either money or age, she filled her home with whatever she fell in love with when on her travels, driving through the countryside or walking around cities. Totally different from the modernity and avant-garde with which she had surrounded herself purposefully on her rise to fame, the house was true to its mistress: unorthodox, organizedly chaotic, slightly irreverent and magnificent: crystal *lampadaires* from Schoenbrunn Palace in Vienna, Boucher chinoiserie tapestries, a pair of raging leopards from the Vatican. It was also most comfortable. Elsa loved it so much that she never returned to it, even after an absence of only a few hours, without visiting all the rooms to make sure they were still there.

The arriving guest was greeted in the entrance hall by Elsa's household gods, two life-size seventeenth-century Venetian figures sculpted in wood. Hypnotic, with enigmatic smiles and snapping blue eyes, they were named Monsieur and Madame Satan. Elsa had made their acquaintance in a second-hand dealer's shop in Edinburgh. Madame Satan had a high bosom and before it raised a slender delicate hand as if in a warning not to betray the house or its mistress. With tiny wings on her shoulders, she wore a high-collared three-quarter length jacket and a laced waistcoat, and Elsa lavished chokers, necklaces, bracelets and rings on her. Monsieur Satan, with his two-pointed beard and horns, wore a shirt with ruffles, a waistcoat over a slightly bulging stomach and a long swallow coat almost hiding the tail which curled round one of his goatish legs. He held out his hand. As at the Fontana di Trevi in Rome, a guest could put a coin into Monsieur Satan's palm if he wished to come back to Elsa's home. Everyone did.

In the house of Schiaparelli's loves, Monsieur and Madame Satan stand guard over the drawing-room (right), a cornucopia of treasures gathered by Elsa in the course of her travels.

Elsa relaxes in the company of one of her Vatican leopards. Note her wedgies, and the somewhat barbaric necklace of gold and cabochon emeralds, a favourite piece of hers.

Many couturiers – Worth, Poiret, Chanel – rose from the ranks and were not to servants, gracious living and the running of large homes born. Elsa's background made it easy for her to become a *grande dame*. Whereas in business she gave young people their heads, she tended to entrust her home to servants who were middle aged, keeping them as long as they cared to stay, no matter how old they became. Once she had given her orders, she let them carry on freely, an appreciable change for them from the French bourgeois mistress, particularly if they came from French colonies in Asia, as did the butler-cook M. Phong and his successor M. Jean, whom Gogo kept until he died. Although Elsa never paid them a compliment any more than she did her Place Vendôme employees, they appreciated her evident respect of them. If they had to cope flawlessly with all the entertaining, they also understood Elsa's desire for privacy when she was alone, and they did not hover over or disturb her. Nor did she trouble them. If she wanted something, she went and got it herself. She served herself if she lunched or dined alone, often in her unusual bath-lounge, which was as large as the drawing-room, could replace a salon, permitted her to rest, read, write and receive, and prefigured a feature of modern living that would catch on in the seventies. A version of this appeared in MGM's *The Woman* (1939) with Joan Crawford and Rosalind Russell, the latter dressed in a strikingly similar version of Elsa as seen in Vertès' drawing for *Harper's Bazaar* for May 1938 (see page 121).

The room that gave Elsa greatest joy was her library. There she felt so secure that she sometimes made appointments with herself to spend the evening alone in it doing absolutely nothing, a turban on her head, something oriental on her back, her little dog on her lap, eating rice and spinach and sipping white wine, surrounded by friends who looked out at her smilingly from photographs in frames scattered on the grand piano, by flowers in vases placed anywhere but on tables, by beloved paintings on the floor, on chairs or propped up against ancient Chinese bronzes, and by books on shelves that mounted to the ceiling, piled up against the walls, littering the tables and chairs. There was a deep sofa upholstered in red and covered with priceless furs. But she had her own special corner, a divan she had dreamed of and had had executed after her dream. Recalling an eighteenth-century *causeuse,* it took the shape of an elongated S, and she and another person could recline on it facing each other with a tray on their laps.

One might eat and drink anywhere and everywhere in Elsa's house, usually French cuisine at lunch and Indo-Chinese for dinner, often on a bridge table, in the library, in the drawing-room, in the garden, even before the open fireplace for 'bath-and-supper' nights in winter in her bath-lounge. Most people, however, begged to dine in the 'Bistro'. This was the picturesque bar in the cellar near the kitchen. Leaving the piping exposed, Elsa had added many of the elements of a typical French café: a real zinc counter and sink unit

The Bistro, complete with zinc counter, bar stools and Chianti bottles.

decorated with small white elephants, a wooden table with vaude-ville posters of the nineties, gilt chairs. Elsa's Bistro saw a great number of world celebrities. Since she invited people to her house only because they pleased her, she treated everyone alike – stars, ambassadors, royalty, society leaders – and never put herself out for one more than another.

To her famous Sunday night suppers in the Bistro, Elsa asked only the chosen few, 'the family', intimate friends who had the run of her house and knew its secrets. Before the servants left for the evening, they set the ingredients out on the kitchen table. Elsa was thus left to cook for anything from ten to twenty people, and she generally used one of her own recipes for spaghetti and salad, or sometimes a more complicated dish like curry or ox tongue with port. Writers, journalist, painters and musicians joined in the fun. Often after a new play or musical comedy had come on, 'the family' would ransack Elsa's wardrobe to stage a burlesque of it, disguising themselves in her precious originals or foreign-bought costumes supplemented with underwear, kitchen utensils and jewels. Actors and singers arriving after a performance would thus be confronted by sudden and unexpected imitations of themselves. Invariably, the members of 'the family' left Elsa's house as they had found it. They did not want Monsieur Satan to throw their coins back at them as they took their leave of him.

Though surrounded by celebrities and herself famous and rich, Elsa never forgot Paul Poiret. With Jeanne Lanvin and Madeleine Vionnet, she was among his staunchest defenders when the Chambre Syndicale de la Couture Parisienne moved to vote him a monthly pension, only to be defeated by the president, Jacques Worth, who had disliked Poiret's published remarks about Worth's illustrious grandfather. Elsa bought some of his paintings at an exhibition organized by his friends to help him. Finally, utterly down and out, Poiret could offer nothing and was to be heard from no more. Time after time Elsa sought him out. She chided him for neglecting her (for all his other women, she would say) and invited herself to dinner, never failing to wear one of the dresses he had pressed on her ten years earlier. He always took her to cheap, picturesque restaurants in Les Halles, where he had lived as a child. Here no son of the area down on his luck was allowed to pay, as Elsa well knew, and they sat into the small hours, sipping wine and chatting.

A rare and regal homage from a celebrated friend: a drawing by Jean Cocteau. The legend in the scarf reads: 'Schiaparelli made this dress for dining and dancing. Jean Cocteau drew it for the readers of Harper's Bazaar.'

Opposite page: Despite the carnival dress there is no mistaking the seriousness of the sitter in this portrait of Elsa by Vertès.

15

Such Stuff as Dreams Are Made On

I N THE middle twenties, manufacturers such as Rodier with woollens, Bianchini with silks and Colcombet with artificial fibres brought about a renaissance in French textiles that led to fabrics becoming more and more fluid. Their new synthetic materials caused the couturiers to reconsider the basic architecture of their clothes. No one understood the new trend better than Elsa Schiaparelli. Ideas, she always claimed, sprang from fabrics. She found new beauty in conventional ones through cut, finish and the skilful addition of original, interesting details, and she enjoyed making innocent fabrics look worldly. On the other hand, she pioneered the use of new and unusual materials, but not simply in order to be eccentric; in them she found a source of inspiration, substituting an unexpected material for a conventional one. Collaborating personally much more closely with textile manufacturers than did any of her competitors, she goaded them into experiments that were not always successful. She demanded to be the first to see new materials in order to launch novelties. 'For thrilling fabrics,' declared *Harper's Bazaar* in April 1932, 'she is a law unto herself.'

Whereas Chanel and later Balenciaga merely experimented with synthetics, Elsa frankly imposed them on haute couture. Her activities in this were closely linked to the Colcombet family and company, whose decision early in the century in St Etienne to apply the technique of manufacturing ribbons to the very different technique of manufacturing silk, revolutionized the Lyons silk industry and gave the Colcombet company a leading place there. Charles Colcombet pioneered artificial fabrics and launched almost all the new ones in France after 1920.

From the moment she went into business, Elsa rejected the silk that was then being used by everyone else, and this for the best of reasons: its high price. As early as 1927 and her 'Display No. 1' she started ordering from Colcombet. With the demand for cheaper fabrics because of the economic crisis in 1929, French textile manufacturers put out more and more rayon synthetics of conventional aspect. Elsa adopted them at once. American *Vogue* for 4 January 1930

In this photograph by Hoyningen-Huené taken in 1934, the jutting-shouldered taffeta jacket is worn over a dress in tree-bark crêpe and the scarf is of cellophane.

Left: Ornate appliquéd bosses, embroidered with sequins and decorated with white china roses, secure the Schiaparelli Lady in a full-length evening coat of black wool. Further protection is offered (right) by a girdle of musical instruments embroidered around the hips.

reproduced her Pinafore Evening Dress in rayon crêpe and ran a full page Saks Fifth Avenue advertisement in which Elsa, already termed 'one of the most notable of French couturiers', presented a sports ensemble and coat in rayon for the first time in Paris fashion, stating in her endorsement, 'Rayon is like the times we live in – gay, colorful, luminous . . . it is so pliable to work with and so luxurious in appearance . . . [and] launders to perfection.'

Almost before Colcombet knew what was happening, Elsa started plotting with him to invent other rayons of non-conventional aspect. In 1932 she did an entire collection in a fine, elastic rayon crêpe, Ribouldingue, that was crushed, and a goffered (tree-bark) rayon crêpe called Mélodie because its raised designs looked like musical notes. She went on to use rayons as thick as crêpe de Chine with the matt finish of linen and the close weave of satin. Other rayons she mixed with wool, satin, flax or cotton. One that she promoted with a vengeance, Filochard, looked like jasper, another like gabardine. Cosmic, a rayon tulle of two layers, black and white, gave a watered effect, and Capricorne, a knitted rayon (1934), could not be distinguished from wool. In 1935 she featured the unusual 'oak-cork' crêpe, and after the war adopted a spun rayon with which Colcombet had saved many French factories from idleness during the Nazi Occupation.

Elsa did not confine herself to rayon. In a revolutionary mood in 1932 she introduced a new and exquisite synthetic *peau d'ange* jersey called Jersarelli, a deeply crinkled, fine-ribbed, reversible synthetic crêpe brilliant on one side and matt on the other, and Jersala, a synthetic silk jersey with a satiny finish. At the London première of Noël Coward's *Words and Music* in October 1932 she caused a stir by wearing the first evening dress in deep mulberry red Jersala. In 1936 she promoted the remarkable fluorescent Rhodia satin.

After the war Elsa immediately adopted Tergal as well as hailing nylon, which she used with great success right up to her final collection in 1954: Dark Allure, so sheer that the Schiaparelli leg seemed barely stockinged, Cracknyl for waterproof coats and swim and sun suits, and Pluvionyl for light, crease-resistant and waterproof clothes of all kinds. Even after her retirement she endorsed a Nomotta Knitters advertisement in American *Vogue* for September 1954, featuring her design for a day-into-evening suit dress hand-knitted in chromespun acetate ribbon indistinguishable from pure silk.

The practical innovation that caused the greatest stir, however, was Schiaparelli's sliding or lightning fastener, better known as the zip. From 1930, Elsa used zips for pockets of beach costumes, and by March 1932 *Harper's Bazaar* was reporting with astonishment that most of her gowns no longer needed to be pulled over the head: they could be undone or stepped into. But not only did Elsa dare impose zips on haute couture in a collection full of them (August 1935), she put them in the most unexpected places. She used them on evening

Schiaparelli's 'glass' cape, made not of glass or even cellophane but of Colcombet's synthetic Rhodophane. The photograph is by André Durst.

Schiaparelli combines black wool with Hudson seal in this harlequin-inspired suit. The buttons are plastic crowns and the hat, also of seal, is crown-shaped.

clothes and even on hats. She had them specially made in plastic and boldly emphasized them by attaching Indian tassels or baroqe pearls to the fasteners and having them dyed in a colour contrasting with the fabric. In scarlet they ran the length of the front of a dressing gown in white brocaded satin or bright blue corduroy and the side of country skirts from belt to hem. They fastened shoulder seams: when zipped up, the dress was informal, when unzipped it was appropriate for lunch or tea. The Schiaparelli Zipper Back also gave another double duty to a gown, up for dinner and down for formal occasions.

American buyers, grasping the significance of the innovation even sooner than Elsa herself, ordered and ordered. But on delivery day a horrifying message was received: 'The dresses cannot be shipped. American trade barriers prohibit the importation of French zippers.' Cables and radio-telephone calls flew across the Atlantic and the Schiaparelli zipper scandal took on the proportions of an international political issue until the US Secretary of Commerce at last relented. 'And ever since,' Elsa purred, 'zipper dresses have remained unchallenged in the States, like Columbus.'

Elsa was fascinated by paper materials and used paper straw for sports jackets, scarves and belts. She experimented with many other unusual substances, none more than cellophane, and she was the first to employ the initial cellulose acetate, Setilose, in 1934. Often embroidering with it, through interweaving sometimes underscored by silver, gold and white threads, she used cellophane to give a glint of taffeta and a shine to coats and jackets of stiff ribbon and other open work. She designed a cocktail suit in cellophane velvet and evening hats in black and silver cellophane, sometimes combined with lace in a bonnet version for day wear. She sent cellophane butterflies and flowers swarming over her wicker Basket Hat, and made cellophane belts with alphabets running round them, a Valentine edging of celluloid with punched holes that looked like lace, entirely transparent cellophane evening bags and cellophane scarves. With Colcombet she promoted Balboa (1932), corrugated jersey made of cellophane and a synthetic silk weave. She replaced sequin embroideries with strips and dots of brightly coloured shimmering cellophane, and used transparent cellophane buttons which were almost invisible against the fabric underneath.

Among Elsa's greatest triumphs must be numbered her famous 'glass' tunics worn over evening dress in August 1934. Recalling a substance used for centuries in Venice for baskets and devised by Colcombet to a secret formula, it was not cellophane although, like the true glass it resembled, it did not contain any silica, lime or potash. Known in the trade as Rhodophane, it was a brittle, transparent, spun synthetic that had to be handled with care but would not shatter and could be used for accessories such as belts as well as for skirts, jackets and even coats. It came in flat, ribbon-like strips sometimes interwoven with silks, rayons or metal threads, and had a strange sheen. The wearer took on the appearance of a Dresden figurine in glazed eggshell china. Mrs Harrison Williams, for years with Daisy Fellowes on the list of the ten best-dressed women in the world, made an unforgettable impact in a Schiaparelli pink glass gown strewn with pink camellias.

Often it was maddeningly difficult to know what a material really was, with crêpe and woven rayon looking like wool, wool like crêpe or feathers, linen a little like either, jersey like herringbone (running, moreover, in two directions), satin like silk jersey and even horsehair like lace or fine net curtains. Into haute couture she brought rough surfaced rubber and also latex, a rubber substance that had hitherto been associated only with corsets and other undergarments. This she intermingled with any number of fabrics, including taffeta and silver thread, to render them elastic, thus being able to eliminate fastenings for, say, skirt waists. She even used latex for gloves. And she so exalted cotton that it could not be distinguished from silk: once everybody applauded a suit of particularly attractive linen that was actually Coutil, a white mattress ticking.

One of her earliest American contracts, with the Westcott Hosiery Mills, led her to sponsor Fabrimode, a revolutionary new fashion in hosiery, and an advertisement including a photograph of Elsa appeared in American *Vogue* for 15 March 1930. The stockings reflected the appearance of a garment by giving an effect of crêpe chiffon, rough sports crêpe, shantung or tweed.

Schiaparelli delighted in 'contradictions' to shock, tease and amuse. She used traditional fabrics for the 'wrong' garments: wool instead of silk, crêpe instead of wool, crêpe de Chine for coats, felt for day suits and evening jackets, horsehair for evening wraps, crinkled and weatherproofed taffeta for top coats, sharkskin for raincoats, jersey for gloves, tent canvas for hats, calfskin (moreover dyed velvety rose) for a three-quarter evening coat, a meshy gold fabric for lumber jackets and oilskin for the flying suits included in her Eskimo Look. Subtly, she related a coat and a dress by adding the basic fabric of one as an element of the other – crêpe and wool, say. For evening dresses she put velvet sleeves on satin, combined a lace skirt and a suede top, substituted thick cord for shoulder straps on all kinds of fabrics and strewed confetti on lamé. Then, to bewilder and excite the more, she combined a fabric and a skin or fur: black caracul and black tweed; Irish crochet and calf; lace and antelope; wool and bulky opposum or seal; a wool sweater and a monkey fur, tweed lined and faced with leopard. She caused a sensation by linking a silver fox cape and muff with twisted satin ribbons. She trimmed suede jackets with serpent and put nutria (coypu fur) on antelope.

To deepen the confusion she played tricks, wearing coarse beige stockings with black day suits, using stitching as an element of a garment like cuffs or lapels, leaving lapels and collars off suits and coats, as if she had simply forgotten them, or lacing them on so they could be removed and the garment given a second look, or

This romantic creation of July 1939, a last defiant fling before the onset of war, has a flower-decked hat with brim of horsehair net.

lengthened to form a peplum over the hips. Once she designed a street dress to be worn back to front. Accused of not knowing how to be demure, she used mantillas to protect the neck from sunburn on the beach, but dyed them in vivid hues. Was that cape a hood, was that scarf a cape? They were both. Did those gloves rise to the shoulders and back of the head to form a scarf, or was that a scarf descending the length of the arms to form gloves? To a simple, innocent-looking white cotton net wedding gown in the spring of 1938 she added a circular white mantilla embroidered in radiating lines of spikes of madonna blue bugles like an enormous starfish.

Elsa was intrigued by British textiles and visited factories all over England, Scotland and Ireland. She haunted Linton in the Borders of Scotland and ranged as far north-west as the Isles of Lewis and Harris. She descended on the crofters of County Wicklow to study linens and ordered variations of her own devising. After the war she was regularly invited to the annual Antostai to judge factory-produced clothes, a new industry for the Irish. So moved was she by the dedication of British and Irish craftsmen that she took to wearing a pair of diamond and enamel clips representing the emblems of their countries – the rose of England, the thistle of Scotland, and the shamrock of Ireland.

She spent days in mills considering colours and studied the different herbs and plants that gave the absolutely pure dyes, seeking explanations of why certain patterns were done in certain ways. In particular, she asked questions about mistakes made on the looms, and often saw more possibilities of innovation in discarded bits of cloth than in a perfect product. Having won the staid weavers over to her ways, she had wools dyed to order and then mixed three or four colours. Once she stayed with the MacLeod of MacLeod on Skye. For dinner thirty-two members of the family, including the children, arrived wearing kilts of the most colourful tartan: pink, blue, periwinkle and lettuce green with topaz and amethyst buttons. Soon afterwards all of these appeared in Schiaparelli designs.

It was in Scotland, too, that she first saw black sheep. She had these shorn and ordered their wool to be made up for her in the most startling finishes, slightly reminiscent of the heavy Arab wools. As for tweed, American *Vogue* for 10 November 1930 was quick to recognize that in her hands it 'has become one of the most fascinating fabrics in existence.' She extended its use from sportswear to cocktail dresses and daytime suits. Sometimes it could not be distinguished from supple wool crêpe, sometimes it had polka dots, sometimes it looked like blotting paper or billiard table felt. Often it seemed to be linen – but then linen could look like tweed, too. She sent fashion reeling with long tailored evening coats and great floor-length evening capes in brightly coloured Scottish tartan tweeds, Irish tweeds from the Vale of Avoca and lamé tweeds lined with elaborate silks and taffetas to match the evening gowns underneath.

As for conventional fabrics, her popular Everfast linen came from

Elsa's pursuit of different types and colours of tweed took her all over the British Isles and established beyond doubt its position in haute couture. Le Jardin des Modes, the French fashion magazine which contained only black and white pictures, devoted the front and back covers of its September 1937 issue to Schiaparelli's colourful tweed ensembles.

flax she found on Skye when visiting the Duke of York (later George VI). Early she took to shirring chiffon and in 1934 dared, in anticipation of the nudity of the seventies, to use one fabric so flimsy that it revealed bared breasts and another so flesh-coloured that it imitated the real thing. She imported Italian Balilla hemp for linen dresses, devised evening gowns of very rare batik from Bali as well as of sackcloth and oil cloth, and made wraps of silky white plush. She used quilted silk and crêpe de Chine widely because she liked the way the light played on their reliefs, as on the 'tree-bark' crêpes, velvets and satins, known as crinkled, crumpled or wrinkled. These were heavy enough to be used for upholstery and so beautiful that the wearer seemed dressed by the fabric alone.

In 1931 she brought out waterproof taffeta, shantung, crinkled crêpe and linen for raincoats that were newly interesting both for their colours, pink, blue and red and black plaid, and for the dressmaker details which she added and that were moreover – of all things in haute couture – washable because, she insisted, the best waterproof fabrics suffer from dry cleaning. Thirty years later, although retired, she recognized the emergence of denim and hailed its possibilities, to be proved right by the universal promotion of blue jeans. In fact the French *Journal de Dimanche*, reporting her death in November 1973, called her 'the first hippie'.

In prints, Elsa let her imagination run riot. Paul Poiret had been the first to induce an artist, Raoul Dufy, to design prints for fabrics in 1911. Long before designer prints became commonplace, Elsa persuaded Salvador Dali, Christian Bérard, Cocteau, Vertès, Drian and other artists to provide her with ideas. Colourful flowers abounded, as did denizens of rivers and seas, swarms of insects and many wild and domesticated animals, all – shades of the Italian Futurists and Art Deco artists – in lively motion. Picturesque elements were borrowed from games such as chess, dice and cards, and from images of childhood like Jack and the Bean Stalk and animal crackers. Wearing a satin evening gown printed with poodles disporting themselves around a typical Schiaparelli lady, Daisy Fellowes brightened up the eerie evening at the Théâtre des Champs-Elysées in 1932 when Kurt Jooss, a striking representative of German expressionism, introduced his ballet, *The Green Table*, which predicted the destructive power of Fascism. That same year Elsa derived one of her most successful prints from a montage of some plaster and netting she had picked up among the rubbish at the Colonial Exhibition. A series of 'Lucky Dresses' in 1935 had the Great Bear or Big Dipper image of Elsa's childhood. The Telegram Print was a joke in itself for the message: 'All is well, mother-in-law in terrible shape.'

When Daisy Fellowes wrote a book, Elsa designed a print that included the title, a sketch of the author and pen and ink illustrations by Vertès. In the same year, 1935, she had the map of Normandy and gambolling pigs printed on crêpe for a midnight supper suit. And in

Vertès was one of many well-known artists to design prints for Schiaparelli. For the bright turquoise blue crêpe evening gown (inset on opposite page, left), worn with shocking pink balloon-sleeved gloves, fairground animals jostle and prance. The pink crêpe evening dress with 'sunburn' back and head-scarf has swallows flying through flowers to deliver billets doux.

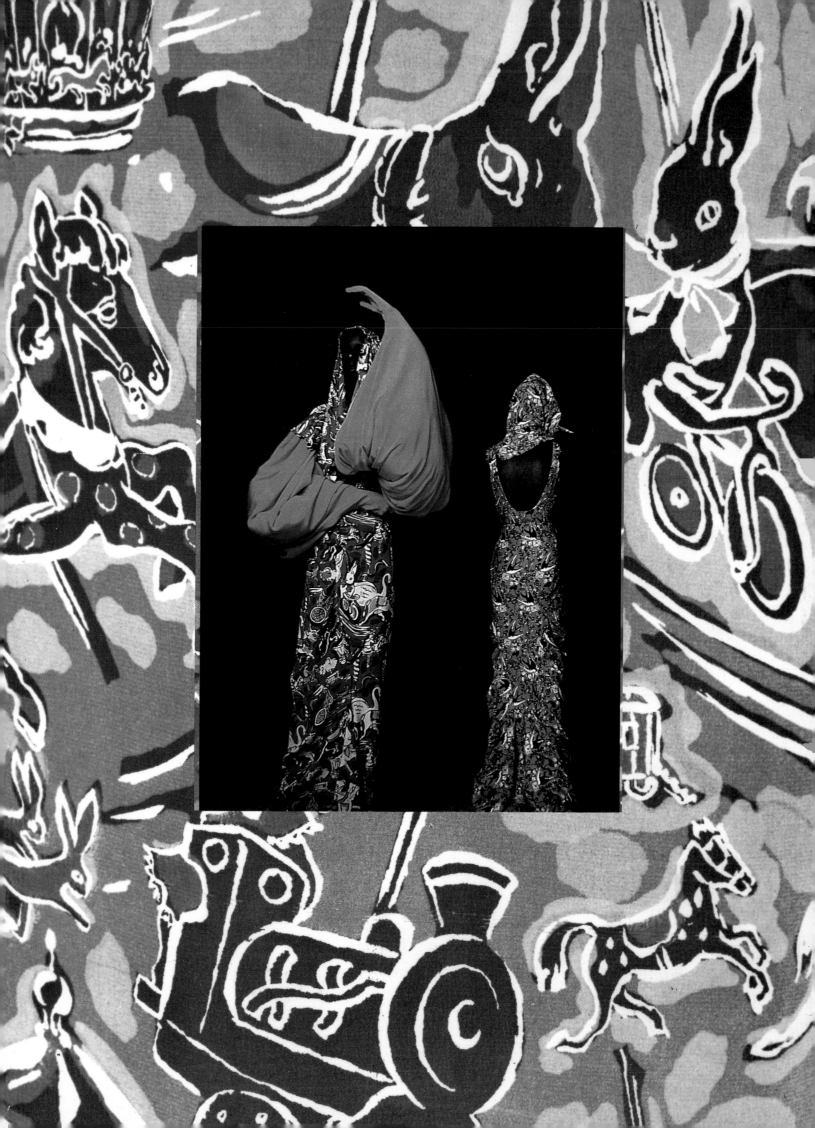

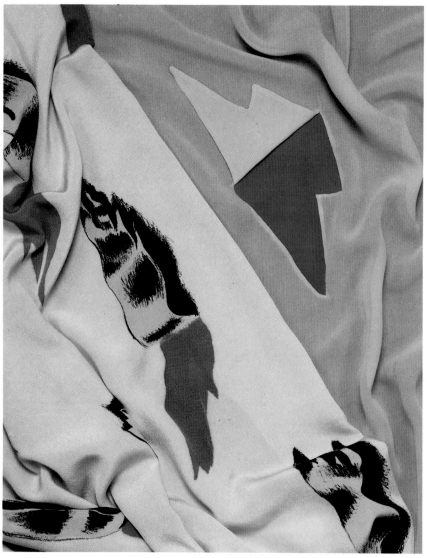

The famous Dali-inspired tear dress in silk crêpe combines a print of peeled bark design with a head-scarf of actual 'torn' fabric. This extraordinary precursor of punk caused a furore when it appeared in 1938.

1938, perhaps in precognition of the destruction to follow, she printed Dali-inspired tears on a hooded evening dress. In 1939 she ordered designs from Plato Cham, a nine-year-old Chinese prodigy whose paintings and sketches had been exhibited in London and Paris since he was seven. Chillingly, her last pre-war print (reproduced by *Harper's Bazaar* for August 1940) represented typically French white windows and green shutters, fastened close.

At the fish market in Copenhagen one summer day Elsa had noticed old women sitting on the banks of the canals wearing newspapers twisted into queer shapes to protect their heads from the sun. Back in Paris in February 1935, recalling a collage Picasso had done with newspaper articles, she gathered clippings of all kinds, including complimentary and adverse comments about herself, in every known language. These she put together like jig-saw puzzles and brought the patterns out for many uses in many different fabrics, even glazed chintz. Never one to miss an opportunity, she was the first of all the couturiers to have her customers publicize her name or initials by printing them on materials.

16

Trimmings and Trappings

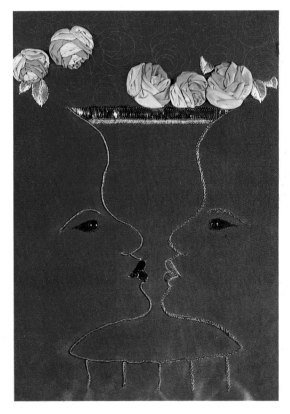

Opposite page: On top of a column defined by gold threads Cocteau places an urn composed of two faces and filled with pink roses. Above is a sample of the embroidery by Lesage. The dress was originally bright blue, as in the detail.

I N *Femina* for February 1938 there was an article entitled 'The Precepts of Mrs. Reginald Fellowes', illustrated by page after page of sketches of clothes by Schiaparelli. 'Were the planet suddenly to bury a large French city,' observed Daisy, 'the archaeologists of future times would find articles of feminine adornment far more beautiful than those discovered in Egyptian tombs.'

If in one sense Elsa's design was strict, almost a protective armour for the woman beginning to succeed in a man's world, with her colours, fabrics, prints, accessories and perfumes she gave women the means to fulfil their desire to assert themselves and enjoy themselves at the same time.

Rarely had a couturier done more to promote embroidery. In so doing, Elsa worked closely with the Maison Lesage, and in particular young François Lesage, who later became the president of the Chambre Syndicale de la Parure. Whereas Vionnet used embroidery to enhance a dress, Schiaparelli designed a dress to enhance embroidery. This was typically true of her boleros and black suits encrusted with gold and multicoloured stones or sequins and gold cord, their lapels embellished with butterflies, dragonflies or sea-horses. Boldly she placed tiny strips of rolled metal, often gold, on sleeves and lapels of suits and used them to form collars, added crystal embroidery to an evening mackintosh and worked red glass into an embroidery of grapes. On a trip to Austria she went to Wattems in the Tyrol to study the development of rhinestones. Soon she poured them over capes and gowns, clipped belts with them and topped enamel hats with plumes of them. Jean Cocteau in July 1937 drew an urn formed by two heads in ambiguously pursed-lip profiles which was embroidered on a blue silk jersey evening coat, and a woman's head with flowing hair for a grey linen jacket. Christian Bérard designed some striking motifs, including those for the magnificent Roi Soleil cape first modelled by Daisy Fellowes. Salvador Dali, whose wife was dressed free of charge by Elsa, provided the

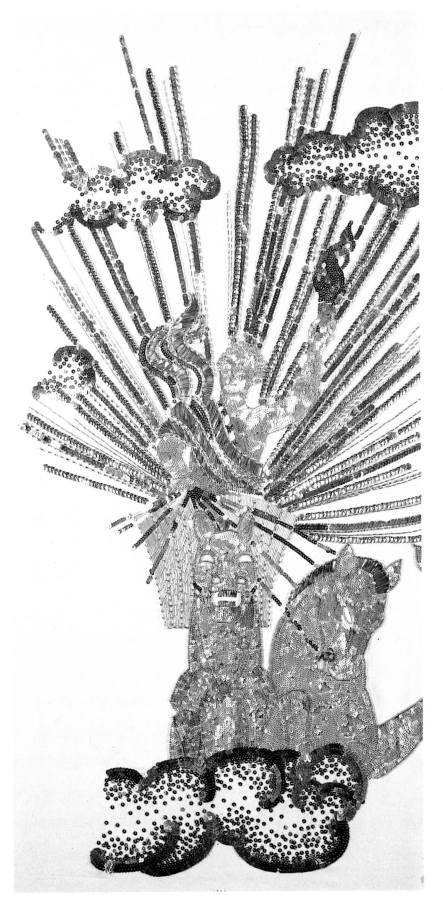

A trial run for an embroidery eventually used on a black silk evening cloak. The design, of a chariot and horses inspired by the Neptune Fountain in the Parc de Versailles, is embroidered in gold sequins, bugle beads and bullion.

Opposite page: This satin jacket in the form of a frock coat has chestnut motifs embroidered in chenille and metal thread embellished with pearls.

surrealistic drawings called 'City of Drawers' and 'Venus de Milo of the Drawers' which were the basis for her Desk Suit (December 1936). It featured a vertical series of true and false pockets embroidered to look like drawers, with buttons for knobs.

Surrealism also left its mark on Schiaparelli gloves. One pair looked like foxes' heads. Another bore the fingernails, veins and lines of the hand. Yet another featured a jewelled finger-ring on one hand. Some gloves could be worn on either hand. One variety for evening wear – precursor of punk – represented metal claws, another a hand with diamond nails. Many sported coloured fingers. Long red antelope and black tulle gloves disclosed the thumb and index finger, black antelope gloves had three fingers in gold kid, handkerchief gloves were tied around the hand, leaving the fingers free. The wearer of her suede smoking glove removed a safety match from the cuff and struck it on the wristband.

Other accessories, often called Schiaparelli 'witticisms' or 'conceits', were just as fanciful and paradoxical. She dictated velvet bow ties for shirts, promoted Viennese-inspired *petit point* luggage, insisted on stockings coloured to match dresses, and favoured kerchiefs even for evening wear. She also promoted fans: they could be of feathers, clear glass set with diamonds and rhinestones, milky glass with mirrors in the handle, or grotesque painted Grecian types. Masks abounded in Schiaparelli designs, occurring to Elsa naturally from her memories of the Commedia dell'arte. Some were held on a gilded stick. For evening wear she offered white plaster variants with red leather or red feather eyelashes, while for mountain sports she made a version in wood and added a visor. Some masks covered the forehead, some were pushed on to the top of the head, while others masqueraded as hats in black velvet with eyes, nose and bright red lips.

Parasols came in blue taffeta and red straw ribbon, umbrellas could be slipped into scabbards, and some were shepherds' crooks. Based on roller skates, her widely banded evening sandals of blue kid piped in gold had three revolving gold balls under the instep. Yellow shoes with gilded nails were to be worn in the country, while old-fashioned high buttoned boots of butter-yellow and pale blue kid accompanied lamé evening dresses, and Tartar boots came in violet felt with red kid feet or in wine-coloured felt with pale blue kid soles and sides. In 1936 she bared the toes, and *Harper's Bazaar* in April announced: 'The astonished foot . . . is wearing Schiaparelli's curious lattice-work elastic suede sans buckles or buttons.'

Ordinary buttons symbolized utter boredom for Elsa and she persecuted them with the zeal of a reformer. She never bought a single one. Most were fashioned by Jean Clément, who baked them in a tiny electric oven. None looked the way a button was supposed to look. Many were found where never a button should be – on a hat, say – and each one took on the importance of a carefully selected ornament. Elsa exploited her natural gift, sharpened by Art Deco, for

The Schiaparelli Lady goes to the office (or the beach?) in the Desk Suit, based on a drawing by Dali and here photographed by Cecil Beaton, 1936.

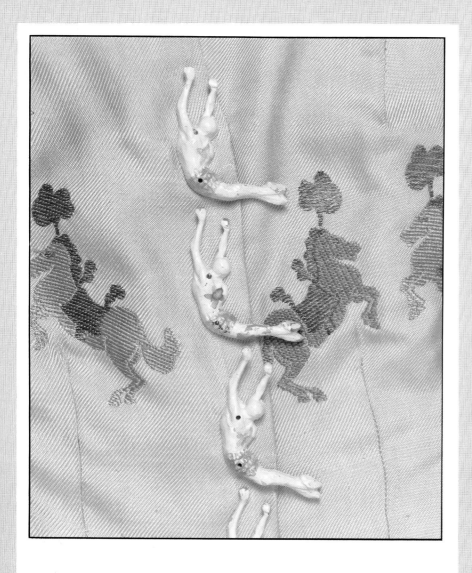

Elsa abhorred ordinary buttons, and never lost a chance to make them enhance the over-all effect of a design.

seeing beauty in lowly objects which had hitherto escaped special attention. Lacquered button-substitutes became one of the most striking features of her house. They were made of everything under the sun: hand-carved wood, aluminium, china, celluloid, metal, amber, coloured crystal, white jade and sealing wax. She initiated the use of ceramics as fastenings for suits and coats. She had terracotta objects dyed to represent lemons, grapefruits, egg-plants and oranges. A great many button substitutes were of plastic substances, Jean Clément being more at home in this media than anyone. On wood he sometimes employed a manual pyro-engraving technique used in Central Europe to decorate little boxes.

Schiaparelli rendered the mundane delightful with buttons in the form of shoelaces, flower-filled crystal paperweights, spinning tops, spoons, padlocks, lollipops, Christmas tree bells, coffee beans, fish hooks, the bobbins and weights of a fisherman's net, safety pins, paper clips and cinnamon that was edible. At one point she thought of the fun to be derived from magnets, but they proved to be too heavy. For Edward VIII's accession in 1936 she featured little gold crowns. She was never more waggish, and probably never more commercially in earnest, than when she launched the dollar sign button in 1933, only to see the dollar collapse.

When it came to belts Elsa was, as ever, innovative. She was the first to use a wide curved belt, perfectly adapted to the body (which was to be re-launched by Christian Dior in his New Look). She adapted polo player and peasant waistbands into belts and pioneered the importation of Australian kangaroo leather. She was also the first to varnish belts, and directed Jean Clément to stain them in special colours to ensure a perfect match with the garment. She enjoyed belting dresses in aluminium and cellophane and in coloured lacquer string. She featured vivid braided patent leather belts, and in 1936 designed belts with hollow daggers containing a comb and lipstick, others with pockets, and still others that as a buckle had a policeman's club out of which, when unscrewed, popped a bridge pencil. At times she used fabric cables or silk and metal ropes as belts. For making leather belts (and some buttons), Clément had an assistant who was originally a saddler. Since Elsa sometimes exaggerated stitching as a feature of a design, Clément had him stitch by hand, using two needles instead of one, which gave an irregular and individual effect. Thus saddle-stitching was born into fashion, lending a primitive look to the belt suitable for sports clothes and foreshadowing the post-war fashions taken from the American Far West. Since Elsa also liked mixing leather and fabric, the ex-saddler made frogs and buttons of crocodile skin for black wool dresses.

Handbags, before 1932, all contained a separate section inside in the tradition of coin purses, and usually the fastenings were of leather covered with silk or suede. That year Elsa invented bags without any visible closings. She also made diamond, rhinestone, gold and enamel mesh varieties that glittered under the evening lights. There

were others in waffled rubber. Bags were shaped like an old-fashioned portmanteau, a suitcase, a flat-bottomed satchel, a flower pot or a lifebuoy.

Soon after starting in business, Elsa had introduced beach bags with cord straps just long enough to be slipped up the arm to the shoulder. Later she modified these bags for town wear. Then, in 1938, she asked Jean Clément to adapt the French railway guard's bag into a small bag at the end of a strap. She lengthened the strap, slung it over her shoulder, brought the article out in a rigid, tortoiseshell version for day, in soft leather for sports and in lamé for evening, and called it the *bandolière*, or shoulder-strap bag. This, adopted at once by Arletty, symbolized the Occupation when women took to bicycling, and became a universal rage after the war; it was even adopted by men in the seventies. Taking her inspiration from the pouches of tram and bus conductors, Elsa made evening bags to hang around the neck. In the eighties such bags became popular as a way of discouraging pickpockets.

In 1932 Elsa gave an early fillip to her career with an evening dress that was ermine from the waist up. From then on her use of furs was most unexpected. She worked beige stone marten in vertical zigzags (Christian Dior would remember these), brought out a rabbit's hair fabric for her Football Frock (August 1935) and promoted stoles so long that they fell to the knees.

When Daisy Fellowes made a grand entrance into the Ritz for dinner one evening in the first Schiaparelli gold-embroidered black monkey-fur cape (later also a jacket), diners clambered on to the chairs and tables to have a look. And the tricks Elsa played with silver fox! Heads peered down from forward-tilted hats, paws gripped pockets, tails fluttered from mittens, coiled bodies protected necks. Her Persian lamb Trinity wrought fashion havoc: a scarf, vest and muff cut in one piece and clapped over a wool dress. Her innovative use of dyes was perhaps most apparent in her furs: red, green and bright blue fox, burgundy red sheepskin, pastel ermine, marten bewilderingly dyed to resemble mink. Of a sealskin cape dyed the colour of old port, *Harper's Bazaar* for October 1934 predicted that it would 'make winter the most exciting in years'.

Wearing imitation jewellery in the nineteenth and early twentieth centuries was just not done. Between the two world wars jewellery design changed radically, thanks largely to René Lalique, who popularized decorative jewellery by substituting crystal and enamel for precious stones. At the same time Koloman Moser and other designers of the Wiener Werkstatte were making decorative jewellery of silver materials and conditioning the public to semi-precious stones like coral, opal and lapis lazuli. Price and carats gave way to craftsmanship and design. Cubism, Futurism, Surrealism, the Bauhaus, Mondrian, de Stijl, Klee – all influenced modern jewellery design, and they were followed by such artists as Braque, Arp, Man Ray, Max Ernst, Dali, Picasso, Giacometti and Cocteau.

The famous Bettina, one of the outstanding models in haute couture, wears a sumptuous Schiaparelli fur in this moody photograph by Henry Clarke.

In the early twenties Chanel had glorified 'costume jewellery', intended as adornment in its own right, and by the late twenties fashionable women had adopted the style of wearing frankly false, or 'fake', jewellery during the day. Elsa, appropriating the trend, transported it to dizzying heights. She claimed justifiably that it was more of an art to create what she did not hesitate to call 'junk jewellery' than the real thing, since the latter had intrinsic beauty of substance and did not require skill in combination. But she always took care to moderate the effect of her more outrageous jewellery by placing it on severe clothes. In being daring and sometimes pugnacious, junk jewellery, she understood, allowed women to assert their individuality.

To divert, shock and amuse, but also genuinely to adorn, she began by creating a fad for pseudo-barbaric jewellery, partially inspired by black African art. She then went on to endow simple beads and other classics with new excitement and glamour by using substances hitherto unassociated with jewellery: china, porcelain, the lightest possible aluminium, plain glass, crystal, plexiglass and plastics. Her Butterfly Brooch became a rage, and she herself often wore her Lucky Brooch, a phoenix with a large baroque pearl for the body and diamond legs and wings. One of her most charming ideas was to pin a little diamond brooch to the centre of a fresh rose, a habit adopted by chic women the world over. The first famous Schiaparelli clip came from the fastenings on French mechanics' overalls. On its heels came nautilus shells, fir cones, mushrooms, musical boxes, caterpillars, mermaids, swallows, coats-of-arms, ducks. To please Elsa, her great friend Cecil Beaton designed the Heart Clip, pierced by a rose and dripping iridescent rubies, and the Galatea's Head clip, alabaster-like with a bower of flowers cascading over the gilt hair and face. Another friend, Giacometti, designed two bronze clips, but they were too heavy to be commercialized. Besides phosphorescent flowers, to guide women in the darkened streets of Paris at the beginning of the war, there were luminous torches attached to real batteries on suit lapels and, maddest of all, a lamp-post or candlestick on which was seated a cherub holding a tiny electric light bulb.

There followed processions of necklaces and bracelets. Louis Aragon, the Surrealist poet, and his wife Elsa Triolet, once designed necklaces that looked as if they were made of aspirins. Elsa herself launched the somewhat terrifying viper necklace and bracelet set: the serpent's black body was white and gold plated and dotted with rubies, while the head was crowned with large rubies set in diamonds. The Schiaparelli jangle of gold and enamel coins on an evening dog-collar of white grosgrain ribbon became almost a cliché. Leeks, cauliflowers and egg-plants formed the Vegetarian Bracelet. Other bracelets could be factory cogs or saw-toothed tools, featherweight discs and flattened metal balls: 'Mechanical splendour,' cried *Harper's Bazaar* for May 1935, 'the bolder the better, the crueller the more chic.'

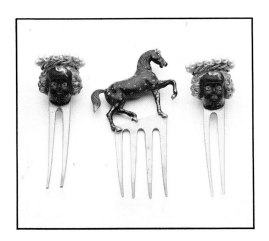

Jean Schlumberger used animals and coiled serpents to decorate his combs (used for securing snoods) and collar ornaments, while Lesage gave Elsa her head with this hypnotic snake embroidery.

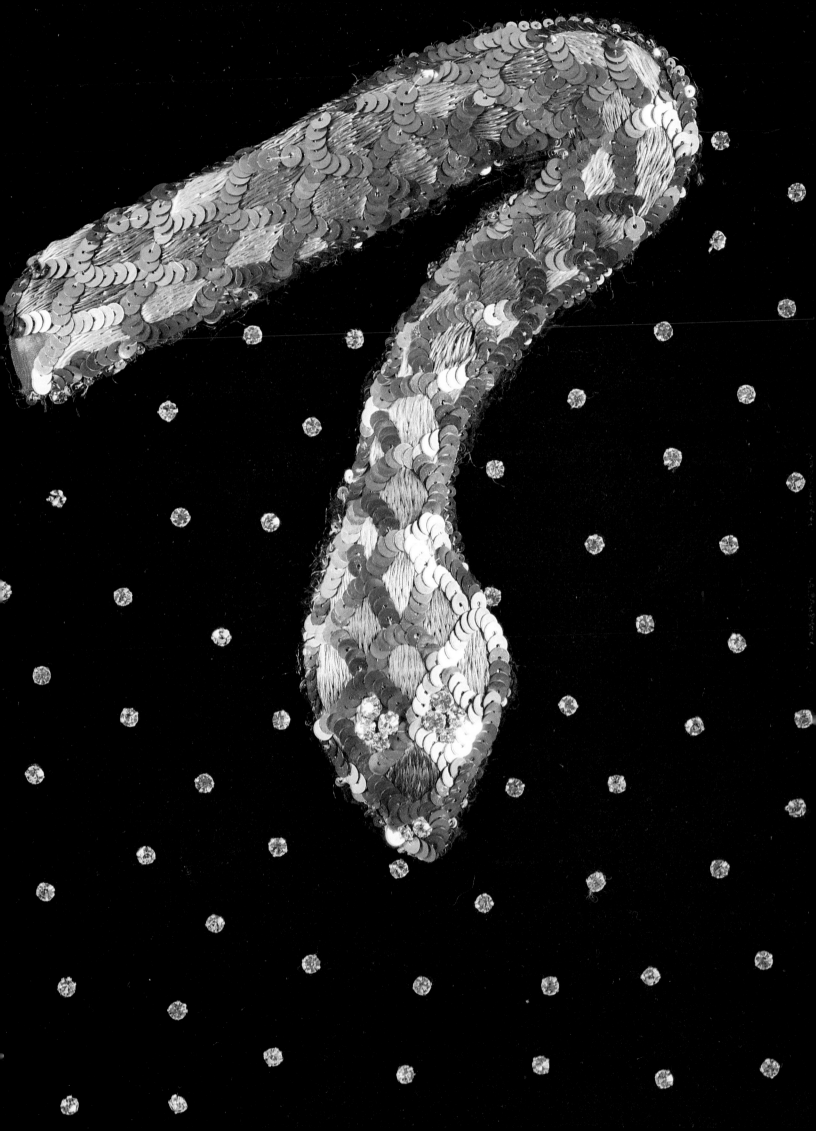

A cork lifebuoy served as a vanity case, a medieval helmet and a gold-metal shell as powder boxes, an earthenware powder box had a big red mouth on the lid. One compact was a gilt and pearl birdcage matching a boutonnière, another, in July 1935, a black enamel and chromium telephone inspired by Dali which opened when a number was dialled. Pins came in the form of a scarlet kilt, gold pomegranates studded with ruby seeds, and weathercocks gyrating on a hat as the wind blew.

Of her singular style-setting rings, in 1938 one was worn at the base of the little finger, the second just above the middle joint of the ring finger and the third cupping the tip of the next finger like a thimble. A three-jointed diamond ring covered the nail.

Schiaparelli set the trend for amusing earrings. From the Hindu chains of topaz that accompanied her saris in 1935 to the post-war diamond daisies with emerald stems piercing the ears, she was always on the lookout for new ideas. Daisy Fellowes, at the Interallié Ball in 1937, wore the most unusual earrings ever seen: one cluster of emeralds clipped at the top of the ear, another on the lobe. Double earrings were to become the rage in the eighties, as were one-ear clip earrings – Elsa put these on sale in 1937.

Early that year Elsa's eagle eye fell upon a pair of earrings worn by Marina, Duchess of Kent, who had been voted the best-dressed woman in the world two years before; they took the form of golden flying fish with diamond fins. She discovered that they had been designed by a young man from Alsace, Jean Schlumberger, who had refused an assured fortune in his prosperous family's textile business and, in the rue de la Boetie apartment he had taken over from Picasso, was working as an artisan for a tiny set of stylish and artistic society leaders which included Daisy Fellowes and Mrs Harrison Williams. Pouncing on him forthwith, Elsa asked him to make some jewelled buttons – Chinese pink starfish, a d'Artagnan plumed hat, speckled pebbles, ostriches.

Schlumberger for Schiaparelli made cuff-links for women's shirts in the form of bagpipes, roller skates, ostriches and other animals for the Circus Collection, 1938.

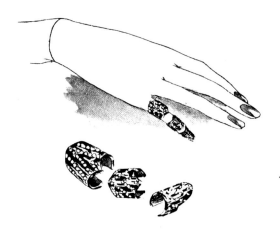

A three-part diamond ring for the little finger.

They sold like hot cakes. Both Schlumberger and she agreed that modern jewellery had gone flat and could only be given new dimensions by combining semi-precious stones with precious ones. Soon 'Schlumberger for Schiaparelli' jewellery became the rage and was copied at all prices. *Harper's Bazaar* in January 1938 proclaimed that Jean Schlumberger had 'Cellini versatility', while the San Francisco *Examiner* of 3 March 1938 called him a 'pace maker', and the *Atlanta Georgia Journal* of 3 April 1938 declared: 'Costume jewellery is perhaps the biggest news in the world of style this spring.' In New York City *Mademoiselle* for November 1938 described this 'artistic find of the ebullient Elsa Schiaparelli' as a 'Galahad in a dinner coat . . . tall, darkly fascinating . . . handsome and charming.' In no time he was the toast of New York and London as well as of Paris.

'Schlum', fully attuned to the Futurist-cum-Art Deco movement translated into fashion by Schiaparelli, interpreted the trend of modern art in his designs as Elsa did in hers. 'I try to make everything look as if it were growing, uneven, at random, organic, in motion,' he said in *Connoisseur* for April 1982.

Schlumberger for Schiaparelli started off with a coral-fringed tassel necklace streaking almost to the knees and a delightful brooch made of two roller-skating feet. The Cupid clips and earrings, fat little neo-baroque gilt cherubs each brandishing a rhinestone torch, and the Louis XIV clips and earrings, golden sunbeams studded with rhinestones, were so successful that Elsa and he launched a gold rush. A lapel pin represented a golden ear of corn with a few missing kernels replaced by rhinestones; another, a golden vase from which emerged sprays of amethyst, sapphire and ruby leaves. A gilded metal choker necklace composed of water-lily leaves had gold frogs perched on various petals. Schlumberger for Schiaparelli necklaces of gold cord and silk, of gold bowknots, strands of golden fish and exotic seashells, a string of Victorian hands and wrists, a cortège of swans filing past gilt and white enamelled rushes – they could not be produced fast enough at any price, ten dollars at Bonwit Teller or 59 cents at the Lexington Arcade. Mrs Harrison Williams launched a vogue with the topaz, sapphire and amethyst flower lapel clips worn in staggered groups of two to five. The Duchess of Kent ordered a primitive-looking multicoloured stone necklace and bracelet that caught on like fire. The climax of the Schlumberger for Schiaparelli designs came with the gold cigarette lighter in the shape of a little fish with ruby eyes and rubies set in a tail so flexible that it actually wriggled. Just before the outbreak of war it was to be found in the evening bag of every chic woman on two continents.

Jean Schlumberger fought for the Free French Forces as a liaison officer with the British, afterwards setting up shop on East 63rd Street in New York with one of Paul Poiret's nephews. He was acknowledged as a true artist in 1961 when the Wildenstein Gallery held a retrospective exhibition of his work, and he became a vice-president at Tiffany's where he ran his own department into the late seventies. Undoubtedly the modern world's greatest jewellery designer, he was declared by *Connoisseur* in April 1982 as 'clearly one of the most gifted artists of this century'.

Of all the daring and innovative accessories dreamed up by Schiaparelli, it is perhaps her hats that made the biggest impact. A particularly flattering hat, she reasoned, set a beautiful woman apart from others, while a crazy hat acted as a defence against the insecurity of not having too pretty a face. Whatever the type, she balanced her suits and dresses with neatly proportioned, delicious hats with fanciful motifs, sometimes tipped forward at a rakish angle almost on to the forehead, sometimes even nose diving, topped with feathers, garnished with fur, and with flaps floating behind and adorned with all manner of absurdities and little jokes, such as a yellow and brown quill shooting up the back like that of an Indian chief. Fashionable women practically took to living in puppet-sized Doll's Hats, sometimes called Cocked Hats, and Toy Hats so minute they barely covered a single curl. Her skull caps, now and then contradictorily squared, became all the rage, and American *Vogue* in December 1934 described a variation called the 'snug cap' as 'the smallest head we've seen in ages'. In 1938 there came the Pin-cushion Hat and the infinitesimal gold African peak with emerald drops that she wore herself, as in the Vertès portrait. In mid-1936 every chic woman sported a large pie-dish strewn with long-stemmed calla lilies, only to give it up for, in turn, the tiny black rose-stabbed hat that toppled precariously over one eye, the straw braid hat pierced by a spike hairpin, and the one-jewelled black band wound round the ears and forehead to hold the curls emerging from on top of the head. Berets were perched hazardously on one side of the head, and, called His Honour, could be formed into a judge's toque. Then came the high hats with saucily uptilted brims, the Russian Crown and the Breton Sailor. These were followed by the soaring Scheherazade, the dashing upward and forward shooting Skylarkers ('worn,' said Elsa, 'far ahead of yourself') the Hide-and-Seek Hat, the Lobster Basket brimming with lobster-printed linen, the Berry Garden and the Sea Shell made of layers of pleated organza. Her ostrich caps were immediately popular, and for Edward VIII's accession she presented in October 1936 an interminable rose and plum-coloured affair.

When it came to trimmings for her hats, horsehair dyed white, pink or any colour you like served for brims or visors for both day and evening wear. Fruits, blossoms, grasses, vegetables and metals abounded. She stuck a pencil into the crown of one hat in case of urgent need to note something (and wore it herself to the races), and to the brim of another attached a fisherman's fly. She brought out hats in black lacquered kid, sometimes combined with felt or antelope, golden winged white panama, black plaited straw and black patent leather. She did visor-peaked Botticelli pageboy hats (August 1935), Monkey Hats and the dreamily romantic Merry

"Mirror, Mirror on my suit——"
Schiaparelli

Huge buttons in the form of hand-mirrors adorn this jacket, worn with a nose-diving hat.

'There was a young woman who lived in a shoe . . .'

Widow Hat. Reversing all the present trends, she ordered 'Hair brushed up!' To intensify the heated disputes over the new coiffures she launched the crushed top hat, the tiny fedora and (May 1935) the Tangle Hats – flat like pancakes, poker chips and saucers – that customers fought to procure, and an Hour-Glass Hat inspired by Mae West. Anticipating the new practicality necessary during the war years, she brought out cowls remembered from illustrations in her father's books – in jersey for the country, velvet for the city, with flap ends that could be tied into a scarf or lifted to form a turban.

In the history of costume, hats had not generated such fun and games since the times of Marie Antoinette. All over the world newsreels sent audiences into gales of laughter with Elsa's adaptations of realistic objects: chimney pots, three-bladed aeroplane propellors, ventilators, igloos, windmills, ships' funnels, a bird cage containing a singing canary. She attained a high point in headgear folly even for her with the Surrealist hats: the anticipatory Television Hat (February 1935) and, in the autumn of 1937, a black hat in the form of an upside-down shoe with a velvet heel sticking up like a small column, which only Daisy Fellowes and she had the courage to wear. But Elsa alone in the same autumn dared to wear a beret shaped like a mutton chop sporting a perky patent leather white frill over the bone – perhaps her ultimate claim to eccentricity.

17

'Shocking' : Pink and Perfume

FROM her earliest presentations Schiaparelli managed to make even black a different colour. Her blacks, taken from childhood images of the clothes worn by people in Campagna Romana under the rich Latium sun, were warm and joyous, even spicy. As American *Vogue* said on 15 September 1936, they were 'consummate, eternal, irreplaceable'. The first true colour shock she introduced was ice blue in 1932, and thereafter startling colours became a hallmark of the House of Schiaparelli. Elsa's designs were infused with the scarlets and violets of the ceremonial priestly garments imprinted on her mind as a child at St Peter's, to which she added the bright, striking colours of the Fauves, Cubists, Futurists and Surrealists, all put together like a Matisse plume. She introduced as well innumerable 'firsts', shades that had never been seen before and that set the fashion world spinning.

In this she also broke new ground technically. To devise a new shade according to her wishes, Jean Clément used a procedure hitherto associated with the automobile industry, which was to remain unique to Schiaparelli in haute couture but was widely adopted by painters a generation later. Manipulating an airbrush, Clément projected droplets of tinted cellulose varnish, normally used for the bodies of custom-built motor cars, on to sheets of white paper. While spraying, he varied the mix of components in the brush to create a complete range of the colour. From this Elsa selected what corresponded best to her idea and then gave the ingredients of the 'dose' to her fabric, embroidery and fur suppliers so that their dyers could reproduce it. Oranges, browns, yellows, greens, blues, greys, reds and even whites – she renewed them all. She put as many as five shades together to dazzle the eye with her Barber Pole evening gown. Among the unusual dyes she ordered were a wet-moss green and a rose lavender, but most striking of all was sunlight golden: it stained some satins a faint honey colour, others orange-red, and played over the blues, violets and pinks as at the edge of an evening sky.

A Lesage butterfly embroidery for the Music Collection 1937 and (inset) a Medusa head in gold tweed and sequins on a short cape of shocking pink wool, 1938.

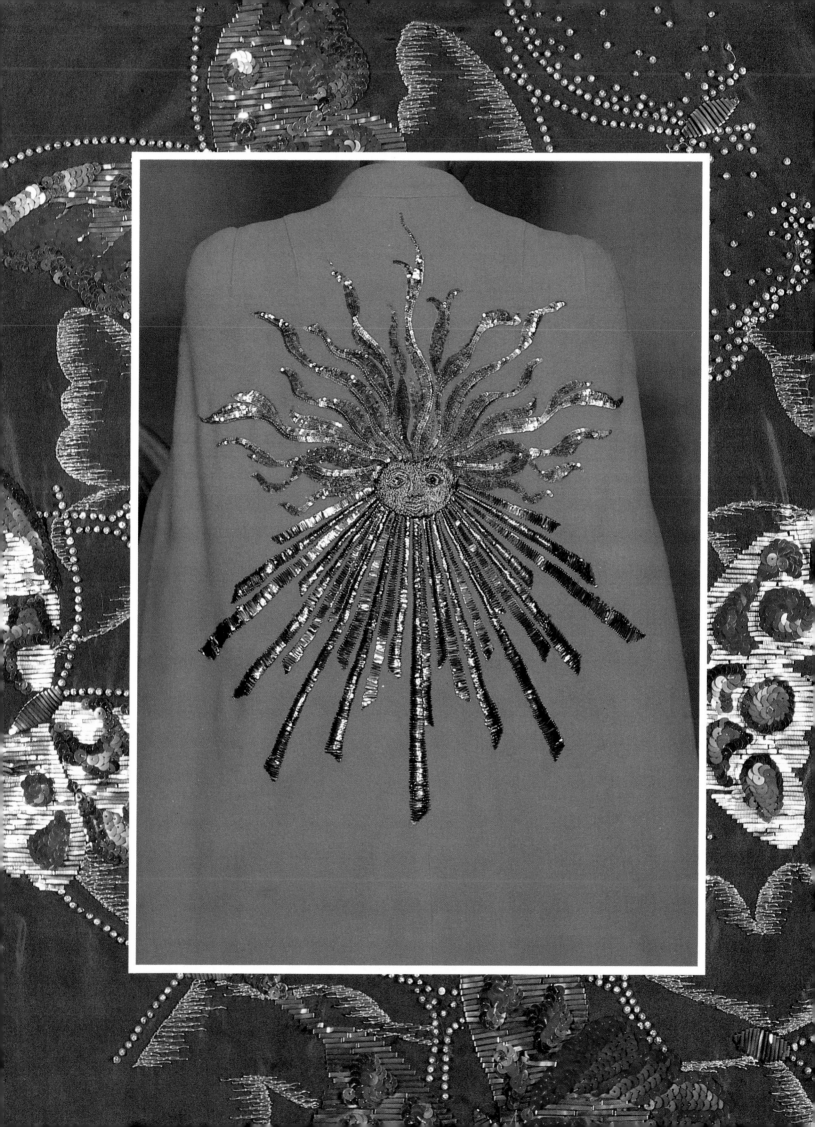

Inevitably, the day came when Elsa asked Jean Clément to come up with something astonishing to recall the scarlet robes of the princes of the Vatican and the vibrant pink of the Peruvian Incas that she had seen in the illustrated books at Palazzo Corsini. This request led to one of her greatest achievements. First Clément toyed with 'cameo' pink, desert rose pink, pink ruby and mauve rose. She accepted them, but indifferently. Then he combined parlour pink with mauve and a pink-violet dear to Christian Bérard's heart. She used these too, but without any great enthusiasm. Then one day in 1936 Clément added magenta to pink, creating an iridescent cyclamen colour. At the sight of it Elsa nodded, and dressed an entire collection in what was promptly dubbed 'shocking pink'. The presentation was shocking, and most of the gowns and accessories were shocking. To underline the colour's instantaneous success, Salvador Dali dyed a large stuffed bear shocking pink and put drawers in its stomach. Elsa dressed the bear in an orchid satin coat and loaded the drawers with jewels. Then she gave her dachshund, which accompanied her everywhere, a shocking pink collar and leash. Dali also used shocking pink for a divan he designed in the form of Mae West's lips for Elsa's interior decorator and friend, Jean-Michel Frank. *Harper's Bazaar* for November 1937 did a whole page on Schiaparelli's shocking pink 'Peruvian Magic': beret-like montera; puños, lavishly embroidered armlets to accompany black evening dresses; and chullos, hoods worn high in the Andes. The colour became one of Schiaparelli's most famous trademarks and the predominating colour in the world of fashion, no matter how many other names its copies and variations assumed, until it was edged out by red in the fifties. A shocking pink sheath worn with a shocking pink skull cap was 'Schiaparelli's loveliest dinner dress', according to *Harper's Bazaar* in October 1940. What an image with which to begin the blackout in Paris.

After the war Nieman-Marcus, one of Elsa's best customers, invited her to Dallas, Texas, where the mayor himself was to make her an honorary citizen. As her plane landed, it taxied into a twenty-foot-high reproduction of the Eiffel Tower built of shocking pink roses, while thousands more were scattered from a helicopter circling above. Her hosts outdid the city's legendary extravagant hospitality at a cocktail party for three thousand guests in an immense garden planted with shocking pink carnations.

The development of organic chemistry and the creation of synthetic laboratory fragrances opened vast horizons to perfumes, and it was Paul Poiret, before the First World War, who was the first fashion designer to bring out scents and beauty products under the name 'Rosine'. Notably Lanvin, Chanel, Patou and Molyneux furthered the idea in the twenties. Early in the thirties, while fickle fashion was still a money maker, Elsa invaded the market. Her first fragrances and their eaux de cologne and eaux de toilette were made in England by George Robert Parkinson, who benefited from the

In typical Schiaparelli contradiction, innocent cherubs frolic around a sensual Mae West mouth advertising 'Shocking Radiance' lipstick.

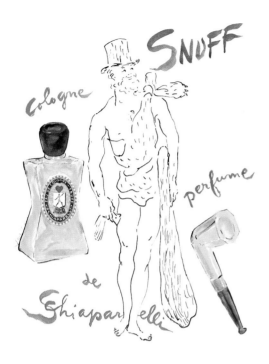

Macho advertising for 'Snuff', the first perfume for men.

renown of her recently opened branch house in London and also ensured American distribution. In 1934 three Schiaparelli perfumes were put on sale. 'Salut', a fragrance for evening, gave the impression of a valley of white lilies by the light of a silvery moon. Daytime 'Soucis' was a delicate sandalwood scent presented in a heart pierced by an arrow. 'Schiap', an updating of the early 'S' for sports, had a madonna lily and hyacinth base, was both fresh and bittersweet, and – years in advance of its time – aimed at men as well as women. By 1937 the production of couturier scents had gathered such momentum in Paris, the Schiaparelli offerings were so successful, and the Place Vendôme house had caused such excitement that Elsa decided to produce new perfumes in France and set up a separate British-based company, again wholly owned by herself. To assist her she hired a young and brilliant Frenchwoman, Paulette Laperche, who grew so much in the job, as did the job with her, that ultimately she became the manager of the company and remained with it until well after Elsa's death.

In Bois-Colombes, a northwestern suburb of Paris, Elsa set up and equipped an entire perfume factory. It was not, of course, in some dismal shed or hangar, but in a small mansion surrounded by verdant grounds. Here the scents were manufactured in all stages, from laboratory experiments to the mixing of basic oils and the wrapping, packing and despatching of the articles to customers all over the world.

For advertising Elsa turned almost solely to the pictorial artist, Marcel Vertès, whose sketches were infused with a whole new note of gaiety and freshness. To translate her ideas for bottles, glassware, labelling and boxing into realities, she relied on the designs and dummies of D. Guerycolas, perhaps the greatest perfume designer of all times, who later signed an exclusive contract with Christian Dior. 'Sleeping' (1938), heavy, sugary and with a touch of vanilla, came on a blue background in a Baccarat crystal candlestick with a lighted taper and a cone-shaped extinguisher. One 'Sleeping' box represented an eighteenth-century drawing-room of which the doors were opened by two lackeys, while another, a royal canopied bed, accommodated two snuggling bottles, and in yet another the gloved hand of the Statue of Liberty held the candlestick-taper aloft. Three 'Sleeping' bottles nestled in the cradle of New York in 1940. And when you opened the door to a cuckoo clock to remove the 'Sleeping' bottle, the cuckoo called out. 'Snuff', a sober, dry scent and a revolution in 1939 since it was for men alone, was packaged in yellow with a cork stopper topped by a crystal pipe. In 1946 came 'Le Roi Soleil', a jasmine scent in an extravagant bottle designed by Salvador Dali, representing a radiant gilt sun with flying seagulls (the Sun King's face) and a wavy gold and blue sea in a golden shell. 'Succès Fou' (1953), for which the advertising, sketches by Paynet, featured a pair of shy young lovers, came in a green ivy leaf protected by a dazzling pink heart. To use 'Si' (1957) you uncorked a straw-

For 'Sleeping', a gentler image with the young girl dreaming of her sweetheart.

enveloped Chianti-type wine bottle packaged in fluorescent orange. To open the new 'S', Elsa's last fragrance (1961), described as calling forth meadows and woods, warm and ferny, you wound a large opaline fob watch.

Which brings us to 'Shocking'. The greatest triumph of the House of Schiaparelli, Elsa's first scent produced in Paris, 'Shocking' (1937) was a voluptuous, sweet bouquet of Mediterranean flowers, as impudent as shocking pink, with which Elsa at once ingeniously associated it in the interests of promotion and publicity. She asked young Leonor Fini to take her inspiration for the design of the bottle from a dressmaker's dummy with Mae West curves, broad Schiaparelli shoulders and a small waist. She herself draped a dressmaker's tape-measure around the neck so as to form a V-shaped décolletage fastened over the waist with a button-initial 'S'. The half-length figure-bottle required a very delicate assembly, performed in the Schiaparelli factory in Bois-Colombes, of over twenty separate pieces after more than thirty employees had supervised each of the operations required for their manufacture.

To advertise 'Shocking', Elsa incited Vertès to do sophisticated, suggestive, even erotic sketches, very daring for the times, thus creating a new seductive approach to the sale of scents and anticipating the erotic advertising that popped up everywhere half a century later. She brought out 'Shocking' in a wide range of beauty products and toiletries and combined it with jewellery and accessories. She devised perfumed clips, stick pins, hat pins, hairpins, metal and ivory buttons, rings, bracelets, seashells and other gadgets. Fashioned out of enamelled filigree gold metal, they contained tiny pieces of absorbent material on to which the fragrant essence could be poured. They immediately became a craze. One day in 1938 Elsa combined shocking pink and 'Shocking' in a lipstick, but the colour did not suit unmade-up cheeks, so she added rouge for the cheeks in the same colour as the lipstick, thus initiating matching beauty products.

In no time the sales of 'Shocking' roared past the new couturier fragrances – Lanvin's 'Arpège', Chanel's and Molyneux's 'No. 5', Patou's 'Joy' – because Elsa kept it accessible in price to women of modest means, especially in the British Commonwealth and the United States. It was followed in 1948 by the bittersweet 'Zut', presented in a bottle formed like a woman's hips and legs, the complementary lower half to the 'Shocking' bust.

Schiaparelli Perfumes employed forty people, did two million dollars' worth of business annually and was prevented from expanding further only because of the difficulty of obtaining the basic ingredients – Elsa would not settle for substitutes. In the end this undertaking proved to be the more profitable of Elsa's two major activities, for hundreds of thousands of women who could never aspire to a Schiaparelli original bought her scents. After the war, with an American branch, Schiaparelli Perfumes lent money to the declining fashion business, and, when hard times arrived, would prove to be Elsa's salvation.

'Zut' provided the complementary half to the erotic 'Shocking' torso (opposite).

18

Star of the Show

IN 1935 French couture was showing a two billion franc deficit. Whereas unemployment in the trade had been unknown until five years earlier, there were now ten thousand people in the fashion world out of work in Paris alone. At 4 rue de la Paix, however, the premises had become too small. Elsa claimed she could hear the walls groaning under the impact of the teeming crowds, and luck now made it possible for her to fulfil her wildest dream. January 1935 marked the start of the four 'blind years' described by Winston Churchill as 'the long, dismal, crawling tides of drift and surrender, of wrong measurements and feeble impulses.' But for Elsa it marked the start of her great period, for on New Year's Day 1935 she carried her screens a few yards down rue de la Paix to a 98-room mansion at 21 Place Vendôme.

'Nothing is in fact more tragic and vain than fashion,' Salvador Dali wrote in his autobiography.

The House of Schiaparelli, 21 Place Vendôme.

> The war which was to liquidate the post-war revolutions was symbolized . . . by the dressmaking establishment which Elsa Schiaparelli was about to open on the Place Vendôme. Here new morphological phenomena occurred; here the essence of things was to become transubstantiated; here the tongues of fire of the Holy Ghost of Dali were going to descend. And (since unfortunately I am always right) the German troops were to swoop down on Biarritz, just a few years later, camouflaged in the Schiaparelli and Dali manner, wearing cynical and mimetic costumes, with branches of leaves freshly torn from the soil of France bursting from their sandy animal hair like the Nordic buds of a crucified Daphne.

Throughout the centuries Place Vendôme, designed by Mansard at the end of the seventeenth century in accordance with Louis XIV's instructions, had preserved all its integrity and dignity. Originally, there were to be noble structures to house the Royal Library, the Royal Mint and various royal academies, but money ran out when only the façades had been built, and the Sun King leased the land to the city of Paris. A century later, Napoleon erected in the centre a column to the glorious memory of his triumphant *Grande Armée* and topped it with a statue of himself in the toga of a laurel-wreathed Caesar. Elsa acquired the mansion from Madame Cheruit, the couturier who forty years before had given the teenager Paul Poiret his first encouragement there.

On the low-ceilinged mezzanine were three inadequate little front rooms in which Elsa set up her studio. It was level with the stockroom, and this saved the young women from having to carry heavy rolls of fabric up and down stairs. Elsa did most of her work either in semi-darkness or by electric light in this excellent observation post, for she could see and hear everything that went on in Place Vendôme from there.

Upstairs on the grand first floor were the salon serving as Elsa's office and the large and small salons used as showrooms. All overlooking Place Vendôme and its column, they were notable examples of early eighteenth-century decoration: beautiful high-ceilinged rooms decorated in off-white and gold, lined with gilt-framed mirrors and above them lovely murals in dark colours, almost all depicting cherubs. Elsa upholstered the Louis XIV chairs and divans in blue and white, while her cherished screens, covered with blue chintz, formed dressing-rooms. She stood white plaster vases or candelabra on the mantels of the great fireplaces and scattered about padded cushions of the latest avant-garde designs.

At a time when photographers were outlawed from collections, both Raoul Dufy and Christian Bérard did drawings of the sensational Schiaparelli openings, which generated all the excitement of the première of a long awaited and highly publicized new play and had to be repeated three times a day to accommodate the crowds. Around Michèle Guéguen and her school-uniformed *vendeuses*, seated as usual behind their desks at the entrance to the showrooms, the winding staircase up and down was packed with artists, writers, architects and musicians, joined after the war by women pilots, women Army and Navy officers, air hostesses, decorators, and teachers and students from art schools. These crowds resented being crammed into the hot downstairs hall while waiting for the lift or for the congestion on the stairs to ease. Cunningly, Elsa placed her little 'Schiap' annexe to the left in a three-roomed shop with three large windows giving on to the broad pavement. In one was an inviting glass door, which also attracted potential customers too timid to enter a great mansion under the watchful eye of a liveried doorman. The mansion's main entrance was barred, forcing the customers to pass through the shop to gain access to the lift or stairs. While they waited there, they looked – and bought.

'Bouticle', a thirteenth-century word, signified that part of the façade of a house where a merchant or craftsman displayed and sold his wares. Preceded by Paul Poiret's 'Chichis' and Patou's and Lanvin's ready-to-wear shops, the iconoclastic and amusing Schiap

The Schiap Boutique.

Boutique, the first of its kind, became instantly famous because of the new formula, 'Hand-made and ready to be taken away immediately, even with minor alterations'. Elsa filled it with startling pictures and unconventional gadgets. On Louis XIV sphinxes she strewed evening sweaters, skirts, blouses, lingerie and accessories previously scorned by haute couture. On impertinent straw figures she displayed bags, shoes, scarves and fake jewellery, along with her inevitable interchangeable separates. In a gilded cage she set out items of her expanding perfume and beauty product business and lavished feathers and frills on a life-sized donkey. As a good-luck piece she bought in Pascal, a golden-haired wooden figure of pure Greek beauty, tall, slim, dignified and unutterably glamorous, soon married to Pascaline, good and inconspicuous. Pascal never protested about being shown in the most outlandish and esoteric get-up and always contemplated the gaping crowds with calm indifference, whether in Paris or representing his mistress abroad.

The impudent Schiap Boutique became one of the sights of the City of Light as tourists flocked to photograph perhaps the most famous windows in the world. Possibly the best testimonial to it was by Elsa's employees: they all bought there. After the war, Christian Dior extended the idea almost to the bazaar, and by the seventies couturiers were selling chocolates, watches and bed linen in their boutiques, by the eighties, scooters, carpeting and food products.

After her arrival at Place Vendôme one of Elsa's most spectacular innovations was to give each collection a theme. For practical purposes this lent greater overall harmony and encouraged a more precise creativity. It also allowed her to streak off on unprecedented flights of imagination, humour and theatricality. For these collections she designed gowns of special fabrics, appropriately printed or embroidered, with corresponding buttons, jewels, trimmings and accessories, all reflecting and contributing to the theme.

'Most of the women I see – on the street as well as in my own showrooms – have too many clothes,' Elsa declared in the open letter to her daughter requested by the London *Daily Express* for 21 May 1936. 'Each outfit, whether you have one or a dozen, must be thought out, not chancily flung together – shoes, hat, handbag, belt buckle, buttons, all building up an especial effect.'

Duly, Schiaparelli was the only house that presented its manne-quins completely dressed from head to foot, with hat, gloves, scarf, jewellery and shoes, and carrying an umbrella and a handbag. In many cases Elsa now refused to sell the elements of a 'number': you had to take the entire ensemble or nothing. 'Of a Parisienne you can never say exactly what is pleasing in her toilette,' Thérèse de Caraman-Chimay quoted her as saying in the first article she prepared for the press in 1931. 'The search for an overall effect is so instinctive with her that details seem natural. A painting is not beautiful because of the treatment of one tree, and the attraction, although made up of details, is as indefinable as the charm.'

Raoul Dufy

The Schiaparelli opening at Place Vendôme, 1936, as drawn by Raoul Dufy

Schiaparelli's presentations were like parades or shows, complete with music, lighting effects, dance steps, grouped appearances, stunts and jokes. Customers flocked to her collections to be stimulated, entertained and scandalized. Paris fashion, even when it goes eccentric or foolish, often tends to retain some relation to politics. Elsa staged her 'Stop, Look and Listen' collection in August 1935 'to meet the uncertain political temper of the times'. According to the Associated Press on 29 September 1935, 'While the world is divided between kingdoms, republics and dictatorships and European statesmen weigh the problem of threatened Italo-Ethiopian war, Schiaparelli has launched both royalist and republican clothes.' To commemorate George V's Silver Jubilee there were royal blue and imperial violet afternoon and evening garments, for the Left red French Revolution capes matched with a Gallic rooster-crest hat. To show her anti-Fascist feelings, she designed a black evening dress in the form of an Ethiopian warrior's tunic to be worn with trousers of purple honouring Emperor Haile Selassie, and she put long-coated pyjamas over Ethiopian pants. One of her tailored coats in Grenadier Guards cloth was cut as for a soldier, causing American *Vogue* on 1 October 1935 to proclaim it, because of its colour, Revolutionary red, 'the smartest swing left of the decade'. In a vibrant effort to support a lost cause, she dressed the window of the Boutique as a 'peace' window featuring a big world globe with flying white doves and a bird sitting on it with an olive branch in its beak.

The Eskimo Collection launched in October 1935, though deemed extraordinary by the press, was one of the few pre-war Schiaparelli looks that did not catch on. The reason was undoubtedly that it made the body appear too bulky all over, not only at the shoulders. The forearms were shielded by gauntlets in husky fur recalling those of an ice-hockey goalie or in embroidered wool and velvet in the Peruvian style. Hands were protected with suede-lined fur gloves as hefty as a cab driver's – these, according to American *Vogue* 1 October 1935, 'the most exciting accessory of the year'.

Following the Parachute Collection in February 1936 came the Current Events Collection in August of that year. It was the time of the Front Populaire, so Elsa brought out Rabble hats and cravats with long French Revolution streamers. She celebrated the accession of Edward VIII with Coronation velvet and felt, fur and velvet hats in the form of crowns and a lord mayor's hat.

The Music Collection in February 1937 had butterflies fluttering throughout, singing birds and buzzing bees woven on summer prints, and buttons, necklaces and clips in the shape of violins, drums, bagpipes, mandolins and horns. Sheet music was imitated with ribbons for bars and roses for notes printed on a white silk crêpe, while words, staff and scales were printed on coloured silk and a suede belt was twisted into a treble-clef buckle. When you opened one bag, a musical box tinkled a melody, another was shaped like an accordeon, a third had piano keys on the frame.

Music provides the theme and variations for the collection of February 1937.

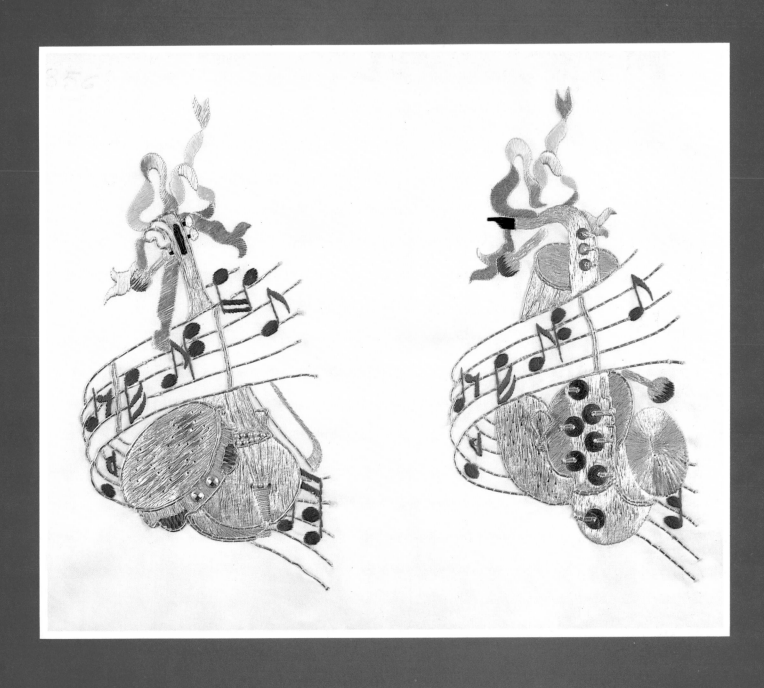

Christian Bérard sketches the opening of the Schiaparelli circus for Vogue, *April 1938...*

The year 1938 provided perhaps the greatest excitement Paris fashion has ever known. Schiaparelli produced four of her most imaginative shows. In February she let loose her Circus Collection, sent the performers skipping up and down the imposing staircase and leaping on and off the *vendeuses'* desks in her dignified showrooms, had them jumping in and out of the windows overlooking Napoleon's Column and Place Vendôme by means of ladders propped up on the pavement against the Louis XIV façade. This was the most riotous and swaggering show that fashion had ever seen. Here you paraded in a tall hat and a ringmaster jacket with a high collar, or in tights worn under long narrow black skirts. You pirouetted in bright satin boleros embroidered with ponies sporting diamond bridles and coloured plumes. You jumped through hoops in intricately cut acrobat skirts, balanced like a daring bareback rider in the sketchiest of tutus, glided with the stately grace of a mandarin's lady, or pranced in Daliesque 'torn chiffon'. You toed the line – and looked taller and more slender – in 'footstools', based by shoe designer Perugia of Padua on evening sandals from eighteenth-century Venice, modified by the Arab shoes Elsa had brought back from Tunisia. Composed of thick cushioned cork soles and kid straps

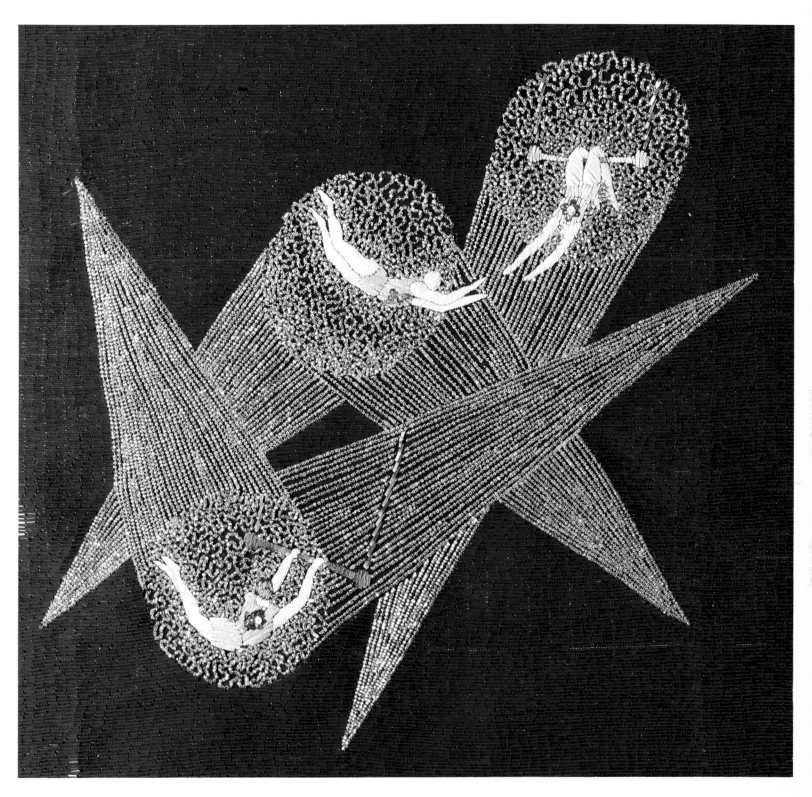

. . . and Lesage spotlights the acrobats.

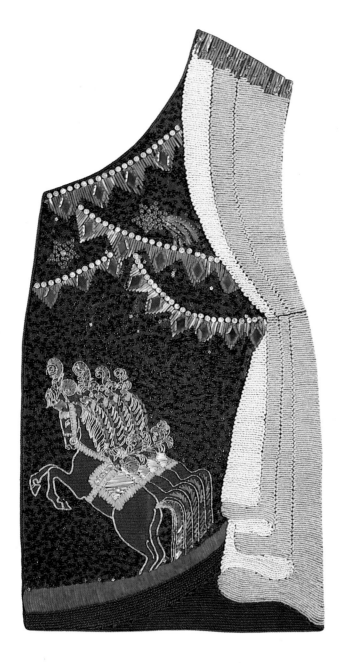

of a contrasing colour, these were later vulgarized as the universally worn clog shoes, or 'wedgies'. Here came the Skeleton Man in furs and the Fat Lady in a tiered cape of stiff puce satin. The grimacing face of a clown, liquorice all-sorts, peppermint sticks, candy floss, slices of gingerbread – buttons in these shapes fastened your jackets. Gold fringe or flashy pompons decked your bosom, pastel feathers or an organdie stock encircled your neck, black silk gloves up to the biceps were held in place by shocking pink velvet garters. Round your neck, acrobats swung from trapezes. An ice-cream cone, a sitting hen with buttons for eggs, an inkpot with its quill, a chariot wheel of lacquered straw, a beret of tufted upholstery, an osprey duster, a Punch with ostrich feather flowers: these were among the models for your hats. A 'tent' snood of printed silk hid your hair by day, one of rhinestones matching the embroidery on your gown or coat by night. Schlumberger made for Schiaparelli lapel clips and brooches of circus horses' head, jewels in gold and jade or sparkling

Elsa plays the ringmaster with performing elephants and horses for evening boleros in the Circus Collection.

Venetian glass, balloons as bags, gloves looking like spats or sporting a bow on one finger.

To present the Pagan Collection, also referred to as the Forest Collection, in April, Venus after Venus stepped out of Botticelli paintings in capes covering simple, clinging gowns embroidered with wreaths of leaves and delicate flowers. Pan, prancing, piped in fabrics as soft as thistledown. The earth, grass, trees and wild life of field and forest came surging up to Paris from Elsa's Campagna Romana and the Alban hills. Wood nymphs wore jackets buttoned with owls, stags' heads, nuts, brightly feathered birds and insects. Belts of supple foliage encircled their waists, bright twigs entwined their bosoms as embroidery, wound about their arms forming multiple bracelets, and nestled in their hair as clips, while ferns adorned their lapels.

The Astrology (or Zodiac) Collection in August 1938 was aglitter with the stars, the moon, the sun. Horoscopes printed on coats and jackets foretold the future, as minor planetary influences were visible in lights flashing from jewels, and in gadgets like a clip in the shape of a fish with a power-batteried eye that lit up in celebration of the Pisces sign.

In an attempt to relieve the anxiety over the deteriorating political situation by bringing some poetry back into life, Elsa produced in October 1938 what would be her last great collection, the Commedia dell'arte, introduced by the strains of Scarlatti, Vivaldi, Pergolese and Cimarosa. Harlequin wore a suit half of Hudson seal and half of black wool. Columbine, in love with Harlequin, was radiant in a ballet dress with fan-skirted tutu, a wreath of small roses in her hair, her legs showing to great advantage in shocking pink Schiaparelli tights. Pedrolino (taken from French Pierrot), so hopelessly enamoured of Columbine that a tear always glittered on his face, sported a large white ruff flopping around a whitened face. Comediennes entered, balancing mischievous hats on a lock of hair. Wandering troupers masqueraded in big, bulky topcoats of rough and tawny colours with linings in sharp contrast, and in long evening coats of felt patchwork. Underneath were suits or dresses that fitted like tights. Bells tinkled on the belts of troubadors and minstrels or dangled merrily from zips. Although now and then Elsa could not prevent a blue or purple velvet from casting its shadow on black or brown, no tragic muse invaded this scene.

Schiaparelli was never at a loss. For the 1937 International Exhibition of Arts and Techniques, the Chambre Syndicale de la Couture Parisienne, in its Pavilion of Elegance, had devised a series of displays of evening gowns by all the great designers. Elsa complained that the over-long dummies with featureless heads and melodramatic poses provided by the Chambre were too hideous. She was rebuked. Very well: she laid the dreary plaster mannequin allotted to her, naked as the factory delivered it, on some turf outside the Pavilion and piled flowers over it 'to cheer it up'. Then she stretched a rope across an open space and, as on washing-day, hung up a wide range of smart women's clothes even to panties, stockings and shoes. Gendarmes had to hold back the crowds.

In 1947 strikes stopped work before she finished preparing a collection. Nothing daunted, she turned the showing into a sensational publicity stunt by displaying items with one sleeve, bringing to life half-finished evening dresses with costume jewellery, and pinning to them explanations about cut written in her bold hand with swatches of fabric and sketches to show where buttonholes would be, the kind of buttons to be used and their colours. This was the cheapest collection she ever designed, and it sold very well.

In 1952 she was too late with her official request to the Chambre Syndicale to obtain a suitable date for the presentation of a collection. So she scheduled it at midnight in her home, asking a film company to transform her courtyard into a showroom out of a fairy tale. A long dais stretched its length, vivid tartan covered the glass marquee and life-sized Chinese animals attired in her new ball-gowns stood looking out of the windows of the house against a sky-blue background. The show took place with the mannequins swaying to the strains of Brazilian music played by the Scola da Samba, the foremost orchestra in Rio de Janeiro.

At her height Elsa had 600 employees making, promoting and selling 10,000 items a year, some of these costing as much as $5000 each. In two major and two minor collections she presented 600 models annually and inaugurated the custom of distributing bulletins to the press before a showing to draw attention to the *nouveautés*. Cunningly she grabbed a lead on her rivals by ignoring the practice of disclosing darkly veiled fashions only in a big collection. In her mid-season showings she hinted broadly at the goodies to come a few months later, and this forced buyers into 21 Place Vendôme four times a year instead of the usual two.

And how they flocked! For a show, the small salon would contain the press, literally sitting one on top of the other. In the gold and white grand salon the best seats were reserved for the smartest people, royalty past and present, leaders of society, wives of presidents, colonial governors, ambassadors, generals, admirals: Lady Elsie Mendl, Mrs Winston Churchill, Eve Curie, Mrs Cole Porter. World-famous actresses included Constance Bennett, Myrna Loy, Fay Wray, Norma Shearer, Merle Oberon, Annabella, Danielle Darrieux, Michèle Morgan, Vivien Leigh. Marion Davies, mistress of the newspaper magnate William Randolph Hearst, was there, and Mrs Randolph Hearst Jr, his daughter-in-law. Greta Garbo sat inconspicuously in a corner pondering which raincoat to buy. And there was Marlene Dietrich trying on hats, her famous legs crossed, smoking the inevitable cigarette as if she were posing for a still. Dietrich always remembered upon her next visit to present a rose to an employee who had rendered her any special service. Here sat Claudette Colbert, mischievous and twinkling. (As early as 1937,

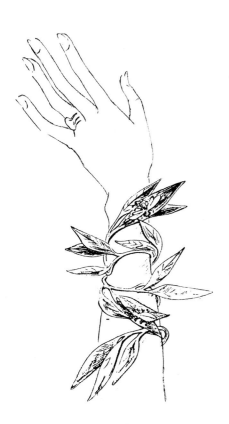

Leaves and flowers abounded in the Pagan Collection of April 1938. Note the beetles and bees on the bracelet of green metal leaves.

Paramount considered making a film on Elsa's life starring Colbert. After the war Joan Crawford and then later Lauren Bacall were mentioned. After seeing *Moulin Rouge,* Elsa wanted John Huston to direct, but the film was never made.) Elsa's most poignant customer was Helen Keller, the deaf-mute American whose sensitive fingers could appreciate quality of texture better than most. She dedicated a photo to 'Madame Schiaparelli, whose hand calls beauty into being'.

The most famous customer of all was, perhaps, Mrs Wallis Simpson, who married the Duke of Windsor, formerly Edward VIII. She was a very Schiaparelli type: dark, crisp, tapering. For Mrs Simpson's cosmopolitan trousseau, the American Mainbocher, the French Paquin and English Molyneux collaborated with the Italian Schiaparelli, who provided notably a black crêpe day dress printed with little white turtles, an evening dress with yellow butterflies printed on Wallis blue (actually Windsor blue, colour of the ribbon worn by the Knights and Ladies of the Garter) and repeated on the lapels of a blue tweed jacket, and a variation of the Dali Painted Gown, a white evening dress printed with a bright red lobster crawling from waist to knee.

This was Elsa's heyday, and from 1935 to 1939 she was the undisputed queen of Paris fashion. It was one of the most glittering periods in French history, both economic and social, yet one of the most harrowing for Europe as a whole. By 1939 the export of one gown designed by a great couturier enabled France to buy ten tons of coal, and the export of a litre of scent paid for two tons of crude oil. During these 'blind years', though catapulting towards what was to be its blackest time, Paris was more frivolous and scintillating than ever. The world of elegance and refinement whirled giddily on the edge of the rumbling volcano at lavish parties and brilliant balls intended to beguile the senses and intrigue the wit.

Against this background, Elsa urged women to dare to appear publicly in theatrical clothes, not only to assert their independence but to provide glamour, fun and romance in their daily lives. 'Wear the smartest of what is conventionally permitted, yes, but also be the most exciting of your own unique self while remaining fashionable.' So, along with her masculine styles, she drew the fancy dress and masquerade balls out of private mansions and on to the streets.

The world was divided between kingdoms, republics and dictatorships, Adolf Hitler was on his chilling ascent, assisted by the British sell-out at Munich, European statesmen were gauging the consequences of the Italian invasion of Ethiopia, the Spaniards slaughtering one another, the Japanese massacring the Chinese. Elsa went all out in her military effects. But these were not dour, glowering or severe. Continuing to soften the early pugnaciousness of her look, she now dipped into the make-believe world of musical comedy and operetta as set to martial airs from Strauss. These military styles were intended to be worn with the swashbuckling confidence of all those smiling lieutenants who ever waltzed at the

A long evening coat in harlequin patched felt for the Commedia dell'arte Collection of October 1938.

Featuring prints: (far left) a Dali-inspired lobster creates a splash on this white evening dress, c.1937, while Vertès gives a Gay Nineties background to a white crêpe dress with flaring collar forming cap sleeves, also 1937. Schiaparelli uses another Vertès print (right) for an evening dress extravagantly draped to give the bustle effect popular just before the war in 1939.

Tuileries or dined at Maxim's. Longer and more theatrical than her earlier version, Elsa's grand capes sent shock waves through the great soirées in capital cities all round the world: a dramatic swirling Dracula version with high shoulders and a high-standing collar, a giant strawberry-coloured petal dropping in huge folds to the ankles, a billowing one summoned up from her childhood recollections of the capes of the Campagna Romana shepherds guiding their flocks through moonlit Rome on Via Nazionale, and another recalling the capes of friars on pilgrimage to St Peter's.

If the Sentry Cape paid a dramatic tribute to ordinary soldiers, there were also officers' full-backed coats slit up the back, and an Ethiopian warrior's tunic transformed into a black evening dress over purple trousers. The military influence extended to accessories, from gauntlet gloves to the famous Schiaparelli Roman helmets. Other head-coverings with martial overtones included the Dryad's headdress of tumbling cock feathers, Dragoon, Grenadier and Field Marshal hats, American doughboys' fatigue caps, Hussar toques and the rooster-feathered Bersagliera Cap, named after the famous Italian regiment. Schiaparelli's military look anticipated the women's uniforms of the Second World War. She also designed a policewoman's uniform which she sent to Scotland Yard. Although it was rejected, it predated by thirty years the invasion into uniform designing by all the big fashion names. Conventionally uniformed policewomen were glamorized after the war in American TV serials. During the late seventies, women traffic wardens writing out parking fines on Paris streets were dressed in a fetching version in periwinkle blue, designed by Carven with a nod to Schiaparelli. In the early eighties the Fendis for basics and Gucci for leatherwear collaborated on the uniform for the Women's Police Corps in Rome. Then, with Giorgio Armani and Gianni Versace doing uniforms for women's military service in Italy, the designers branched out: Guy Laroche, the hostesses at the Paris city hall; Oscar de la Renta, the American Boy Scouts; Bill Blass, the executives and maintenance crew at New York's Kaufman Astoria Studios; Ralph Lauren, TWA air and ground staff; Calvin Klein, SAS; and Issey Miyeke, not only the Ground Self-Defense Force Band but also Japanese working in such companies as Sony, Shiseido and Coca-Cola.

'Madame Schiaparelli has taken literally the expression: the theatre of the mode,' Jean Cocteau wrote in *Harper's Bazaar* for April 1937. He continued:

> Whereas in other times only a few mysterious and privileged women dressed themselves with great individuality and by the violence of their garb destroyed the 'moderne' style, in 1937 a woman like Schiaparelli can invent for all women – for each woman in particular – that violence which was once the privilege of very few, of those who might be called the actresses in this drama-outside-theatre which is the World.

A Surrealistic setting for this Sentry Cape with embroidered epaulettes, modelled here by Bettina Bergery and photographed by Henry Clarke.

Schiaparelli is above all the dressmaker of eccentricity. Has she not the air of a young demon who tempts women, who leads the mad carnival in a burst of laughter? Her establishment in Place Vendôme is a devil's laboratory. Women who go there fall into a trap, and come out masked, disguised, deformed or reformed, according to Schiaparelli's whim.

In August 1939 fashion collections were presented during a week full of terrifying war scares. All the dress houses reported extraordinary orders from private clients. At Schiaparelli all sales records for a five-day period were broken.

Products of Elsa's 'mad carnival' — masks, tricorne hats, and (right) a cape of circus stripes in pink satin on pink and olive satin velvet.

179

19

The 'Drôle de Guerre' and American Lecture Tour

AT 5.45 am on 1 September 1939, Adolf Hitler, without troubling to declare war, ordered the Luftwaffe to bomb Poland into submission prior to exterminating the Polish race. At last, with no choice left, Great Britain and France announced their entrance into the hostilities – and steeled themselves for the expected Nazi onslaught. Paris was quickly arrayed in battle dress: sandbags blanketed precious statues and monuments, gigantic anchored balloons billowed over the Tuileries, a State-issued gas mask in a tin can dangled from the shoulder of every French citizen and schoolchild (foreigners had to buy one), and orphans were evacuated to the countryside with name-tags around their necks. Sugar, tobacco, coffee and petrol were rationed – and hoarded. The black market flourished. Queues which included smart, newly servant-less society matrons doing their own shopping, formed in front of butcher's shops, bakeries and dairies.

One of the first streets to feel the effects of the war was rue de Berri, where Elsa lived. Refugees besieged the Belgian Embassy next door to her house in such droves that the staff was unable to offer proper shelter and food. Elsa turned her concierge's lodge into a bivouac and kept hot coffee and bread and butter ready at all hours. In no time the Bistro in her cellar became a meeting place for the steadily arriving stream of British officers, volunteer American ambulance drivers and women of the French Mechanized Transport Corps, Elsa's daughter Gogo included, who were driving six-wheeled trucks between Paris and the mythical front on the Maginot Line, which the French were wistfully hoping would halt Adolf Hitler's advance. When able to get away from work, Elsa personally helped the Salvation Army in its canteens and rest homes near the front and visited the camp of the famous regiment of Zouaves so often that the men adopted her as their 'godmother'.

The fashion designers all realized the importance to France of the dressmaking industry – second only to metallurgy – as a continued source of income and morale. Except for Chanel, who closed, and Mainbocher and Molyneux, who returned home, the shows went

Goodbye to all that . . . The French maid, never to be seen again, lends her apron to the stylish Parisienne in March 1940.

on; but the difficulties quickly mounted. With all the men mobilized, Elsa's employees were reduced to 150. She had no tailors, the little school desks occupied by her saleswomen were half-empty, only three mannequins were left and most of her customers had fled. Yet in three weeks she built up a mid-season presentation for October 1939 which proved, if proof were needed, that she was not one to let catastrophe curb her inventiveness and which showed all her usual awareness that changed lifestyles demanded practicality. This was her Cash and Carry Collection, featuring jackets with huge pouch pockets to enable a woman to take essentials with her, retain the freedom of her hands and yet manage to look feminine. Since the lack of servants was becoming an acute problem in current life, Elsa offered gardening dresses and kitchen clothes so that her customers might mow lawns, prune roses and do their own cooking – and still look attractive. As early as 1928 she had extended the wrap-around skirt from beach clothes to town wear. Now over her gown the elegant hostess could slip an apron of light, rubberized crêpe de Chine so that she might mix her cocktails and scramble her midnight eggs with impunity. This was developed into the style of a charming French maid's apron, in March 1940 part of the final Schiaparelli pre-war silhouette. Since a simple life meant shorter and less complicated underwear she minded Dorothy Parker's injunction, 'Brevity is the soul of lingerie', ignored pleatings, real lace and pure silk and introduced much smaller items which women could wash themselves and wear with a minimum of ironing.

Next she designed skirts which brought the old country bicycling costumes into town, and insisted on the wrap-around skirts as worn over gaily printed bloomers and matching blouses, thus preparing for the new mode of transport to be imposed by wartime restrictions (eleven million bicycles were registered in France in 1942). She adapted camouflage techniques and launched the Transformable Dress. When the woman of the world, deprived of her Hispano or Bugatti, emerged from the Metro to attend a formal dinner party or to dine at Maxim's, she merely had to pull a ribbon to lengthen her short-skirted day dress into an ankle-length evening gown, release a hook so that a pleated edge around the waist fell to form the decoration of a tunic, lower the bustle drapery of an afternoon dress to mould the hips for a lengthened evening dress, remove a plain or embroidered yoke from a short dress to turn it into a low-necked *grande soirée* gown, or unfasten a patch of slip-over material to reveal a stunningly embroidered collar or pocket. She also folded a woollen boiler suit on a chair next to her bed in case a nocturnal air-raid drove her down into the cellar. The fabric of one white coat supposedly withstood poisonous gas. The first drip-dry dresses in haute couture had also arrived. As for colours appropriate to the times, you could choose between Maginot Line blue, Foreign Legion red, trench brown and aeroplane grey.

Autumn went, the Germans did not attack, everyone started to

With practical pleats for ease of movement and an 'apron' tied at the back, the wartime Parisian lady still manages to look chic.

become accustomed to the *drôle de guerre,* or phoney war, which continued throughout what Winston Churchill called 'the winter of illusion'. At the behest of Lucien Lelong, head of the Chambre Syndicale de la Couture Parisienne, the Paris couturiers joined forces to keep unemployment from hitting their sector and to show that French morale was still high. In the bleak February of 1940 they announced as usual a week of elaborate, dazzling collections of new summer clothes. To demonstrate their solidarity, leading American reporters and buyers, laden with food parcels for friends, crowded on to the *George Washington* to cross the submarine-infested Atlantic to Genoa, struggled through complicated customs formalities, mined areas and bitter snow and ice up to Paris, where they checked without complaint into unheated hotels. So successful – and highly publicized – was the combined effort that in London the *Daily Telegraph* for 6 March 1940 enquired with annoyance, 'Do the Parisians happen to know their country is at war?' Of Schiaparelli *L'Officiel de la Couture* for March 1940 remarked, 'There is so much youth and character in the models one feels their creator must have taken pleasure in creating them.'

Significantly using Legion of Honour red as a colour motif for the entire collection, Elsa exhibited clothes for Florida and California, including a startling bathing suit made of kid and skirts fitted with elastic belts adaptable to both the fat and the lean years. She again placed capacious pockets everywhere, and especially where least expected. For warmth she introduced broadcloth spats in many colours, stocking caps that covered the head and wrapped the neck, and a soft coverall hood, 'the type of hat that Paris has been searching for,' announced *Harper's Bazaar* for February 1940, 'a hat reduced to its bare definition of a head.' In a vehement protest against the Soviet Union's invasion of Finland she featured Finnish embroideries, and in the Boutique, Finnish aprons and wedding belts. Her sewing girls, shivering in the now unheated workrooms, made clothes for Finland's babies in their spare time.

While emphasizing the new importance of bicycling by splitting tweed skirts up the side and pushing short trousers, later to sweep the entire sports world as Bermudas, Elsa also did flying skirts and smart air-raid ensembles and ordered slacks out of country homes and on to the city streets. To facilitate that other new necessity, walking, she dictated flat patent-leather shoes. The Salvation Army asked her to design a uniform for women volunteers, and she did one in blue with a red collar and a blue apron. Because of the scarcity of buttons and safety pins she used dog chains to close suits and hold skirts. To big flat colonial hats and Bali straw boaters (1940) she added sheer linen 'slip covers' that could be removed and washed. On one scarf she printed Maurice Chevalier's latest song, on another the restrictions Parisians were enduring: 'Monday – no meat. Tuesday – no alcohol. Wednesday – no butter. Thursday – no fish. Friday – no meat. Saturday – no spirits. But Sunday – *toujours l'amour*'.

In spring 1940, the quiet deepened ominously. Suddenly in April, Hitler pounced on Denmark and Norway and in May struck down Luxemburg and neutral Holland and trampled over Belgium. His stukas and Panzer divisions outflanked the Maginot Line and hurtled towards Paris. Within one week France was lost. During the early days of June, exceptionally hot to add to all the horror, the northern French joined their shattered neighbours streaming south in a tragic exodus and the Parisians now also took wild flight.

What remained of fashion had been idle for months already but Lucien Lelong, determined to hold the profession together come what may, united with Elsa and a few other designers in making for Biarritz, where Molyneux had put his estate at their disposal, with what staff and working supplies they could muster in order to present a semblance of the winter collections in August. In locking up 21 Place Vendôme, Elsa confined her perfume business to her attorneys-at-law and left her rue de Berri home to the Quakers for the benefit of refugees. Crammed into cars and vans, the little group braved the heat, dust, thirst and indescribable disorder of armies, government officials and refugees fleeing under incessant enemy strafing of the teeming roads. No sooner had they reached the streets of Biarritz on 10 June 1940 than the radio announced that Mussolini, like a jackal ever ready to batten on a kill, was allying himself officially with Hitler; Italy had stabbed France in the back with a declaration of war. Elsa, unable to receive the shock standing up, dropped on to the pavement and wept. Tears were to fill the next few days. The French Government, convening in dismay in Bordeaux, declared an Armistice. From London, General de Gaulle made his moving appeal for unity in action, sacrifice and hope. Then, in profoundest humiliation, the Third French Republic capitulated to the Third German Reich. Biarritz was not to be the showcase for Paris fashion's winter collections.

Historically, French couture had already served as a political instrument several times. During the French Revolution the first dictator of styles, Rose Bertin, travelled back and forth to Germany ostensibly on business but actually to beseech rich French émigrés to help her best customer, Marie-Antoinette. During the First World War the French Government had commissioned Paul Poiret, Master Tailor of the French Army, to design a collection that it sent on tour of the United States as part of its propaganda thrust to persuade the Americans to come to the aid of France. In 1939 it knew it had to renew this persuasion, but now America had barricaded itself in isolationism. Who was the Paris fashion figure best known to the American masses? Elsa Schiaparelli.

She had already removed Pascal, her famous wooden figure, from the Boutique and sent him to the Schiaparelli stand in the French Pavilion at the San Francisco Fair of 1938. To show French interest in sports events, she dressed him as a cyclist in red, white and blue satin, had the words 'Paris–San Francisco' embroidered in diamonds on his blouse, added boots by Perugia, and – to enable him to read the latest edition of *Paris-Soir* every day in peace and quiet – sat him on a plot of grass and propped him up against a gold bicycle with a bouquet of jonquils tied to the handlebars. Pascal remained in the United States throughout the war. As well as representing Schiaparelli products and French sportsmanship, he became an image of the French spirit under duress and the hope for the survival of Liberté, Egalité, Fraternité.

After lengthy negotiations Elsa had signed a contract in January 1940 with the Columbia Lecture Bureau: to audiences in American

Pascal in masquerade.

women's clubs and large department stores she would, at some future date to be agreed, deliver a series of lectures, 'Clothes Make the Woman', to be illustrated by a collection of dresses that she undertook to send over on a ship soon to sail. Early in July 1940 it was clear that the moment had arrived, and M. Lelong urged Elsa to leave Biarritz for New York immediately. Teaming up with three American friends, she crossed Spain in a packed and filthy train. Once in Portugal they had to get off at Coimbra because the authorities could not handle the mobs fleeing to Lisbon. After weeks of waiting in vain for a permit, Elsa packed her friends and their luggage into a taxi, badgered the Lisbon police into letting them stay in an abandoned casino in the Estoril and waged an unrelenting and finally successful fight to obtain priority seats on the Yankee Clipper plane. Waiting for her in New York on 1 August 1940 was Gogo, who had met her future American husband, Robert Lawrence Berenson, on the last ship out of Genoa.

Meditating alone in her suite at the St Regis Hotel in New York, Elsa faced squarely the problems of her coming tour. She could not claim to be either a writer or a lecturer, and indeed had never written any prose professionally or done any public speaking in any language, much less English. But even if she could practise a speech until she was sure of it, what about answering impromptu post-lecture questions? She did not have the backing of an official mission and was cut off from all material or moral support from any French source. She was aware that the America she loved and admired – and was grateful to – saw the events in Europe from the point of view of an uninvolved young nation. She understood that Americans could only partly grasp, and without feelings of personal loss, the tragedy of the French defeat, and that because of their rampant isolationism they were not deeply touched by the French anguish and pain. With memories of the First World War losses still bitterly fresh, the Americans could not comprehend why they should be expected to spill their sons' blood again for a lot of foreigners who could not keep a peace for more than twenty years. Nonetheless, Elsa determined to make them understand that it was impossible to replace Paris in the realm of her particular creative endeavour and that they must not allow France and what it represented to perish.

In the Rockefeller Center office of Schiaparelli Perfumes Inc. she designed her own wardrobe of twelve outfits, had them reproduced by Manhattan manufacturers and authorized them to be sold throughout the country with special labels that cost a dollar apiece on the condition that the money thus raised would go into a fund administered by the Quakers for unemployed Paris fashion work-room girls. Painting competitions had been held among French children, and she helped to organize exhibitions of the works, which were sold by the Red Cross for its own benefit. She also arranged with a philanthropic group headed by former President Herbert Hoover, with whom she had worked briefly twenty years before at

Left: Memories of the Wild West: a bucking bronco embroidery by Lesage in progress.

the American Relief Association, to use all the profits of her forthcoming tour on food to be sent through the Quakers, the Red Cross and French welfare organizations to the 'free' southern zone of France. Suddenly, disaster hit. The ship bringing her originals to New York for the tour was sunk. Dismayed, she appealed to Bonwit Teller, which opened its workrooms to her at once, and thanks to the goodwill and ability of the employees, though without the fine fabrics she usually had at her command, she managed to reproduce the collection in a record few days.

Shortly before her first lecture, in September 1940, Japan joined Germany and Italy in the Tripartite Pact, pledging mutual assistance in the case of an American declaration of war on any of the signatories. The lecture tour was enlarged to include forty-two towns in eight weeks, ending in November 1940. Elsa began in front of a wildly enthusiastic crowd of five hundred at Lord and Taylor in New York. Then, dressed in what *Harper's Bazaar* for December 1940 called 'the most revolutionary coat of the decade' in militaristic Rocket red, without any padding and hanging like a sack, she plunged west into the heart of the United States for what she

Elsa, wearing her revolutionary coat of Rocket red, is given a cowboy's welcome during her lecture tour of America.

afterwards referred to as the biggest love affair of her life – with the American people. Everywhere she was received with sympathy, interest and affection. Audiences struggled to hear her and to give her little mementoes. No one would dream of allowing her to stay at a hotel, and she was entertained in gracious houses whose friendly atmosphere bolstered her courage. At the Kentuckian Institute, Louisville, she drew the largest attendance since the institute was founded. In Oklahoma City she was met by a Red Indian chief and a princess who took her around in a streamlined car decorated with enormous shocking pink bows. In Phoenix, Arizona, after visiting the famous red and orange canyons, she spoke in a university built into the side of a mountain. In Hollywood, following a lecture in an auditorium so full of stars that you might have thought it was Academy Award Night, the police drove her through the town, with sirens screaming, to a distant station where the train to San Francisco had been stopped to wait for her.

She went up to Canada where, in Victoria, British Columbia, she lectured in an old store that had been closed for some time; everything was covered with white sheets. Here three poor young stranded French sailors sought her out: with their last penny they had bought her a flower. The Montreal Railway Depot was filled with French Canadians in Alsatian dress wanting to embrace someone fighting for the racked mother country. Down to Minnesota she went. In St Paul the weather was so bad that traffic came to a halt and she arrived late at the stadium where she was to speak. Waiting patiently were 25,000 people. They had braved snowstorms and ice not only to see Elsa Schiaparelli but to hear about France. At a moment when statesmen and other promoters of European interests were struggling to be heard and believed in the face of American isolationism, here, as everywhere, a representative of a so-called frivolous art was able to touch the hearts of ordinary people with a tale of work and of faith.

20

M. Lelong Said, 'Non!'

BACK in New York in December 1940, Elsa announced her decision to return to Paris. War or no war, Occupation or no Occupation, she had a country, two businesses, hundreds of employees, friends and a home to defend personally. The Quakers entrusted her with $60,000-worth of vitamins and medicine for the children in the non-occupied zone of France, and into her high fur hat she sewed several thousand dollars that Americans had given her for old friends left destitute in Paris. She embarked on a ship that had not a scrap of furniture – the passengers had to sit on the floor – and so old that water poured in from every side. The crossing to Lisbon took two weeks, and then because of the need for travel permits she spent over a month in and out of trains before reaching home.

A million Parisians, she found in January 1941, had returned from the June 1940 exodus and were coping with new restrictions as best they could. The air in the capital had become pure: there were no motor-cars to release exhaust fumes. The pigeons had disappeared, for no one had an extra crust of bread to feed them. Losing weight was no problem either on a diet of rutabagas, herbs, ersatz flour, coffee, oil and mustard. Still, the Nazi presence was keeping on a pleasant mask – for the moment. The misery of ordinary citizens, the martyrdom of the Jews, the political persecutions and the sacrifices of members of the Resistance were but a matter of time.

All was well at the house on rue de Berri; it had been under neutral diplomatic protection. At 21 Place Vendôme, work was going on. Elsa had left huge stocks of tweed, and Irene Dana, a Finnish neutral whom Elsa had put in charge of her showrooms, was using these to keep the Boutique business alive while manoeuvring to obtain other fabrics and to present new collections, even if these were greatly reduced. In general, it was the major houses that were hit first. Much of their private clientele had been composed of North and South Americans. These were not only absent but had left behind large unpaid bills, and the drop in professional foreign buyers was also significant. However, a new type of clientele was developing, and the couturiers were rallying.

In the spring of 1941, Elsa could reasonably feel that her American lecture tour had made some small contribution to the Allied cause, when the American Lend-Lease Act became law and the United States started to help all countries vital to its defence. But her personal situation in Paris became more and more uneasy, and her return there was to prove short-lived. Though she was naturalized French, both Germans and Italians considered her Italian, and they did not forget her widely repeated denunciations of Mussolini and Hitler before the hostilities broke out. One day in May 1941, soon after the Nazis had occupied Greece and dismembered Yugoslavia, the American consul informed her that he and his staff were leaving France and urged her too to get out straight away. She entrusted her valuable furniture to Jansen and her jewels to Cartier (these two houses secretly kept safe many a fortune during the Occupation) and placed her home at the disposal of the neutral Brazilian Embassy. She turned her fashion business over to M. Meunier, assisted by Irene Dana, Michèle Guégen, Jean Clément, Mike and Yvonne Souquières. As Paulette Laperche was still very young, Elsa reasoned that she might not be able to cope with the Germans, so she named as general manager for perfumes M. Cavaillé-Coll, a man experienced in the field and already used to dealing with the Germans, when Patou agreed to let him go to her.

Before leaving, Elsa worked out the elements of a new winter collection, to be shown in August. Notably, it included a variant on her ingenious transformation games: sleeveless knee-length quilted wool waistcoats which added to the heat of the basic garment in winter and could be slipped under a non-lined redingote in spring. Her last instruction was to package 'Shocking' in a box that represented a cage containing a bird – '*Shocking chante l'espoir*', Shocking sings of hope. Commenting on this collection, *Comoedia* for 17 September 1941 was rhapsodic: 'At Schiaparelli's, while watching the collection, you are attending an art show, an exhibition of elegance and good taste. Because of the penury of raw materials and the restrictions, it was to be feared that the new autumn mode in Paris would be melancholic and without lyrical flight. Schiaparelli has completely reassured us. This house proves that French creation and quality continue in the direction of beauty, refinement, youth and grace.'

Elsa had not entrusted her showrooms to Irene Dana witlessly. Married to a prominent Russian nobleman, Irene had been a *directrice* at Molyneux's before dressing the crowned heads of Greece and Scandinavia in her own establishment in Paris and then joining the Paquin branch in London. As a neutral Finn, she was not viewed unfavourably by the German authorities. Aided by the premières and taking a leaf from the design drawings carefully accumulated over the years by Elsa's studio, she contrived to maintain the dashing Schiaparelli spirit of colour, fun and the avant-garde, while carefully preserving the inimitable cut and fit. On 29 September 1942

Schiaparelli faces the drôle de guerre *with a woollen suit, leather bound and buttoned, a large pouch pocket on the hip. The cover-all hood in turquoise blue jersey matches the hidden blouse.*

Comoedia reported: 'It is not surprising to find the role of creator of fabrics still in Schiaparelli's hands, particularly in her printed summer suits.' The same newspaper remarked in February 1944: 'This collection is of a striking youthfulness.' And just before the Allied landings in Normandy in June 1944 it asserted, 'Everything is new, imaginative, amusing, original, sparkling. Each model possesses a secret, offers a discovery and charms by a piquant seductiveness. The striving for gaiety is very likeable.'

As no one had a proxy signature, throughout the years of Elsa's absence salaries could not be adjusted to changing money rates. The employees could barely live on what they earned – Michèle Guéguen for one spent all her savings – but they remained faithful to 'Madame' and to the house. Since they were forced to economize on light and heating, they kept the overheads down. Only once did a serious menace hang over them, when the Nazis made a move to send the Schiaparelli First Tailor to Germany. Irene Dana went to Nazi Headquarters and remonstrated with the officials: if they took the man, she contended, they would ruin business, the employees would starve and the scandal would not help their cause. The First Tailor remained where he was.

During the four years of the Occupation the Nazis systematically ruined and exhausted the 'French State', which they divided at first into two zones – the northern half occupied, the southern half 'free' – with a new capital in Vichy and a puppet government headed by eighty-four-year-old Marshal Pétain. They increasingly took over French industry, and Paris fashion was one of the first on the list. Intent on freeing the Axis world of the domination of French fashion and the French textile industry revolving around it, they used information stolen from *Vogue* to promote their own German-language periodicals and the French periodicals they were either founding or taking control of. When Michel de Brunhoff, editor of French *Vogue*, refused to collaborate with them, they forbade *Vogue* all publication rights in France. At that, M. de Brunhoff closed *Vogue* down to avoid being forced to serve the Nazi plot, had all the Condé Nast files and archives buried in the Chantilly Forest, and lent Lucien Lelong every secret assistance possible until the Nazis were routed.

Meanwhile the Germans had ransacked the premises of the Chambre Syndicale de la Couture Parisienne and filched all the files, including the entire list of foreign buyers and documents dealing with the professional schools and the creation of models for export. Next, they announced that they had decided the fate of French haute couture. It was to disappear. The fashion houses would be absorbed by a German organization with head offices in Berlin, the cultural centre of New Europe. The professional schools were to be disbanded and set up in Berlin and Vienna to train young German talent. The couturiers would also be transferred to these cities. So would their workshops and the people employed in them, to supply the skilled labour lacking in the German workshops. Of course, the couturiers would be 'free' to supervise them.

Lucien Lelong, on behalf of the Chambre Syndicale, said no to the invaders: 'Impose whatever you like on us by force, but French fashion cannot be transplanted either as a whole or in units. No nation in the world has the power to expatriate the creative genius of Paris, which is not only a spontaneous outburst but the result of a tradition cultivated by skilled workers in many different trades and professions. French fashion exists in Paris, or it does not exist!'

It takes ten years to train newcomers to expertise in fashion, so small wonder that M. Lelong was resolved to oppose any scattering of skilled workers, and to ensure the continuity of their training through enrolment in the professional training schools and subsequent experience in fashion houses. Lucien Lelong was relying on the knowledge that coercion must destroy the climate in which such a creative art as fashion designing can flourish. Faced with this resolute resistance, the Germans agreed (but secretly only for the moment) to leave French fashion in Paris and let it keep its skilled labour. However, they moved swiftly to curtail production: only fourteen clothes manufacturing companies were authorized to remain in business. Undeterred, M. Lelong contrived to increase the list to thirty-five by January 1941, and six months later there were eighty-five.

In the following years of the war the fashion business lived dangerously, lurching from one reprieve to another. Closely watched, it had to elude traps at every turn. The Nazis calculated that a ban on showing collections abroad, an increasing lack of choice in materials and textiles, the necessity of submitting all photographs to the Censor, and intensified oppression in general would gradually destroy the profession through the loss of foreign markets. Berlin, Vienna, Milan and Rome stooped to any ruse to woo foreign capital cities over to the National Socialist styles and force contracts on foreign buyers. Paris no longer knew what quality paper looked like and its specialized magazines were severely rationed, especially the fashion reviews.

In the spring of 1942 Lucien Lelong, exasperated by the Nazi machinations, countered with a bold act of faith to maintain prestige abroad. Slyly, he seized upon the excuse of assisting National Emergency Relief (a fund which in fact was pocketed by the Nazis) to send mannequins from eighteen houses down to Lyons – significantly, in the Free Zone – to present the latest models at two gala evenings shared with the Paris Opéra ballet company. Designers were thus enabled to renew contacts with provincial dressmakers, from whom they had been separated by the zoning, and with more than three hundred foreign buyers who managed to reach Lyons from Switzerland, Spain, Portugal, North Africa, Hungary and Turkey. Since the couturiers had no extra materials to spare they sold paper patterns which were snapped up at high prices. As they were prohibited by the Nazis from advertising in French periodicals, they arranged for a series of illustrated albums to be put out in Monte Carlo and distributed abroad. The presentations – culminating in a range of stunning evening gowns which M. Lelong had inveigled the Nazis into authorizing on condition that they were not sold – were an electrifying success from both the financial and pro-French propaganda points of view. The Nazis exploded with fury. They retaliated by ordering the immediate suppression of all publicity and outlawed all exportation, even of paper patterns.

In times of crisis luxury products always flourish, and such was the case during the Occupation. But how did Paris fashion stay alive, and who kept it going? It would be a mistake to conclude that German women were dressed by Paris. First, they did not come to the French capital, and second, they were forbidden to buy French and had to buy National Socialist styles. Throughout the Occupation, Paris fashion did not receive one order from a German civilian manufacturer and not one model was reproduced in German workshops. How then did the French clothing business, numbering 30,000 companies depending on Paris fashion houses, survive? And how did these fashion houses, including Schiaparelli, with only 100 tons of material officially allotted each year, manage to maintain 97 per cent of their labour force?

There are several answers. The wives of officers of the German High Command in France ordered and ordered. Many of these, and other German officers, had French mistresses with expensive tastes who bought, as did the wives of well-remunerated French collaborators, wealthy Frenchwomen in general and, as usual, personalities in the public eye, especially film and stage stars. Then, in 1943, a new phenomenon emerged which would gain momentum until a few years after the Liberation: the BOFs. These were the women from bakeries, dairies, butchers and sausage shops whose husbands and lovers, collaborating with the Nazis and selling to their French compatriots on the black market, trafficked in *Beurre, Oeufs* and *Fromage* (butter, eggs and cheese). With the tremendous sums gained from their profiteering the BOFs could not in time of war buy de luxe cars, nor frequent glittering resorts and spas, nor set off on world cruises. Consequently, while the men vied with the Nazis in buying modern paintings for astronomical prices at public auctions and ate in wildly priced restaurants which charged as much as they pleased by giving ten per cent of the bill to National Emergency Relief, the BOF ladies vied with one another to show off in expensive clothes, furs, jewellery and scents.

The ingenuity of Paris designers was perhaps never so striking as during the Occupation. Desperate shortages of materials led to such items as 'wedgies', a vulgarization of the Schiaparelli evening 'footstool' sandals. Their thick soles were composed of straw or wicker, the famous wood version being trimmed with raffia ribbons. These anchored the wearer to the ground, permitting only long and unfeminine striding, and made even the most dainty of women appear to be club-footed. An enormous bulky look resulted from an extension of the Schiaparelli shoulders and a tightening of the Schiaparelli waists, combined with a new amphora line, peasant styles and balloon sleeves. Over short, gawky coats called Canadiennes, very short skirts, originally intended to flare, actually billowed like a kite when the wearer was bicycling, sometimes exposing ultra-practical trousers, sometimes leaving nothing to the imagination.

Fashion designers cut blouses in rayon, woollen jersey and Vichy, and ordered their customers to paint their legs with make-up base to imitate silk stockings and to add a seam traced with a soft pencil. The hair-do was a complicated progression of the Schiaparelli mode, piled high on the middle of the head with a Pompadour front and tresses waving loose at the back. Since the Nazis for some reason let milliners go untaxed, headgear became the most typical item of the times, dominated by voluminous turbans that towards the end of the Occupation soared as much as a foot high. Huge berets, made of musketeer felt and other fabrics which could not be used for skirts, were loaded with floating veils, bits of feathers, artificial flowers and false ribbons made of varnished wood shavings, even newspapers. The Germans were forced to pass a law restricting feathered birds on hats to a single one.

It was all hideous, heavy and unbecoming. Ever more extravagant as the Occupation continued, the fashions of the time denoted a Paris trampled but still defiant and possessed of a sense of humour, a Paris intent on creating an illusion of luxury that deliberately approached the ridiculous. Joking sadly, Parisian women claimed that their hats would confound the enemy. 'What would they have worn,' wondered the German soldiers, gaping at them, 'if they had won the war?'

In November 1942, when the Allies attacked North Africa, the Nazis occupied the whole of France in retaliation and dropped whatever pretence of pleasantness they had preserved. From January 1943 a kilo of wool could be obtained only in exchange for old clothes donated to National Emergency Relief – from which, of course, no French person benefited. During the following month the Nazi officials demanded that the Chambre Syndicale should hand over lists of employees in the fashion houses with a view to reassigning a certain number to war-priority jobs. At this juncture Lucien Lelong felt it would be imprudent to continue a strong open resistance, but he somehow never managed to supply the lists.

In January 1944, to set an example, the Nazis closed Grès and Balenciaga. While the Spanish Government interceded successfully in Balenciaga's favour, Grès was able to reopen only by agreeing to reveal to Nazi style experts the secrets of her technique which had accounted for the marvels of her designing and brought her worldwide fame. She never made the disclosures. In May 1944 the

Nazis, closing in, announced that German citizens who were no longer physically capable of contributing to the war effort at home would be brought to Paris to replace the skilled employees in the fashion workshops. Come what might, M. Lelong said, 'Non! Non! Non!' Whereupon the Nazis decreed that all Paris fashion houses had to close down within eight weeks – that is, by mid-July. Only one month before that, on 6 June 1944, Allied forces stormed across the English Channel towards the Normandy coast.

Elsa's daughter Gogo driving for the Red Cross in Paris, 1939–40.

21

The War Years in New York

At this point in her autobiography *Shocking Life* Elsa placed a quotation from *La Divina Commedia* by Dante:

> In the middle of the journey of our life
> I came to myself in a dark wood,
> where the straight way was lost.
>
> Ah! how hard a thing it is to tell what a wild,
> and rough, and stubborn wood this was,
> which in my thought renews the fear!
>
> So bitter is it, that scarcely more in death!

After an interval of twenty years, in mid-1941, Elsa settled in New York for the second time. Once more she was alone there, for Gogo, with her husband in the service overseas and true to the spirit of adventure and dedication of her forebears, had volunteered as a nurse in the American Armed Forces on the Burma–China border.

Elsa found herself in an alien land again, for New York was no longer her New York. As it had been after the First World War, it was crowded with refugees from many different nations and walks of life, and in greatly differing circumstances. But, she was dismayed to observe, the mass of Americans, still furiously protectionist and isolationist, and the French exiles – urging the States to go to war, yet themselves divided into two aggressive camps, pro-Pétain and pro-de Gaulle – viewed each other with hatred and suspicion. She became truly upset when, conducting an auction of jewellery at the Stork Club, she was informed that people outside were hurling rotten eggs and tomatoes at the entrance in protest at money being raised to feed French children, those products of immorality and perversion. Needing quiet to gain courage and to pray for help in finding a way of living under these tragic circumstances, she rented a tiny cottage on Long Island for a month and went there alone. Perhaps here, by the sea, she sensed echoes of a previous crisis in her life, when she had paced the promenade in Nice nearly a quarter of a century before. Solitude, she always found, was the best way for her to regain possession of herself.

Elsa dressed for her work in the American Red Cross, 1943.

Obviously, she wanted action. She had been receiving offers to design and direct new dressmaking ventures, but she accepted none, feeling that she had to remain removed from the profession in the States; in this sphere her only duty and loyalty could be to Place Vendôme, even if that meant remaining silent. How could she possibly compete with any small activity that might still be flickering over there? A whirlwind trip to Central and South America to promote her perfumes only strengthened her conviction that merely earning more money could not meet her spiritual need to make a humanitarian contribution to improving the present state of things.

Relief work was a solution, and she offered her services to American Relief to France, a charity which numbered 15,000 volunteers in 300 communities all over the country. The head-quarters had been set up in New York in the former Whitelaw Reid residence at 457 Madison Avenue. Although Elsa was perfectly willing to join the all too few clothes packers in the cellar or go from door to door raising funds, the heads of the organization agreed to her project for transforming the many vast empty rooms in the mansion into a centre of French culture and art as represented in the United States at the time. Commuting from a rented house in Princeton, which recalled the noble and peaceful atmosphere of her father's library in Palazzo Corsini, she devoted the first show to Jean Pagès, a French artist who had done covers for *Vogue*. The paintings she presented narrated the story of a French soldier who had escaped from France and managed to get to New York. This show earned a

The French Canteen expresses its gratitude to Elsa 'for services rendered', 31 March 1945.

great amount of sympathy and won over many new people to the cause. The chain of volunteers in the cellar increased every day, and French and Americans – writers, princesses, millionaires, secretaries and waiters – toiled anonymously for hours together in long assembly lines, packing, packing.

Next Elsa transformed the rooms into a garden for an exhibition by Malvina Hoffman called 'Men of the World' and designed to illustrate the non-isolationist view of the unity of mankind, affirmed in a quote Elsa took from John Donne: 'No man is an island ... Any man's death diminishes me because I am involved in mankind.' Soon afterwards she started bringing together artists who, now in the United States, had helped to make Paris a capital of culture, thus accentuating the theme of unity of thought and continuing in the creative tradition.

Her next undertaking was a calendar, 'France in America', resembling a similar effort by Paul Poiret during the First World War. In it she attempted to reflect the different trends of artists in the United States at the time, choosing a thought for each day from a French refugee writer or sympathizer – such men as Paul Claudel, Julian Green, André Maurois and Saint-Exupéry. The pages of 'France in America' were specially illustrated by such artists as Dali, Lipchitz, Fernand Léger, Kisling, Vertès and others who had chosen Paris as their centre of inspiration.

Then, to deal with the present and the future, she organized a show that was completely modern and avant-garde, persuading her old friend Marcel Duchamp to come out of seclusion to help her and enlisting Tanguy, Miró, Masson and Max Ernst, himself supported by Peggy Guggenheim. The most famous of contemporary artists were represented, and many of the canvasses, such as the Picassos of 1937-38, had never been shown in the United States before. Comprising eighty works hung on screens placed between ropes stretched to form a labyrinth, the exhibition demonstrated the influence of American life on transplanted French artists, was a riotous success and brought in a load of money.

American fashion designers, consciously taking advantage of the war to detach themselves from their Paris mother, were developing an original feel for the sportswear they had inherited from Patou, Chanel and Schiaparelli, turning to Red Indian braves, to ranches and Mormons for their inspiration. After 1938 the Nieman-Marcus Fashion Award was international, but in 1943 (the year in which beautician Elizabeth Arden deemed it opportune to invade the dress business, aided by Charles James), American fashion interests established the Coty Award. Judged by seventy or more editors from the American fashion press, this was bestowed annually on one or a group of American designers who 'have had the most significant effect on the American way of dressing'. The winner received a 'Winnie', a small bronze figure designed by Malvina Hoffman. The first went to Norman Norell, with special mentions for milliners Lily

Madame Schiaparelli dons an apron in her role as money-raiser for the Quakers' Milk Fund in New York.

Daché and John-Fredericks. While Elsa was in the States the award was also won by Claire McCardell and then the pro-Schiaparelli Gilbert Adrian.

In this effort to cast off the French yoke, American designers started a theme that they would sound throughout the decades to come: French couturiers imposed fashion on women, whereas American designers suited clothes to a woman's lifestyle. They were forgetting that French designers had recognized changing lifestyles immediately after the First World War, and that well before the Second, Elsa Schiaparelli, realistic and practical, could not have been more sensitive to the need to adapt. Take for example her interchangeable separates, which the American designers liked to think of as their own. American *Vogue* for 1 April 1949 featured ten pages of them for day wear, then on 15 December 1949 for evening wear, without the slightest allusion to their originator. Fortunately, Elsa reasserted herself with some new separates for her Boutique –

'brilliants' as American *Vogue* for 1 November 1951 called them. But that was that. By the late seventies and early eighties there were no more references.

The *International Herald Tribune* stated on 8 August 1982: 'What is needed today is not a re-hash of clothes developed originally for rich women in the past, but fashion planned especially for the contemporary woman who juggles work, family and social life. In this, American designers, with their stress on interchangeable separates for both day and evening, have a head start.' On whom? Not on Elsa Schiaparelli.

By 1941 the American Relief to France headquarters had so many volunteers who wanted to do something more than just pack that Elsa felt she could turn over her exhibition duties to some of them. Pearl Harbor had been attacked (7 December 1941) and the United States was officially at war with the Axis powers. These events had reinforced Elsa's desire to serve humanity, and in January 1942 she enrolled in the school at the American Red Cross to become an auxiliary nurse. How to take a temperature, treat a burn, bandage a broken leg, stop a wound bleeding, solve the geometrical problems of making a hospital bed – it was an entirely new experience, and the sight of Elsa Schiaparelli, the Queen of Paris Fashion, walking through the streets of New York at 6 am in flat white canvas shoes, white cotton stockings and a blue cotton apron had its funny side. She was assigned first to the Bellevue Hospital, where poor and desperate cases were brought, then to the New York Hospital. She did all the humbler jobs, washing diseased bodies, listening to endless tragic stories, going on errands to the morgue, watching major operations. Her nursing gave her new courage and made the war years tolerable; it helped her to find a semblance of peace and fed her soul.

Meanwhile, the French Seamen's Foyer had been opened on 44th Street. This canteen was decorated to look like a Paris bistro, the walls painted with Parisian street scenes. In addition to the nursing Elsa offered her services as a senior hostess, bringing in her wake Charles Boyer, Jean Gabin, Annabella and Marlene Dietrich to receive and entertain.

Early in 1943 she gave up her hospital and canteen work when she signed up for the Rochambeau unit of women volunteers for service in the Allied liberation of North Africa and France. While waiting to move out, she went to stay with friends in Washington, where she was invited to the White House by President Roosevelt. When the Rochambeau unit was put on the alert, she learned that her name had been struck from the list. The reason given was that she could not drive a car, but the true one was that she was too old, something she had never thought of before and would never face. Moved by her distress, two friends – the commander of Quonset, the naval base in Rhode Island, and his wife – invited her to go and stay with them. In the camp nursery she looked after the babies of the young officers in training. Becoming restive after a time, she returned to New York to raise funds for the Red Cross. In May 1943 she organized an exhibition at the Wildenstein Gallery, taking her inspiration from the image of Dr Maria Montessori, whose dedicated efforts in schools for deprived children had influenced her adolescence in Italy. She enlisted the assistance of the doctors and nurses of the children's ward of the New York Infirmary to illustrate the treatment of children's diseases (including infantile paralysis, with which she had lived so intimately) and the ways of preventing them. She herself gave a lecture. Later she arranged a series of concerts of mostly French music with, notably, pianists Robert Casadesus and his wife Gaby, Giovanni Martinelli of the Met, and violinists Zino Franchescatti and Nathan Milstein. The most memorable concert, in late May 1944, filled Madison Square Garden.

On 25 August 1944 the Allies liberated Paris. Elsa, picking up the *American Journal,* stared at a front-page open letter to her written by a reporter who had gained admittance to her home on the rue de Berri, gave her news of it, and transmitted greetings to her by name from her staff at Place Vendôme. At once she applied for a permit to return to France, but trouble arose on the French side. She soon found out why, when a mission from the Chambre Syndicale de la Couture arrived in New York to revive relations between the countries. At the request of the visitors, Elsa was not included in any festivities organized by the various fashion magazines for them, and in due course she was summoned to what seemed like a court-room trial in their suite at the St Regis.

'We are aware,' they said, 'that because of the isolation of Paris, American designers have created a look of their own – greatly based, it is true, on aspects of the Schiaparelli styles – and have turned New York and Los Angeles into clothes centres. We know that in 1942, with the help of *Vogue,* the American Garmentmakers' Union raised a million dollars to promote American fashion through advertising. To what extent have you contributed to this activity, potentially so detrimental to our own?'

Angrily, Elsa informed the strange, self-appointed tribunal that she had avoided any involvement in American dressmaking to the point of refusing invitations to attend the Coty Award presentations. 'I have defended the good name of French fashion from beginning to end,' she declared. 'I have always maintained that inspiration can only, and will only, be rooted in Paris.' She showed them a copy of a newspaper article reporting her lecture tour in 1940. It noted a question put to her: 'Do you think New York could become the world centre of fashion in the place of Paris?' and her reply: 'Paris pays no attention to quantities, distribution, or prices. All thoughts are concentrated on beauty, new fabrics, designs, accessories. Unfortunately, American designers (because of imperatives of mass production) do not enjoy the same liberty of expression.' These beliefs, she told her interrogators, she had firmly upheld in public and private wherever she had been in the States over the past years. And she wrung from them the admission that this defence might be construed as a form of courage and was indubitably an expression of faith. Quickly, however, she perceived in the eyes of these emissaries from a starving, devastated and bankrupt country an accusing look that she would encounter for years: 'It was easy to be in New York during the Occupation.'

This was just one of the reasons why, from then on, she almost always seemed to be on the defensive.

22

The Tolling of the Bell

I MMEDIATELY after the Germans' unconditional surrender in May 1945, Elsa sailed from Boston to what was left of Le Havre in an overcrowded ship that took two weeks to make the crossing. Miraculously, her rue de Berri home, which had been successively occupied by the Italians and the Germans, was practically intact. In a downstairs desk drawer she found visiting cards of numerous French celebrities who had been received there by the occupants, and she never invited one of them again. At Place Vendôme she took her staff, looking pinched and apprehensive, by surprise, walking in one morning unannounced. She found M. Meunier's accounts up to the minute and in order to a centime, as were M. Cavaillé-Coll's for the perfumes. In fact, the four-year operation showed a healthy profit. Yet she did not utter a single word of thanks to anyone. On the other hand, without having to be asked, she instantly doubled the wages that had been frozen since her departure.

Everywhere she looked she saw a universe of moral apathy. France and the rest of Europe, exhausted by Hitler's evil, instead of being restored by a sense of peace were now paralysed by the fear of nuclear annihilation and the stalemate of cold war. St Germain-des-Prés was the new shrine of intellectual youth, and Sydney Bechet, Juliette Greco and Boris Vian were its idols. Elsa understood the radical change that had overtaken this youth, because the change had come from America with the troops of the Longest Day. Into the cellars and cafés where the young French gathered, the American GIs had introduced bebop and 'le jazz hot'. Although Maurice Chevalier had bridged the years, Charles Trenet, Edith Piaf and Yves Montand were taking over from Mistinguett, Josephine Baker and Jean Sablon. Scenting the veering wind, the ageing Jean Cocteau scribbled on a wall in St Germain-des-Prés, *'Je vous dis adieu'*.

With Simone de Beauvoir, Jean-Paul Sartre could reign over the St Germain-des-Prés cafés, Le Flore, Les Deux Magots and the Montana, because the post-war generation found comfort in existentialism, based on the concept of 'The fault dear Brutus, is not in our stars but in ourselves, that we are underlings'. Basically austere, this philosophy became in Sartre's hands a demand for positive and responsible individual action. Such a call to arms rallied no more enthusiastic a supporter than Elsa. Did Sartre sense a moral kinship with her? At all events, he insisted that Schiaparelli design the myriad historical costumes for his most ambitious and costly play, *Le Diable et le Bon Dieu*. His insistence was considered curious at the time, for Schiaparelli had not hitherto been associated with that sort of enterprise.

While working on the designs, Elsa started marshalling her troops once again. She not only launched the preparations for her comeback collection but, keeping a promise made in New York to Quaker Aid, she set up workrooms at Place Vendôme where second-hand clothing could be repaired and new clothing made for people in northern France, which – to add to all the misery – had just been through the worst winter in living memory. She also gave shows for American GIs in hospitals, collected layettes for the unusual number of babies that were suddenly being born, and sent her best fitters to the villages and hamlets of ravaged Alsace to help dress the children. Learning of Paul Poiret's death the previous year, she put on a black ensemble he had given her twenty years before and went alone to Montmartre Cemetery to pray at his grave.

The final scenes of Elsa's career were enacted within the setting of the French post-Liberation reconstruction programme. A vital phase of this programme was the recovery of foreign markets, and the export companies immediately went to great lengths to prove that France had lost none of her creative powers or versatility. Inevitably, Paris fashion remained a major export item. At the request of the Minister of Industrial Production, the Provisional Government of the French Republic empowered Madame Schiaparelli to go to New York in the interests of 'the development of exportation in America and the resumption of commercial relations'. At her suggestion, Elsa paid her own expenses.

Simultaneously, to raise money for the rehabilitation of shattered villages, the Chambre Syndicale sent a display, the Théâtre de la Mode, to gala showings in capital cities all over Europe and the United States. The brainchild of Jean Cocteau, the Théâtre de la Mode was a collection of doll-sized figurines placed in intricate and imaginatively lit miniature sets. Christian Bérard drew up the plans; fourteen stage designers did the sets; fifty-three leading couturiers, including Schiaparelli, dressed the dolls to scale in their latest fashions, complete with jewels and other ornaments, coiffures and accessories – and all was described in a de luxe brochure by famous writers. The display was meant to prove that despite the rigours of the Occupation, Paris fashion designing still reigned supreme.

In fact, nothing seemed less certain. There was little activity in the field. None of the pre-war luminaries was showing any leadership. Nor did the restrictions help. A woollen coat could not be lined with wool, there was no fur, no dress could be composed of more than

Elsa photographed by Irving Penn in New York, 1948.

three yards of material, and only sixty models could be shown. Moreover, the awful styles that were the legacy of the Occupation – boxer shoulders, flat hips, turbans like towering storks' nests – made women look like inflated caricatures of Elsa at her most aggressively pre-war masculine. Paris was waiting to be brought back to life.

'There seem to be strong currents of thought absolutely demanding certain fashions, certain conceits, at certain times, and equally strong currents turning them down absolutely at other times.' Thus Paul Poiret in *Harper's Bazaar,* back in May 1914. The currents of the opening of the twentieth century demanded a Poiret, but the war had forced him to quit the Parisian scene and he had lost his psychic sense of touch; the twenties had turned him down. In an exact parallel, the currents of the twenties and thirties had demanded a Schiaparelli, but she had been forced to leave Paris by the Second World War and had likewise lost her sense of touch; now the late forties and fifties turned her down.

'Modern', as represented in fashion by Elsa Schiaparelli in the thirties, was now passé. 'Contemporary' was in. While continuing to answer the need for new forms for the burgeoning technologies, the contemporary concept aimed to increase efficiency, comfort and visual enjoyment by outlawing whatever had been strange and pugnacious in the preceding decades. Elsa never lacked inspiration, her designs remained beautiful and she never betrayed women, but she was not in tune with the prevailing mood, and even felt uneasy in the new context; her approach of calculated shock and frivolity no longer corresponded to the spirit of the day.

American *Vogue* on 1 November 1945 reported that the American standbys, the box-jackets and box-coats which Elsa had inaugurated before the war, looked new in Paris, which proved, as usual, how foresighted she had been. Now everyone in Paris expected her to reflect a decided American influence because of her stay in the United States. How wrong they were. While in the States Elsa had not thought seriously about clothes. Her mind had been on other things, and now, as she herself admitted, she fell into step not with what was happening in 1945 but with herself back in 1939 – as when she produced in August 1947 the gimmicky Broken Egg Silhouette of ridged gown backs, and in mid-1948 the over-narrow Arrow Silhouette.

Of course Elsa realized the need for change. She did attempt a complete turnabout, renouncing her 'furled umbrella' silhouette for the 'overturned tulip' then coming into vogue. In a reaction to all the padding, but continuing with her particular vision of women dressed in a practical yet elegant way, she opted for simplicity. She reversed the Occupation caricaturing of her former self by launching a new style with shoulders that practically drooped, flat dresses with sloping lines, unadorned hats that sculpted the head and brightly coloured blouses worn with flannel skirts. Wavering as to what silhouette to introduce, she went back into history, all the more ill-

The Broken Egg Silhouette, seen (above) on a short dress of black silk ottoman worn with a black satin skull cap, and (opposite) with eleborately swathed bustle on a long silk evening dress.

advisedly when she attempted to revive her masculine look. For her return in August 1945 she brought out the Talleyrand Silhouette, involving tightly buttoned frock-coat jackets, voluminously ruffled shirts and, most notably, high stiff collars recalling the *minerve*, an orthopaedic device for holding up the neck following vertebral lesions – and moreover associated unfortunately in French minds with Erich von Stroheim playing a German officer in Jean Renoir's pre-war film *La Grande Illusion*. Charitably, on 15 October 1945 American *Vogue* murmured, 'Schiaparelli's entire collection is intensely pictorial.'

In January 1947 the Gibson Girl look also seemed too old-fashioned for a throwback style, with its boned neck, high shirtwaist and flat-boned cummerbund, although it was to become a popular American resort idea in the early fifties. In April 1947 the tightly bound Mummy Silhouette was an embarrassment, while in early 1948 the Riding-Habit Line and the Impressionist fashions were true errors. A return to geometrical conceptions and then the testing of an asymmetrical line both flopped, as in August 1948 did the jutting collar and peg-topped skirt of the Dandy Look. In January 1949 she brought out her anticlimactic backswept Hurricane Line, just after Balenciaga had produced his sensational Blown-Back Line, itself based on her pre-war Stormy Weather and Typhoon Silhouettes.

Throughout these first years after the war Elsa thought it might still be useful to protect her woman (it wasn't); in her August 1946 collection she drew out the shoulder area from arm to arm with the look of collar upon collar and a little continuance of collars on the sleeves. A failure then, it later developed into the cape-sleeved suit adopted by the fashionable world in the fifties. Then in 1947 she did capes and capelets as collars and sleeves for coats: as 'collar capes' these caught on wildly – but years later. In the same year she produced the apron skirt, a development of her pre-war apron designed to cope with changes in methods of travel, which was featured in all the couturiers' collections in 1950. She revived her 'contradictions': in 1946 gilt-embroidered felt jackets that were comfortable enough to wear at home with corduroy slacks, and the short, bust-enveloping American Civil War Northerner cape in blue that could be thrown back over the shoulders like huge lapels, revealing its yellow lining. She conjured up more 'witticisms': in 1947 she tinted rhinestones and cut them square for a necklace. In mid-1949 she did a spectacular, long, diamond-shaped shawl of black fox with a hood; Paris disdained it but the Americans brought it into vogue six years later in many multi-purpose fabrics. Early in 1950 she put white dots on a blue lapin stole. At the same time her lamé-bound cellophane X-ray cardigan and sheath dress was noticed by no one except Chanel, who brought it out in overskirts as an 'original' several years later.

The hats Elsa designed were meant to be exciting, and they would have been before the war: the black felt and grosgrain toque

Schiaparelli's first post-war look in autumn 1945 was the arrogantly suave Talleyrand Silhouette.

accordeon pleated at the back (December 1951); the magnificent shocking pink velvet off-the-face beret embroidered with sequins and rainbow-coloured pearls, and the three-tufted Elfish Topknot (both February 1952); the Robin Hood hat (October 1952), a variation of her early Mad Cap in that it could be worn in any number of ways and, folding easily, could be put into a bag or suitcase; and the Bali Ballets in lacquered black and white cellophane (August 1953).

Elsa was as practical as ever. For air travel – taking into account the 30 kilo luggage limit on a transatlantic flight – she produced a straight shoulder-to-hem Constellation travel coat (plus Constellation Bag) that American *Vogue* on 1 April 1946 instantly dubbed prophetic, and another coat with 'suitcase' pockets. For travel by land or sea she brought out in early 1947 the accordeon pleated Carry-All Bag, the longest bag in Paris, with stepladder compartments, and for obvious purposes the Commuter's Bag with two huge flaps on either side. That same year she made up an entire trousseau in a specially designed leather bag that opened like an envelope and weighed less than seven pounds but contained six dresses, a pair of shoes and three hats, while toilet accessories could be placed in the large pockets of a reversible coat for day and night wear. All this represented the natural answer to the new lifestyle facing modern women, but the Jet Wardrobe belonged fifteen years ahead; it found no place in the years immediately after the Liberation.

The truth was that post-war Parisian women were weary of everyday problems. A certain coarseness prevailed: logic and practicality were out of the question. Great Britain might be bravely facing austerity, but France, in her attempts to recapture foreign markets, still believed that sumptuousness and glitter were necessary. French life, like yeast, rose again towards a devoutly desired state of illusion, and fashionable women, who at the outbreak of the war had feared to lose irrevocably what was left to them of youth, now breathed freely again and determined to show up the BOFs, whom they scorned – and routed.

In the immediate post-war social context, though, there was no vital change in the status of women for fashion to anticipate, mirror and support, no message to deliver, no battle to wage. It is not surprising that no truly innovative Messiah of Fashion burst on to the scene, but only dictators of styles – exquisite, smart and exciting, certainly – who would keep women in a rigid mould of convention for years. Pre-eminent among these was Christian Dior, previously assistant to Lucien Lelong, who was backed by the cotton king of France, Marcel Boussac, as part of the renewed export effort. Dior's new kind of fashion house represented for Elsa, as she herself put it, 'the tolling of the bell'.

The post-war New Look was a logical reaction to the pre-war Old Look, the Schiaparelli Look, which had gone haywire during the

Occupation. A new look – younger, more romantic, softer – was in the air before it became *the* New Look. Cristóbal Balenciaga had announced it as early as 1937, when inaugurating his Paris house. American *Vogue* for 15 July 1939 noted that 'Schiaparelli amplifies the hip theme', and then queried in a headline soon after the Liberation (in May 1945): 'What's the New Look in Paris?' The fledgling post-war couturiers – Fath, Balmain, Piguet, Dessès – all reflected the need to restore unforced femininity to women after the dreary years of utility, but with his first collection on 12 February 1947, Christian Dior was proclaimed the creator of *the* New Look because he had sniffed the breeze best at just the right moment, had a broader view of tomorrow than the others, was supported by untold sums of money, had access to brilliant planners and unlimited amounts of breathtaking fabrics (all supplied by Boussac), and was promoted by the greatest din of publicity ever known to fashion. But in truth his was an inspired continuation of the rounded line that had been seen since the first post-Liberation collections: no revolution, rather a new use of themes which had been crystallizing for seasons past and which now seemed fresh and inviting.

Elsa had measured the threat of Dior well before he first unveiled his wares, and – having kept only for a short time in her *atelier tailleur* (tailored suits) a promising twenty-three-year-old cutter from Venice, Pierre Cardin – she cast about for a brilliant young junior designer to help her stand up to the imminent challenge. Irish-born John Cavanagh, Molyneux's assistant, preferred to join Balmain before opening his own fine house in London. Thereupon, Elsa secured the services (particularly for the Boutique) of Hubert de Givenchy, barely twenty years old, who remained with her until going into business on his own, despite Elsa's expressed desire to leave her house to him. (He was succeeded briefly by Philippe Venet, just twenty-one.) In August 1949 Schiaparelli's winter collection showed so much of the old mastery that *Newsweek* gave her its cover on 26 September 1949, extolling her in comparison to 'Dior and his immediate imitators, who are falsifying good taste with creations simply meant to attract publicity.'

That same month, at 530 Seventh Avenue, New York City, Elsa opened a branch of her fashion company for the mass-production of suits, dresses and coats to be marketed throughout the United States, but with no more than one outlet per city to maintain the aura of 'exclusivity'. Schiaparelli here featured little brightly colourful and young-looking jackets called 'shorties' with pockets in the form of camera cases and stiffened for greater emphasis; she inundated America with dyed furs used as coat linings and suit trimmings; she used shock colours of blue, red and yellow for suit and coat collars; she introduced afternoon dresses with detachable décolletages of interchangeable colours to harmonize with hats and gloves; she came up with buttoned sashes to wear long or longer, depending on which set of holes were used; she launched the Pyramid Line for coats,

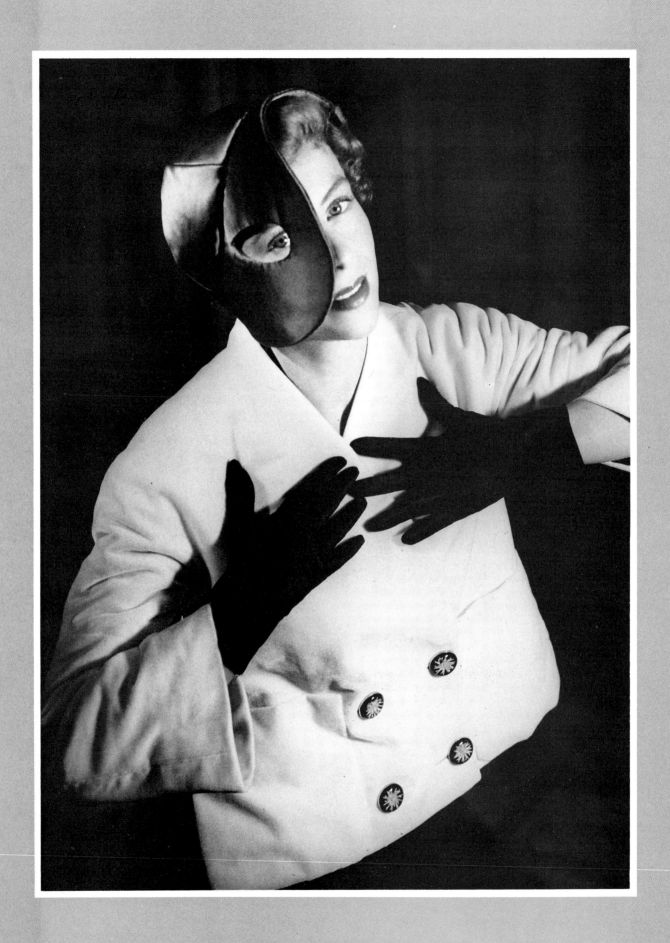

including the big Duster Coat and the Dolman Greatcoat with secret pockets in the sleeves – 'one of her wonderfuls' reported American *Vogue* on 15 March 1951; and she inaugurated a range of lingerie featuring quilted housecoats lined in shocking pink, others with shocking pink shoulders and embroidered with strass, and ermine-collared dressing gowns. To capture public fancy the more, Elsa revived the eighteenth-century method of publicizing Paris styles abroad: she marketed Schiaparelli dolls, fashioned, dressed and coiffed in fourteen different ways, for display in shop windows. In October 1950 a survey carried out at the corner of 42nd Street and Fifth Avenue revealed that the Paris name best known to passers-by was still Schiaparelli.

Unfortunately, the success of the new American venture did not help Elsa solve the problems of the mounting cost of her collections (on which she refused to economize), of increased wages and social benefits, and of declining sales at Place Vendôme. Gamely, season after season, she fought to regain the ground she couldn't help but see she was losing. The Shape Line (August 1951) was supposed to represent the rolling of sea waves; Shocking Elegance (1952) was achieved through manipulating the 'open heart of the bosom', a daringly plunging neckline on a narrow, sleek silhouette; the Chinese Pagoda effect (1952) was obtained by means of stiffened ruffles on the skirt of an evening gown; the Caressing Line of August 1953 had shoulders descending almost to the elbows and armholes beginning below the natural waistline. Yet none of this caught on: it seemed contrived and it was inappropriate.

Truth to tell, was Elsa's heart really in it? The Shelf décolletage, the surrealistic Profile Hat cut after the wearer's profile with a diamond brooch to simulate the eye, the face-covering straw hat with a cellophane window to see through – all gave an impression of leftovers. So did the new 'Schiaparelli-isms': a belt conceived to contain a bottle of sun-tan lotion, sunglasses in braided straw continuing over the ears to form pigtails, hand-painted dressmaker details on plain dresses, eyeglasses that looked like enormous eyelashes in black cellophane. The thrill was gone.

Finally, Elsa lost so much money that M. Cavaillé-Coll, about to retire and preparing to turn the management of the perfume business deservedly over to Paulette Laperche, made Elsa understand that this company could not go on paying for what she owed to her fashion suppliers, most of whom were refusing to grant any more credit, although it was greatly thanks to her that they had made fortunes. While she agreed to close, she never ceased to maintain that couturier perfumes need a fashion house and a great name designer to be kept before the public for any length of time, and she adamantly refused to sell. By coming to an agreement with her creditors she avoided going into bankruptcy, and in the years to follow she personally honoured every single one of her debts with what she earned from the perfumes.

Schiaparelli attempts to reintroduce a Surrealistic theme with the post-war Profile Hat.

Elsa with Ginger Rogers and Earl Blackwell of Celebrity Service at the Winter Collection shown in Elsa's home, 1952.

At the age of sixty-three, in February 1954, Schiaparelli showed her farewell collection, featuring the free and elegant Fluid Line. While Michèle Guéguen carried the last bolts of fabric out of the stock room, Elsa shut herself up in her home for a month to master her chagrin. As an added humiliation, that same year Chanel Perfumes hauled their septuagenarian originator out of fifteen years' retirement to save them by lending her fabled personage to fashion once more. Did Elsa derive some consolation from the catastrophic reviews hurled at the new Chanel collections? In any case, Chanel soon recovered all her old aplomb. Elsa, too: to the annoyance of her detractors, she did not fade out of the picture at all. Celebrities continued to seek her company, and she went on receiving them as always, in Paris and now also in her house in Hammamet, Tunisia. She travelled all over the world for her own pleasure, doing promotional appearances for the perfumes and accessories; Schiaparelli earrings were featured in American *Vogue* as late as 1 March 1965. She accepted innumerable honours, was to be seen at theatres and concerts everywhere as usual, adored going to the cinema, read avidly and attended all the big fashion shows.

'Young designers – and it is most regrettable – can no longer do what they like because of pressures on them to produce lines that sell for a certainty,' she remarked in an interview. 'The daring is gone. No one can dream any more.' Consequently, she bought almost exclusively from her friend Balenciaga, the only designer, besides Saint Laurent, who could still afford to follow his dream and dare to do what he liked. The young newcomer Yves Saint Laurent, determined to uphold the grand tradition of Parisian beauty and elegance, Elsa appreciated and supported from his first collection, and she bought at least one model from him a year.

Did she derive any satisfaction from outliving Chanel by a few years? At all events, during them she suffered several strokes. After the first she fought valiantly to recover her former vitality, but the second one reduced her to a physical dependency offensive to a woman so jealous of her privacy and so proud. But she did not relinquish her hold on her fashion or Paris perfume interests until faced with the fact of imminent death.

To the very end, fully or partially conscious, she was always ready for the day. No one ever visited her, even when she was bedridden, without finding her properly coiffed, made up, dressed in exquisite lingerie, scented in 'Shocking' and surrounded by flowers and photographs of her family and friends. Elsa Schiaparelli died in her sleep at her home on 13 November 1973, aged eighty-three. A mass was celebrated for her on 1 December nearby at St Philippe-du-Roule, where she drew crowds for the last time. She had given up her place in the family tomb in Rome in favour of a relative, preferring a simple plot in the graveyard of a small church in the village of Frucourt in Picardy, near the home of some treasured friends. She loved this graveyard because of its simplicity and profound quiet. Her grave was marked by a bare Picard cross and a plain graphite slab with the florid signature she had herself traced in gold. Standing beside the grave during the simple burial ceremony was Gogo, with Gino Cacciapuoti, her second husband, an intuitive, humane Neapolitan nobleman. Also there were the truly loyal: Mike, Michèle Guéguen, Yvonne 'Faith' Souquières, Roger Jean-Pierre and Paulette Laperche. The sun shone brightly through the branches of the trees, which were still wearing their vividly Schiaparelli-coloured autumn leaves for her.

It was not thoughtlessly that, as an epigraph to her autobiography, Elsa placed a quotation from Chuang Tzu, who declared in 400 BC: 'Birth is not the beginning, death is not the end.' She had always believed that her existence, however successful in wordly terms, was a means to some other end. During her busy career – creating, commanding, routing competitors, amassing a small fortune, basking in her international reputation – she did not have time to find out what this end was until the autumn of her life brought its true harvest.

Unlike so many of her rivals, Elsa did not feel compelled to go to great lengths to prove to them and to herself that she was not a has-been, and she did not have to combat boredom or loneliness.

For one thing, she had the ever-present care of Gogo, she could contemplate with joy her two granddaughters, Marisa and Barynthia, and was able to reflect that she had secured beauty, gracious living and wellbeing for them for ever. More important, she had herself, her rich inner self, a self she had protected from all

aggression and kept secret and inviolate.

As the darkness gathered around her she passed peaceful hours in the company of Gogo and her husband. With Gino the wheel came full circle: she reverted to the Italian language and, in so doing, to the noble beauty and order of the Roman setting of her childhood and youth. With a gesture usually foreign to her, she would gently place her hand on his. 'Pino,' she would murmur, 'Pino.'

'No, Elsa, I'm Gino.'

'Well, you remind me of Pino. He was my first love, you know.'

Elsa with her granddaughters.

Bibliography

Agron, Suzanne, *Précis d'Histoire du Costume* (Librairie J. Lanore, Paris, 1970).

Antoine-Darriaux, Geneviève, *Les Voies de l'Elégance* (Hachette, Paris, 1965).

Assailly, Gisèle d', *Les Quinze Revolutions de la Mode* (Hachette, Paris, 1968; translated as *Ages of Elegance: Five Thousand Years of Fashion and Frivolity*, Macdonald, London, 1968).

Baines, Barbara B., *Fashion Revivals* (Batsford, London, 1981).

Ballard, Bettina, *In My Fashion* (Secker and Warburg, London, 1960).

Barthes, Roland, *Système de la Mode* (Editions du Seuil, Paris, 1967).

Battersby, Martin, *Art Deco Fashion: French Designers* (Academy Editions, London; St Martin's Press, New York, 1974).

Beaton, Cecil, *The Glass of Fashion* (Weidenfeld and Nicolson, London, 1954).

Beaulieu, Michèle, *Le Costume Moderne et Contemporain* (Presses Universitaires de France, Paris, 1951).

Beaumont, G., Vilmorin, L. de, and Cheronnet, L., *Plaquette de Luxe sur l'Exposition 'Le Théâtre de la Mode'* (Aljanvic Publicité, Paris, 1945; exhibition organized by Chambre Syndicale de la Couture Parisienne).

Bertin, Celia, *Haute Couture – Terre Inconnue* (Hachette, Paris, 1956; translated as *Paris à la Mode. A Voyage of Discovery*, Gollancz, London, 1956).

Bibescu, Princess, *Noblesse de la Robe* (Grasset, Paris, 1929).

Boucher, François, *Histoire de Costume* (Flammarion, Paris, 1965; translated as A *History of Costume in the West*, Thames and Hudson, London, 1967).

Butazzi, Garzietta, *La Mode: Art, Histoire et Société* (Hachette, Paris, 1983; translated from the Italian).

Carlier, Freddy and Jean, *Dans les Coulisses de la Haute Couture Parisienne* (Flammarion, Paris, 1956).

Chase, Edna W. and Ilka, *Always in Vogue* (Gollancz, London; Doubleday, New York, 1954).

Colas, René, *Bibliographie Générale du Costume et de la Mode* (Colas, Paris, 1933).

Contini, Mila, *5000 Ans d'Elégance* (Hachette, Paris, 1965).

Delbourg-Delphis, Marylène, *Le Chic et le Look: Histoire de la Mode Féminine et des Moeurs de 1850 à Nos Jours* (Hachette, Paris, 1981).

Delbourg-Delphis, Marylène, and Mauries, Patrick, *Humeur de Mode* (Autrement, Paris, 1984).

Descamps, Marc-Alain, *Psychosociologie de la Mode* (Presses Universitaires, Paris, 1984).

Devlin, Polly, *Vogue Book of Fashion Photography 1919–1979* (Simon and Schuster, New York, 1979; Thames and Hudson, London, 1984).

Dior, Christian, Chavane, Alice, and Rabourdin, Elie, *Je Suis Couturier* (Conquistador, Paris, 1951; translated as *Talking About Fashion*, Hutchinson, London, 1954).

Dior, Christian, *Christian Dior et Moi* (Amiot-Dumont, Paris, 1956; translated as *Dior by Dior*, Weidenfeld and Nicolson, London, 1957; Penguin, Harmondsworth, 1958).

Dorig, James, *La Mode et la Couture – Vocabulaire France-Anglais* (Rossignol, Paris, 1925).

Dorner, Jane, *Fashion in the Twenties and Thirties* (New Rochelle, New York; Arlington House, 1974).

Du Rosella, Bruno, *La Crise de la Mode: la Revolution des Jeunes et la Mode* (Fayard, Paris, 1973).

Du Rosella, Bruno, *La Mode* (Imprimerie Nationale, Paris, 1980).

Etherington-Smith, Meredith, *Patou* (Hutchinson, London, 1983).

Fargue, Léon-Paul, *De la Mode* (Editions Littéraires de France, Paris, 1945).

Faughey, John P., *Information Needs in Fashion Design* (British Library, London, 1978).

Flugel, J. G., *The Psychology of Clothes* (Institute of Psychoanalysis, London, 1930; Hogarth Press, London, 1950).

François, Lucien, *Comment un Nom devient une Griffe* (Gallimard, Paris, 1961).

François, Lucien, *Les Elégances de Paris* (Commissariat Général du Tourisme, Paris, 1946).

Gernsheim, Alison, *Fashion and Reality 1840–1914* (Faber and Faber, London, 1963).

Giafferri, Paul Louis de, *L'Histoire de Costume Féminin Mondial* (Nilsson, Paris, 1925).

Gramont, Elisabeth de, *La Femme et la Robe* (La Palatine, Paris, 1952).

Hall-Duncan, Nancy, *Histoire de la Photographie de Mode* (Editions de Chêne, Paris, 1978).

Horst, *Salute to the Thirties* (Bodley Head, London, 1971).

Keenan, Brigid, *Dior in 'Vogue'* (Octopus, London, 1981).

Khormak, Lucille, *Fashion 2001* (Columbus Books, London, 1982).

Kidwell, Claudia B., and Christman, Margaret C., *Suiting Everyone: the Democratization of Clothing in America* (Smithsonian Institution Press, Washington, 1975).

La Loi du 12 Mars 1952 sur le Contrefaçon (Paris, 1952).

Latour, Anny, *Kings of Fashion* (Weidenfeld and Nicolson, London, 1958).

Latour, Anny, *Les Magiciens de la Mode* (Julliard, Paris, 1961).

Laurent, Jacques, *Le Nu Vétu et Devétu* (Gallimard, Paris, 1979).

Laver, James, *A Concise History of Costume* (Thames and Hudson, London, 1969).

Laver, James, *The Literature of Fashion* (Cambridge University Press, London, 1947).

Laver, James, *Taste and Fashion from the French Revolution to the Present Day* (Harrap, London, 1937, 1945).

Leese, Elisabeth, *Costume Design in the Movies* (F. Ungar, New York, 1983).

Lemoine-Luccioni, Eugénie, *La Robe: Essai Psychanalytique sur la Mode* (Seuil, Paris, 1983).

Lepape, Claude, *Georges Lepape* (Herscher, Paris, 1983).

Les Elégances Parisiennes (Hachette, Paris, 1917).

Lynam, Ruth (ed.), *Couture: An Illustrated History of the Great Paris Designers and their Creations* (Doubleday, New York, 1972).

Lynam, Ruth (ed.), *Paris Fashion* (Michael Joseph, London; Clarkson Potter, New York, 1972).

Marly, Diana de, *The History of Haute Couture 1850–1950* (Batsford, London, 1980)

Morand, Paul, *L'Allure de Chanel* (Hermann, Paris, 1976).

Musée de la Mode et du Costume (Palais Galliera), *Hommage à Elsa Schiaparelli*, exhibition catalogue (1984).

Obalk, Hector, *Les Mouvements de Mode Expliqués aux Parents* (R. Laffont, Paris, 1984).

Packer, William, *The Art of Vogue Covers 1909–1940* (Condé Nast Publications, 1980).

Packer, William, *Fashion Drawing in Vogue* (Thames and Hudson, London, 1983).

Penn, Irving, and Vreeland, Diana, *Inventive Paris Clothes, 1909–1939* (Thames and Hudson, London, 1977).

Picken, Mary Brooks, *The Fashion Dictionary* (Funk and Wagnall, New York, 1973; published in 1939 as *The Language of Fashion*).

Poiret, Paul, *Art et Finance* (Lutetia, Paris, 1934).

Poiret, Paul, *En Habillant l'Epoque* (Grasset, Paris, 1930).

Poiret, Paul, *Revenez-y* (Gallimard, Paris, 1932).

Polan, Brenda (ed.), *The Fashion Year* (Zomba Books, London, 1983).

Praline, *Praline, Mannequin de Paris* (Seuil, Paris, 1957).

Roscho, Bernard, *The Rag Race* (Funk and Wagnall, New York, 1983).

Roubaud, Louis, *Au Pays des Mannequins* (Editions de France, Paris, 1928).

Rouff, Maggy, *La Philosophie de L'Elégance* (Editions Littéraires de France, Paris, 1942).

Rouzaud, Claude, *Un Problème d'Intérêt National: les Industries de Luxe* (Sirey, Paris, 1946).

Salvy, Claude, *J'ai vu Vivre la Mode* (Fayard, Paris, 1960).

Salvy, Claude, *Le Monde et la Mode*, Collection Nouvelle Encyclopédie (Hachette, Paris, 1966).

Saunders, Edith, *The Age of Worth* (Longmans, Green, London, 1954).

Schiaparelli, Elsa, *Shocking* (Denoël, Paris, 1954; translated as *Shocking Life*, Dent, London, 1954).

Schlatter, Christian, *Les Années 80: la Création en France* (Flammarion, Paris, 1984).

Seilhac, Léon de, *L'Industrie de la Couture et de la Confection à Paris* (Firmin-Didot, Paris, 1897).

Spencer, Charles, *Cecil Beaton, Stage and Film Designs* (Academy Editions, London; St Martin's Press, New York, 1975).

Steele, Valerie, *Fashion and Eroticism* (Oxford University Press, 1985).

Tessoneau, Rémy, *Le Luxe est-il une Fleur de Mal?* (Union Française des Industries Exportatrices, Paris, 1948).

Tilke, Max, *Le Costume – Coupes et Formes de l'Antiquité aux Temps Modernes* (A. Morance, Paris, 1967).

Tolstoy, Mary Koutousou, *Charlemagne to Dior: the History of French Fashion* (Slain Publication, 1967).

Torrens, Deborah, *Fashion Illustrated* (Studio Vista, London, 1974).

Vèdres, Nicole, *Un Siècle d'Elégance Française* (Editions de Chêne, Paris, 1943).

Vincent-Ricard, Françoise, *Raison et Passion: Langages de Société: La Mode, 1940–1990* (Colombes, Paris, 1983).

Vingt-cinq Ans d'Elégance à Paris (1925–50), Album composed at the request of Marcel Rochas; introduction by Colette (Tisne, Paris, 1951).

White, Palmer, *Poiret* (Clarkson N. Potter, New York; Studio Vista, London, 1973).

Wilhelm, Jacques, *Histoire de la Mode* (Hachette, Paris, 1955).

Worth, Gaston, *La Couture et la Confection de Vêtements de Femme* (Chaix, Paris, 1895).

Worth, Jacques, 'A Propos de la Mode', *Revue de Paris*, 15 May 1930.

Worth, Jacques, *Rapport du Congrès de l'Expansion Economique* (Association Nationale d'Expansion Economique, Paris, 1929).

Worth, Jean-Philippe, *A Century of Fashion* (Boston, 1928).

Page numbers in italic refer to illustration captions

accessories, 62, 66–9, 81, 140–51; *56, 98, 100, 146*
Adrian, Gilbert, 108, 201
Aeroplane Silhouette, 24, 115
African art, 62, 146
air travel clothes, 212
Alvarez, Lily, 76
American Red Cross, 202, 203
American Relief Association, 42, 187
American Relief to France, 199, 202
Amies, Hardy, 110
Annabella, 171, 202
Antoine, 101
Apollinaire, Guillaume, 32
après-ski wear, 74
apron skirts, 65, 181; *181, 182*
Arab style, 29, 166
Aragon, Louis, 146
Arden, Elizabeth, 92, 200
Arethusa, 29
Arletty, 72, 145
Armani, Giorgio, 176
Armenian knitwear, 59–61
Arp, Hans, 145
Arrow Silhouette, 208
Art Deco, 18, 56, 57, 62, 132, 140; *56*
Arthur, Jean, 109
Astrology Collection, 21, 170; *10, 90*
Avedon, Richard, 85
Aviatrix Coat, 97

Bacall, Lauren, 171
bags, 143–5, 212
Baker, Josephine, 205
Balboa, 128
Balenciaga, Cristóbal, 81, 94, 122, 195, 210, 213, 216
Bali Ballets, 212
Balilla hemp, 132
Ballet Russe, 31
Balmain, 213
Bankhead, Tallulah, 69, 94
Banton, Travis, 108
Barber Pole evening gown, 152
Basket Hat, 128
batik, 132
beach bags, 145
beach wear, 74; *64; see also* swim-wear
Beaton, Cecil, 85, 112, 113, 146; *72, 96, 140, 214*
beauty products, 65, 154–8, 183, 199, 215
Beauvoir, Simone de, 205
Bechet, Sydney, 205
belts, 143
Bennett, Constance, 171
Bérard, Christian, 82, 91, 99, 132, 136, 161, 206; *10, 66, 78, 98, 166*
Berenson, Barynthia, 217
Berenson, Marisa, 217
Berenson, Robert Laurence, 185
Bergery, Bettina *see* Jones, Bettina
Bernhardt, Sarah, 32
Berry Garden Hat, 150

Bersagliera Cap, 176
Best and Co., New York, 66
Bianchini, 122; *31*
Biarritz, 183–4
bicycling outfits, 181, 183
Bird Silhouette, 103
Blackwell, Earl, *216*
Blass, Bill, 176
Blown-Back Line, 210
Le Bœuf sur le Toit, 45, 71
BOFs, 194
Bois-Colombes, 156
boleros, 74, 76, 102, 103; *105, 168*
Bonwit Teller, 185–7
bottles, perfume, 156–7
Bourbon-Parme, Comtesse Sixte de, 72
Bourke-White, Margaret, 85
Boussac, Marcel, 212
Box Coats, 102
Box Suits, 102; *102, 106*
Boyer, Charles, 202
bracelets, 146
Braque, Georges, 145
Brodavitch, 85
Broken Egg Silhouette, 208; *208*
brooches, 146, 149
Brunhoff, Michel de, 192
Butterfly Brooch, 146
buttons, 140–3; *142, 150*

Cacciapuoti, Gino, 217–18
Cacciapuoti, Yvonne ('Gogo', ES's daughter): birth, 38; ES's open letter to, 112, 162; ES's relations with, 89; excels at sports, 110; illness, 43, 45, 66; looks after ES, 217–18; M. Jean works for, 119; marriage, 185, 217, 218; at school, 66, 110; and the war, 180, 185; *196*
Caetani, Princess Cora, 80
Campagna Romana, 21–3, 152, 170, 176
capes, 69, 76, 99, 173–6, 210; *18, 39, 45, 176*
Capricorne fabric, 126
Caraman-Chimay, Princess Thérèse de, 80, 82, 86, 162
cardigans, 57
Cardin, Pierre, 213
Caressing Line, 215
Carry-All Bag, 212
Carven, 176
Casadesus, Gaby, 203
Casadesus, Robert, 203
Cash and Carry Collection, 181
Cavaillé-Coll, M., 190, 205, 215
Cavanagh, John, 213
Celestial Silhouette, 21, 103
cellophane, 128; *123*
Cham, Plato, 134
Chambre Syndicale de la Couture Parisienne, 120, 170–1, 192, 193, 203, 206
Chanel, Coco: closes during the war, 180; copies of ES, 210; costume jewellery, 146; dress design as a profession, 94; and influence of

sportswear, 54; lifestyle, 119; loses customers to ES, 52, 72; perfumes, 154, 158, 216; relations with ES, 92, 94; social position, 91, 119; staff strike, 101; style, 52–3, 94; in the twenties, 52–3; use of synthetic fabrics, 122
Chaplin, Charlie, 54
Chevalier, Maurice, 45, 183, 205
chiffon, 132
Chinese Pagoda line, 215
Chuang Tzu, 217
Churchill, Lady, 171
Cigarette Silhouette, 106
Circus Collection, 166–8; *105, 148, 166, 168*
Clair, René, 109
Claire, Ina, 69
Clarke, Henry, *145, 176*
Claudel, Paul, 200
Clément, Jean, 81, 82, 86, 140–3, 145, 152–4, 190
coats, 48–9, 63, 66, 97, 102, 129, 130, 212, 213–15
Cocked Hats, 150
cocktail dress, 106
cocktail suits, 128
Cocteau, Jean, 45, 82, 92, 132, 136, 145, 176, 205, 206; *46, 63, 120, 136*
coiffures, 101, 151, 195
Colbert, Claudette, 171
Colcombet, Charles, 122, 126, 128; *126*
collars, 66–9, 76, 210
collections, 162–73; *see also individual named collections*
colour, ES's use of, 21, 25, 29, 57, 86, 94, 130, 152–4, 181, 183
Columbia Lecture Bureau, 184
Commedia dell 'arte Collection, 170; *172*
Commuter's Bag, 212
Comoedia, 192
Cooper, Lady Diana, 74
Copenhagen, 134
Cosmic, 126
Coty Award, 200, 203
Coutil, 129
Covarrubias, 116; *113*
Coward, Noël, 112, 126
Cracknyl, 126
Crawford, Joan, 82, 108–9, 119, 171; *109*
Crazy Coxcomb, 69
Cuba, 42
Cubism, 17, 32, 54, 57, 101, 152
culottes, 63, 75–6
Cunard, Nancy, 45, 52, 72
Curie, Eve, 32, 171
Curie, Marie, 32
Current Events Collection, 164

Daché, Lily, 200–1
Dada, 17, 39–41, 45, 54
Dali, Salvador, 148, 200; *24*; designs for ES's home, 91; Desk Suit, 140; *141*; on fashion, 160; influence on jewellery, 145; lobster dress, 106,

173; *175*; scent bottles, 156; Surrealism, 54; tear dress, 134, 166; *134*; use of shocking pink, 154; work with ES, 82, 106, 132, 136–40, 156
Dallas, 154
Dana, Irene, 189, 190, 192
Dandy Look, 210
D'Annuzio, Gabriele, 25–6, 28
Dante, 197
Dark Allure, 126
Darrieux, Danielle, 171
Davies, Marion, 171
Davis, Bette, 109
Delaunay, Sonia, 32, 101
denim, 132
Desk Suit, 140; *141*
Dessès, Jean, 213
Dick Whittington hat, 100
Didrickson, Mildred ('Babe'), 107
Dietrich, Marlene, 74, 102, 171, 202; *76*
Dinner Suit, 104
Dior, Christian, 81, 143, 156, 162, 212, 213
'Display No. 1', 56–7, 122
'Display No. 2', 58, 63–6, 74, 79
divided skirts, 63, 75, 76
dolls, 215
Doll's Hats, 150; *107*
Dolman Greatcoat, 215
Domenitis, Alberto di (ES's grandfather), 20; *20*
Domenitis, Vincenzo (ES's uncle), 20; *20*
Domenitis, Zia (Aunt Lily), *20*
Donne, John, 200
Doucet, Jacques, 91
Dreier, Katherine, 41
Drian, 132
Duchamp, Marcel, 39, 41, 45, 200
Dufy, Raoul, 45, 132, 161; *31, 163*
Duncan, Isadora, 31
Durst, André, 92; *41, 126*
Duse, Eleonora, 25–6, 108
Duster Coat, 215

Earhart, Amelia, 74
Earle, Lady Lionel, *86*
earrings, 148, 149
Edinburgh, 116
Edward VIII, King of England, 34, 45, 143, 150, 164, 173
Elfish Topknot, 212
embroidery, 136; *22, 32, 45, 46, 75, 83, 94, 125, 136, 138, 146, 152, 186*
Erickson, Carl ('Eric'), 82; *68, 115*
Ernst, Max, 145, 200
Eskimo Collection, 164
Ethiopian style, 164
evening gowns, 76–8, 104, 106, 128, 129, 152; *49*
Everfast linen, 130
Everyday's a Holiday, 109; *110*
Exposition des Arts Décoratifs et Industriels Modernes (1925), 56
Expressionism, 54

Index

fabrics, *see* materials
Fabrimode, 129
fans, 141
Fath, 213
Fauves, 17, 152
Fellowes, Mrs Reginald (Daisy), 45, 72, 103–6, 129, 132, 136, 145, 148, 151; *45, 72*
Femina, 136; *45*
feminism, 23, 26, 36–7
Fendis, 176
film stars, 108–10
Filochard, 126
Finland, 183
Fisher, Lilian ('Dinarzade'), *61*
Fitzgerald, F. Scott, 54
Flanner, Janet, 78
Fluid Line, 216
Football Frock, 145
Forest Collection *see* Pagan Collection
Françoise Villon hat, 100
'France in America', 200
Franchescatti, Zino, 203
Francis, Kay, 101
Frank, Jean-Michel, 91–2, 154
Franklin Simon and Co., Fifth Avenue, 66
French Colonial Art Exhibition (1922), 62
French Seamen's Foyer, 202
Frucourt, 217
fur, 66, 129, 145; *68, 114, 128*
'furled umbrella' silhouette, 208
Futurism, 17, 26, 32, 37, 54–5, 57, 85, 132, 152

Gabin, Jean, 202
Gabor, Zsa-Zsa, *110*
Galatea's Head Clip, 146
Garbo, Greta, 74, 107, 171
Gaulle, General de, 184
George V, King of England, 34, 164
George VI, King of England, 113, 130–2
Giacometti, Alberto, 82, 91, 92, 145, 146
Gide, André, 45
Ginsburg, Madeleine, 24
Givenchy, Hubert de, 79, 213
glass cape, *126*
glass tunics, 128
gloves, 130, 140; *132*
Graham, Martha, 107
Great Bear designs, 24, 132; *24, 90*
Greco, Juliette, 205
Green, Julian, 200
Greenwich Village, 39, 42
Greer, Howard, 108
Grès, 195
Groult, Nicole, 41, 43
Gucci, 176
Guéguen, Michèle, 79, 81, 82, 161, 190, 192
Guerycolas, D., 156
Guggenheim, Peggy, 200

Haile Selassie, Emperor of Ethiopia, 164
hairstyles, 101, 151, 195
Hammamet, 29, 216
handbags, 143–5, 164
Harper's Bazaar, 65, 66, 75, 76–8, 97, 102, 103, 119, 122, 126, 134, 140, 145, 146, 149, 154, 176, 183, 208; *53, 61, 120*

Harris, Isle of, 130
Hartley, Mrs, 54, 56
Hartnell, Norman, 110
hats, 63, 69, 99–101, 150–1, 164, 176 183, 195, 210–12; *48, 89, 106, 108, 129, 150, 151, 179, 215*
Hays, Blanche, 44–5, 48–9, 54, 56
Hays, Lora, 44
Head, Edith, 108
Hearst, Mrs Randolph Jr, 171
Heart Clip, 146
Hepburn, Katharine, 109; *69*
Hide-and-Seek Hat, 150
His Honour, 150
Hitchcock, Alfred, 112
Hitler, Adolf, 173, 180, 184, 190
Hoffman, Malvina, 200
Hollywood, 107–9, 188
Hoover, Herbert, 42, 185
Horst, Horst P., 85; *85*
Hour-Glass Hat, 151
Hoyningen-Huené, George, 57, 85; *26, 31, 123*
Hugo, Valentine, *100*
Hurricane Line, 21
Huston, John, 173

Ibsen, Henrik, 25
Indian silhouette, 103; *72*
influences on ES: African art, 62, 146; America, 37; *43, 186*; Art Deco, 57, 62, 132, 140; *56*; childhood, 21; *22, 90*; Dada, 17; Egyptian art, 106; Eleonora Duse, 26; Etruscan art, 106; Fauves, 17; Futurism, 17, 54–5, 57; Gabrielle Picabia, 32, 41–2; machines, 26; Maria Montessori, 26; Cubism, 17; Paul Poiret, 49, 94; *49*; Piet Mondrian, 57; Sonia Delaunay, 32; Surrealism, 140; Tunisia, 29, 166; uniforms, 99
International Exhibition of Arts and Techniques (1937), 170–3
International Exhibition of Modern Art (1913), 39
Ireland, 130
Irene, 108
Italian Academy of Sciences, 29
Italo-Ethiopian war, 163–5, 172

jackets, 65, 74, 97, 102, 104, 181; *31, 32, 45, 47, 66, 75, 78, 83, 94, 107, 123, 138*
James, Charles, 200
Jardin des Modes, 131
Jean, M., 119
Jean-Pierre, Roger, 81, 217
Jersala, 126
Jersarelli, 126
Jet Wardrobe, 212
jewellery, 62, 145–50; *56, 146, 148, 149, 171*
Johnson, Amy, 97
Jones, Bettina, 80; *145, 176*
Jooss, Kurt, 132
jumpsuits, 74

Kahn, M., 56, 57–8, 85
kasha, 57, 65
Keller, Helen, 173
Kelly, Orry, 108
Kerlor, Comte William de Wendt de (ES's husband), 34–5, 36, 37–9, 89; *35*

kilts, 130
Kisling, 200
Klein, Calvin, 176
Knox the Hatter, 61

Lachasse, 110
Lalique, René, 145
Lanvin, Jeanne, 86, 91, 120, 154, 161
Laperche, Paulette, 156, 190, 215, 217
Laroche, Guy, 176
latex, 129
Lauder, Estée, 92
Lauren, Ralph, 176
Lee, Jennie, 115
Léger, Fernand, 54, 200
Leigh, Vivien, 171
Lelong, Lucien, 181, 183, 184, 192, 193–4, 195–6, 212
Lenglen, Suzanne, 53–4
Leonardo da Vinci, 24, 115
Lesage, François, 136; *see also* Maison Lesage
Lewis, Isle of, 130
Liberty, 61
Lindbergh, Charles, 97
linen, 129, 130, 132
lingerie, 181, 215
Linton, 130
Lipchitz, Jacques, 200
lipsticks, 158; *155*
Lobster Basket Hat, 150
London, 34, 36, 75–6, 110–13, 156
Lord and Taylor Fifth Avenue, 61, 65, 187
Los Angeles County Museum, 43
Louisville, 188
Loy, Myrna, 171

McCardell, Claire, 201
MacDonald, Hortense, 80
machines, 54, 57
MacLeod of MacLeod, 130
Mad Cap, 69, 212; *69*
Magaloff, Princess Sonia, 80
Mainbocher, 173, 180
Maison Lambal, 54, 56
Maison Lesage, 136; *83, 90, 136, 146, 152, 167, 187*
Major Pictures, 110
Marco Polo hat, 21, 100
Marina, Duchess of Kent, 148, 149
Marinetti, Filippo, 26, 32
Martin, Charles, 53
Martinelli, Giovanni, 203
Mary, Queen, consort of George V, 34
masks, 141
Masson, André, 200
materials, ES's use of, 57, 65, 69, 99, 122–34
Maurois, André, 200
Mélodie, 126
Mendl, Lady Elsie, 171
Mermaid Silhouette, 106
Mestchersky, Princess Marina, 80
Meunier, M., 85, 190, 205
Meyer, Baron Adolf de, 39, 41, 82–5; *39, 92*
Michelangelo, 20
Mikaëlian, Aroosiag ('Mike'), 59–61, 62, 82, 190, 217
Milan, 23
military styles, 99, 163–5, 172–6

Milstein, Nathan, 203
Miró, Joan, 200
Mistinguett, 205
Miyeke, Issey, 176
Molyneux, 154, 158, 173, 180
Mondrian, Piet, 57
Monkey Hats, 150; *101*
Montand, Yves, 205
Montessori, Maria, 26, 203
Montreal, 188
Morgan, Michèle, 171
Morton, Digby, 110
Moscow, 113–15
Moser, Koloman, 145
Munckacsi, 85
Music Collection, 164; *152, 164*
Mussolini, Benito, 184, 190

Nazis, 189–96
necklaces, 146, 149
New York, 36–44, 57, 185–9, 197–204, 213–15
Nice, 35
Nieman-Marcus, 154
Nieman-Marcus Fashion Award, 81, 200
Nomotta Knitters, 126
Norell, Norman, 76, 200
nylon, 126

Oasis, 46
Oberon, Merle, 171
Oklahoma City, 188
'overturned tulip' silhouette, 208

Pagan Collection, 170; *130, 170, 171*
Pagès, Jean, 199
Palazzo Corsini, 19, 21, 24; *21*
paper materials, 128
Paquin, 173
Parachute Collection, 24, 115–16, 164; *115*
Paramount film company, 109, 171
Paris: ES settles in, 43, 44–5; ES's first visit to, 31–4; ES's home in, 91–2, 116–20, 180, 184, 189; wartime, 180–3, 190–6; *et passim*
Parker, Dorothy, 181
Parkinson, George Robert, 154–6
Parkinson, Norman, *86*
Pascal, 162, 184; *184*
Patou, Jean, 52; and influence of sportswear, 53–4; introduces kasha, 57; loses customers and staff to ES, 72, 79, 190; perfumes, 154, 158; rise of, 53; shops, 161
Paynet, 156
Penn, Irving, *206*
perfume, 65, 154–8, 199, 215
Persian Prince dinner suit, 103; *105*
Perugia of Padua, 166, 184
Philadelphia Art Museum, 24
Phoenix, Arizona, 188
Phong, M., 119
Photo-Secessionist Gallery, New York, 39
Phrygian Bonnet, 101
Piaf, Edith, 205
Picabia, Francis, 32, 39, 45, 54
Picabia, Gabrielle ('Gaby'), 32, 39, 41, 43–5, 46–8
Picasso, Pablo, 45, 91, 134, 145, 200
Pickford, Mary, 92
Pignatelli, Princess, 72

pigskin, 65
Piguet, Robert, 213
Pin-cushion Hat, 150
Pinafore Evening Dress, 126
Pino (early suitor), 30, 218
Pluvionyl, 126
Poiret, Denise, 32, 53
Poiret, Paul, 39, 72, 91, 119, 200, 208;
    49; befriends ES, 49; death, 206;
    ES first hears of, 32; ES first sees
    collection of, 49; ES's devotion to,
    120; influence on ES, 86, 94, 103;
    influence wanes, 52; introduces
    beauty products, 154; notices ES's
    designs, 48; at the Oasis, 46;
    pantaloons, 75; prints, 132; shops,
    161; uniforms, 99; war
    propaganda, 184
Polignac, Comtesse M. de, 72
Polo, Marco, 21
Poniatowska, Princess Paulette, 80
Porter, Mrs Cole, 171
prints, 132–4; *132, 175*
Profile Hat, 215; *215*
Puccini, Giacomo, 25
pyjamas, 74, 103; *32, 65*
Pyramid Line, 213

Quakers, 185, 189, 206
Quintieri, Riccardo, 29

Rabble hats, 164
raglan style, 102
Ray, Man, 39, 41, 45, 82, 145
rayon, 122–6
Red Cross, 185, 202, 203
Reid, Whitelaw, 199
Renta, Oscar de la, 176
Rhodophane, 128; *126*
Ribouldingue, 126
rings, 148; *149*
'Riot', 100
Robin Hood hat, 212
Rodier, 57, 122
Rogers, Ginger, *216*
Roi Soleil cape, 136
Roi Soleil scent, 156
Rome, 19, 20–3, 28, 36, 44, 217
'Rosine', 154
Rothschilds, 85
Rouff, Maggy, 49
rubber materials, 129
Rubinstein, Artur, 45
Rubinstein, Helena, 92
Russell, Rosalind, 109, 119; *107*

'S' perfume, 65, 156, 157
Sablon, Jean, 205
Saint Laurent, Yves, 81, 93, 216–17;
    13
St Moritz, 74, 76
St Paul, Minn., 188; *37*
St Peter's, Rome, 20–1
Saint-Exupèry, Antoine de, 200
Saints' Halos, 21
Saks Fifth Avenue, 63, 66, 126
'Salut', 156
Salvation Army, 180, 183
San Francisco, 188
San Francisco Fair (1938), 184
Sartre, Jean-Paul, 205–6
Satan, Monsieur and Madame, 116,
    120; *116*
Satie, Erik, 46

scarves, 59, 66, 69, 100, 130
Scheherazade, 21, 150; *105*
Schiap Boutique, 80, 86, 161–2, 164,
    189; *161*
'Schiap' perfume, 65, 156
Schiaparelli, Beatrice (ES's sister), 20,
    23
Schiaparelli, Celestino (ES's father),
    19–20, 21, 25, 28, 29, 30, 35, 36, 45
Schiaparelli, Elsa: **career:** enters
    business with Gabrielle Picabia,
    41–2, 43; makes her first dress,
    46–8; sees her first Poiret
    collection, 49; first attempts at
    design, 49; first sweater designs,
    54; puts together her first
    collection, 56–7; moves to rue de
    la Paix, 58; first advertisement, 58;
    expands her business, 62;
    introduces 'Display No. 2', 63–6;
    beauty products, 65, 154–8, 183,
    199, 215; turns to dressmaking, 65;
    appearance of tweeds, 66, 130;
    introduces furs, 66; first major
    collection, 66; success of Mad Cap,
    69; seeks free publicity, 71–2; first
    scandal, 75–6; arrives at the top,
    76–8; as a businesswoman, 79–87;
    work routine, 79; staff, 79–85,
    181; expands at rue de la Paix, 86;
    copies of her work, 87; avoids
    strikes, 101; collaboration with
    Antoine, 101; opens London
    branch, 110–13; trip to America,
    107; moves to Place Vendôme,
    160–1, 183, 189; presentation of
    collections, 162–73; as queen of
    Paris fashion, 173; approaching
    war, 173–9; World War II,
    180–204; lecture tour, 184–8, 190,
    203; business continues in wartime
    Paris, 190–6; post-war recovery,
    205–13; threat from Dior, 213;
    opens New York branch, 213–15;
    declining sales, 215; financial
    problems, 215; final collection,
    216; retires, 217; **designs:** concept
    of clothes, 93–106; design ability,
    86–7; film designs, 107–10;
    military effects, 163–5, 172–6; and
    the New Woman, 96–7; patterns
    and motifs, 57, 132–4; promotion
    of embroidery, 136; sources of
    inspiration, 72–4; *trompe l'œil*,
    59–61; tweed, 66, 130; use of
    colour, 21, 25, 29, 57, 86, 94, 130,
    152–4, 181, 183; use of materials,
    57, 65, 69, 99, 122–34; *see also*
    influences *and individual collections,
    designs and styles;* **early life:** family
    background, 19–20; childhood,
    20–3; at school, 23; starts to
    choose her own clothes, 25;
    interest in theatre and opera, 25–6,
    34; seeks means of expressing
    herself, 26–8; studies philosophy,
    28, 34; composes verse, 28–9;
    early suitors, 29–30, 34–5; first
    visit to Paris, 31–4; stays in
    England, 30, 34–5; marries de
    Kerlor, 35; moves to Nice, 35;
    personal life: in America, 36–44;
    her father dies, 36; disintegration
    of her marriage, 37–8, 89; meets

exiled French artists in New York,
    39–42; poverty, 42, 44, 45; part-
    time jobs in New York, 42; affairs,
    43, 89; looks after Gogo, 44, 66;
    returns to Paris, 43, 44–5; daily
    routine, 79; character, 88–91;
    home, 91–2, 116–20, 180, 184,
    189; love of entertaining, 91, 92,
    119–20; visit to Soviet Union,
    113–15; moves to rue de Berri,
    116; love of Britain and Ireland,
    130; and outbreak of war, 180;
    leaves Paris, 183–4; goes to
    America, 184–5; returns to
    wartime Paris, 189–96; resettles in
    New York, 197; war work in
    America, 199–200, 202–3;
    retirement, 216–17; death, 217
Schiaparelli, Emma (ES's aunt), 20
Schiaparelli, Ernesto (ES's cousin), 20
Schiaparelli, Giovanni (ES's uncle),
    20, 23, 24, 28
Schiaparelli, Giustino (ES's cousin),
    28
Schiaparelli, Luigi (ES's cousin), 20
Schiaparelli, Maria-Luisa (ES's
    mother), 20, 23, 30, 44–5; *20*
Schiaparelli Foundation, 20
Schlumberger, Jean, 148–50, 168;
    146, 148
Scola da Samba, 171
Scotland, 130
Sea Shell Hat, 150
Seed Catalogue print, 23
Sentry Cape, 176; *176*
separates, 25, 57, 65, 66
Setilose, 128
shantung, 132
Shape Line, 215
Shearer, Norma, 101, 171; *108*
'Shocking', 158, 190; *158*
Shocking Elegance, 215
shocking pink, 154
'Shocking Radiance', 154
shoes, 140, 166–8, 194–5
shoulders, 97, 210; *99*
'Si', 156
silk, 122, 132
Simpson, Mrs Wallis *see* Windsor,
    Duchess of
skeleton sweater, 61–2
skirts, 63–5, 74, 106, 181, 183
Skye, 130
Skylarkers, 150; *71*
Skyscraper Silhouette, 97, 101–2
'Sleeping', 156; *157*
sleeves, 97–9
'Snuff', 156; *156*
La Société Anonyme, 41–2
Les Soirées de Paris, 32
'Soucis', 156
Souquières, Yvonne, 79, 190, 217
spectator sportswear, 56–8
sportswear, 53–4, 56–8, 63–5, 200;
    54
Stalin, Josef, 113, 116; *113*
Stanwyck, Barbara, 109
Steichen, Edward, 39, 41, 82–5; *109*
Stieglitz, Alfred, 39, 41, 43
stockings, 126, 129, 140, 195
Stork Club, 197
Stormy Weather Silhouette, 103,
    115, 210; *104, 114*
Stratospheric Silhouette, 24, 115

Stravinsky, Igor, 45
Stroheim, Erich von, 210
'Succès Fou', 156
Surrealism, 18, 54, 61, 140, 151, 152;
    41
Sutherland, Duchess of, 72
sweaters, 54, 57, 58–62; *56*
swimwear, 63–5, 183
synthetic fabrics, 122–6

taffeta, 132
Talleyrand Silhouette, 210; *210*
Tangle Hats, 151
Tanguy, Yves, 200
Tchelichew, Pavel, 92
Telegram print, 132
Television Hat, 151
Tergal, 126
Théâtre de la Mode, 206
Tivoli, 23
Toy Hats, 150; *106*
Transformable Dress, 181; *49*
Trenet, Charles, 205
Triolet, Elsa, 146
trompe-l'œil, 59–61
trouser-skirts, 74–6
trousers, 74–5; *32, 75*
Tunisia, 29, 166
turbans, 62, 100
tweed, 66, 130; *66, 75, 131*
Typhoon Line, 103
Typhoon Silhouette, 210
Tzara, Tristan, 45

uniforms, 99, 176, 183
University of Rome, 28

Van Dongen, Kees, 82
Vanity Fair, 116
Vegetarian Bracelet, 146
Venet, Philippe, 213
Versace, Gianni, 176
Vertès, Marcel, 82, 119, 132, 150,
    156, 200; *101, 110, 120, 132, 175*
Vian, Boris, 205
Victor Emmanuel II, King of Italy,
    19, 20
Victoria, B.C., 188
Victoria and Albert Museum, 24, 34
Vionnet, Madeleine, 86, 120, 136
Vogue (American), 61, 66, 69, 71, 72,
    78, 94, 97, 100, 102, 122, 126, 129,
    130, 150, 152, 164, 201–2, 208, 210,
    213, 215, 216
Vogue (French), 57, 58, 66, 72, 78, 192

Wall Street crash, 71
Walska, Ganna, 42–3
Wanamaker's, 61
Wattems, 136
wedgies, 166–8, 194–5; *29, 118*
West, Mae, 109–10, 151, 154; *111*
Westcott Hosiery Mills, 129
Westminster, Duke of, 91
Wicklow, County, 130
wigs, 101
Wildenstein Gallery, 203
Williams, Mrs Harrison, 129, 148,
    149
Windsor, Duchess of, 34, 173
'witticisms', 140, 210
Women's Wear Daily, 56, 61, 66
Wooden Soldier Silhouette, 99
Woodstock, 43, 44

wools, 130
World Fair, Paris (1900), 56
World War II, 180–204
Worth, Charles Frederic, 91, 119, 120
Worth, Jacques, 120
Wray, Fay, 171

Youssoupoff, Prince, 45

Zipper Back, 128
zips, 126–8
Zodiac Collection *see* Astrology
    Collection
Zurich, 39
'Zut', 158; *158*

PICTURE ACKNOWLEDGEMENTS

While every effort has been made to give correct acknowledgement wherever due, this has proved difficult. Where insufficient credit has been given the publishers will be pleased to make amendments in any future edition.

Cecil Beaton: **96**, **141**: courtesy of Sotheby's London; **214**. La Marquise Cacciapuoti: **16** (photo Hoyningen-Huené © Hearst Magazine Inc.) **20**; **21**; **35**; **37**; **48** (photo Toulgouat, Paris); **56**; **60** (photo Bonney, Paris); **80**; **84** (photo Horst P. Horst © Condé Nast, Paris); **116** top and bottom (photo Pierre Jahan); **117** (photo Jean-Pierre Sudre, Paris); **118** (photo S. M. Productions, Paris); **196**; **198** (photo Dick Brugière); **201** (photo Petak, New York); **204** (photo Piaz, Paris); **207** (photo Irving Penn © Condé Nast); **218**. Cinema Bookshop, London: **110**. Henry Clarke: **144**; **177**; **209**. *Daily Mail*, Paris: **91**. Edimedia: **24**. Editions Herscher from *Moments de Mode* 1986 (photos David Seidner): **95**; **105**; **139**. Hachette, *Femina*: **44**; **45**: Feb 1938. *Harper's Bazaar*: **31**: Dec 1939; **32**: Jan 1937; **39**: Oct 1933 (photo De Meyer); **46**: July 1937; **53**: Ixt 1930; **74**: Nov 1937; **75**: Feb 1937; **86**: June 1935 (photo Norman Parkinson); **93**: Sept 1933 (photo De Meyer); **100**: 1936; **101**: Oct 1938; **111**: Jul 1937; **114**: Nov 1934; **120**: 1937 (photo James Maddox); **121**: May 1938; **127**: 1936 (photo André Durst); **150**: May 1938; **151**: Nov 1937; **162–3**: Oct 1936; **180**: March 1940; **191**: Feb 1940. International News Photos, Paris: **216**. *Jardin des Modes*: **131** left top and bottom: Sept 1937. Kobal Collection: **69**; **77**; **108**. Kollar: **160**. Kyoto Costume Institute: **10** (*Vogue* Nov 1938); **124**; **125**; **132**; **133**; **138**; **172**; **175**. Mansell Collection: **43**. Musée de la Mode et du Costume: **50**; **51**. Philadelphia Museum of Art: **47**; **137**; **173**; **174**. Yves Saint Laurent: **12**; **13**; **14**; **217**. Schiaparelli Inc.: **129**; **155**; **156**; **157**; **158**; **159**; **208** (photo Dorvyne, Paris); **214**; **215**. Patrice Stable: 22 top and bottom; **83**; **90**; **136**; **146** top and bottom; **147**; **148**; **153**; **165**; **167**; **168**; **169**; **186**. Studio Anzon: **161**. Union Française des Arts du Costume: **55**: Album 9; **63**: Album 13; **82–3**: Album 19; **131** right; **164**: Album 17; **182**. Victoria and Albert Museum, by courtesy of the Board of Trustees: **18**; **134**; **135**; **142** top and bottom. Courtesy American *Vogue*, copyright © by the Condé Nast Publications Inc.: **33**: Jan 1937; **40**: Jan 1936 (photo André Durst); **64**: 1 Jul 1931 (photo Hoyningen-Huené); **66**: 15 Sept 1937; **67**: 1 Sept 1935; **68**: 1 Oct 1935 (photo Horst P. Horst); **73**: 1 May 1935; **78–9**: 1 Jan 1936; **89**: Oct 1945; **98**: Oct 1935; **102**: July 1938; **104**: Oct 1937; **106**: June 1938; **109**: Oct 1932; **113**: 1936; **115**: 1 Mar 1936; **123**: Apr 1934 (photo Hoyningen-Huené); **128**: Oct 1936; **149**: Mar 1938; **166**: Apr 1938; **171**: Mar 1935; **178**: Dec 1938; **179**: Mar 1939; **187**: 1940; **211**: Oct 1945. *Vogue* Paris, copyright © Les Editions Condé Nast S.A.: **27** (photo Hoyningen-Huené).